SOCIAL MOVEMENTS

SOCIAL MOVEMENTS

Third Edition

Suzanne Staggenborg
Howard Ramos

OXFORD
UNIVERSITY PRESS

OXFORD
UNIVERSITY PRESS

Oxford University Press is a department of the University of Oxford.
It furthers the University's objective of excellence in research, scholarship,
and education by publishing worldwide. Oxford is a registered trade mark of
Oxford University Press in the UK and in certain other countries.

Published in Canada by
Oxford University Press
8 Sampson Mews, Suite 204,
Don Mills, Ontario M3C 0H5 Canada
www.oupcanada.com

Library and Archives Canada Cataloguing in Publication
Staggenborg, Suzanne, author
Social movements / Suzanne Staggenborg and Howard
Ramos. — Third edition.

(Themes in Canadian sociology)
Includes bibliographical references and index.
ISBN 978-0-19-901397-5 (paperback)

1. Social movements—Textbooks. 2. Social movements—History—
Textbooks. 3. Social movements—Philosophy—Textbooks. 4. Social
movements—Case studies—Textbooks. I. Ramos, Howard, 1974–, author
II. Title. III. Series: Themes in Canadian sociology

HM881.S73 2015   303.48'4   C2015-905159-2

Cover image: Blair Edward Kennedy/Getty Images

Printed and bound in Canada

2 3 4 5 — 19 18 17 16

Contents

Contents

Preface and Acknowledgements

Social movements are important means of bringing about political and cultural changes through collective action. The study of social movements, which examines political and cultural opportunities and obstacles, organizational dynamics, resources, collective action frames, and strategies and tactics, helps us understand both how movements achieve change and how they are limited in doing so. The field of social movements is an exciting one; scholars continue to produce new studies of a wide array of social movements in many different countries, while activists regularly provide accounts of their experiences. Relevant to both activists and social scientists, the area is one that students find important and interesting.

Given the proliferation of social movement scholarship in recent decades, it is a daunting task to attempt to capture the field in a short book. Thus, our goal is simply to introduce students and other readers to some interesting history, ideas, and questions about social movements. No researcher can be expert on all of the many social movements that might be covered in such a book, and we have limited ourselves to some of the movements that we have followed for many years in teaching and researching in the area. In this third edition, Howard Ramos, who contributed a chapter on Indigenous protest in the first and second editions, has come on as a second author. We hope that students will find our selection of contemporary protest movements interesting and will learn enough about theoretical ideas and approaches to movements to be able to apply this knowledge to other movements of interest.

We are grateful to Lorne Tepperman and the late James Curtis for inviting us to write the book for their edited series. We also thank the various editors we have worked with at Oxford University Press Canada, including Heather Macdougall, who worked on the third edition, and all of our reviewers. We are grateful to Judy Taylor for reading and commenting on the chapter on the women's movement. We thank Hatem Hassan and Paul Pritchard for their research assistance.

Abbreviations

ACT	AIDS Committee of Toronto
ACT UP	AIDS Coalition to Unleash Power
AFN	Assembly of First Nations
AIM	American Indian Movement
ASP	Assembly for the Sovereignty of the Peoples
ATTAC	Association for the Taxation of Financial Transactions for the Aid of Citizens
CARAL	Canadian Abortion Rights Action League
CBC	Canadian Broadcasting Corporation
COC	Council of Canadians
CUPE	Canadian Union of Public Employees
CUS	Canadian Union of Students
CYC	Company of Young Canadians
DAWN	Development Alternatives with Women for a New Era
DOMA	Defense of Marriage Act
EEOC	Equal Employment Opportunity Commission
Egale	Equality for Gays and Lesbians Everywhere
ELF	Earth Liberation Front
ERA	Equal Rights Amendment
ETAG	Ethical Trading Action Group
EU	European Union
FFQ	Fédération des femmes du Québec
FLQ	Front de libération du Québec
FTA	Canada–US Free Trade Agreement
FTAA	Free Trade Area of the Americas
GLF	Gay Liberation Front
ILO	International Labour Organization
IMC	Independent Media Centre
IMF	International Monetary Fund
ITK	Inuit Tapiriit Kanatami
MAI	Multilateral Agreement on Investment
MAS	Movement toward Socialism
MNC	Métis National Council
MNSJ	Metro Network for Social Justice
MOSOP	Movement for the Survival of the Ogoni People
NAACP	National Association for the Advancement of Colored People
NAC	National Action Committee on the Status of Women
NAFTA	North American Free Trade Agreement

NAIB	North American Indian Brotherhood
NCC	Native Council of Canada
NDP	New Democratic Party
NIB	National Indian Brotherhood
NIC	National Indian Council
NIMBY	not in my backyard
NGLTF	National Gay and Lesbian Task Force
NGO	non-governmental organization
NOW	National Organization for Women
NRDC	Natural Resources Defense Council
NWAC	Native Women's Association of Canada
NWP	National Women's Party
OPP	Ontario Provincial Police
OWS	Occupy Wall Street
PGA	Peoples' Global Action
PPF	Put People First
PQ	Parti québécois
QSF	Québec Social Forum
REAL	Realistic, Equal, Active, for Life (Women)
RCMP	Royal Canadian Mounted Police
SAP	structural adjustment program
SCT	Specific Claims Tribunal
SDS	Students for a Democratic Society
SFU	Simon Fraser University
SMO	social movement organization
SNCC	Student Nonviolent Coordinating Committee
SQ	Sûreté du Québec
SUPA	Student Union for Peace Action
UFW	United Farm Workers
UN	United Nations
USAS	United Students against Sweatshops
USSF	US Social Forum
WMW	World March of Women
WRC	Workers Rights Consortium
WSF	World Social Forum
WTO	World Trade Organization
WVS	World Values Survey
YMCA	Young Men's Christian Association

Introduction

Social movements have used a wide variety of strategies and tactics to bring about enormous social changes, influencing cultural arrangements, public opinion, popular discourse, and government policies. Protest tactics allow people who lack power and influence to gain public attention and force authorities to pay attention and make concessions, sometimes even toppling governments. This was demonstrated dramatically in 2011 during the "Arab Spring" when movements in Tunisia, Egypt, and other Arab countries demanded democracy and overthrew repressive regimes. Those uprisings, along with the global economic crisis, inspired movements in other parts of the world, including the Spanish *indignados*, who brought hundreds of thousands of protesters into the streets of cities such as Madrid and Barcelona to express their indignation at stratospheric unemployment rates and what they saw as "the collusion between bankers and politicians" (Castells, 2012: 111). In North America, Occupy Wall Street was inspired by these protests and fuelled by inequities associated with the economic crisis. After Vancouver-based Adbusters issued a call to occupy the financial hub, the Occupy movement began in New York City's Zuccotti Park in September 2011 and then spread across the country and to cities around the world. Protesters set up camps in public spaces and declared "we are the 99%" in opposition to the wealthy "1%" of the population. Although the Occupy camps were eventually broken up by police, the movement continued in various forms and had an important impact on public discourse about inequality.

Around the world, social movements have mobilized participants, often at great risk, for protests that helped to bring about important social changes. In the nineteenth century, the labour movement in Europe and North America used strikes and other tactics to win collective bargaining rights and concessions such as the eight-hour work day. But movements have never been limited to economic interests; temperance movements, for example, were active in the nineteenth century and a women's movement also emerged. Although not limited to a single issue, the early women's movement produced a worldwide women's suffrage movement that in some places engaged in militant tactics. British "suffragettes"—impatient with the failure of their government to give women the vote— protested in Parliament, marched in the streets, chained themselves to the railings outside the prime minister's residence, and went on hunger strikes early in the twentieth century. Numerous suffragists were jailed and force-fed, and many were beaten by police when they participated in demonstrations. The militancy and bravery of the suffragists inspired movement activists around the world. By the 1920s, suffrage movements had won the vote for women in many countries, but struggles for a full range of women's rights persisted. Today, the women's movement continues to combat problems such as violence against women and to fight for access to education, employment, and citizenship rights for women around the world.

One of the most influential movements of all times took place in the southern United States, where civil rights activists in the 1950s and 1960s used boycotts, sit-ins, mass demonstrations, "freedom rides" on public transportation, and voter registration drives to secure basic rights for African Americans. Activists were jailed, beaten, and murdered as they combated a society in which African Americans were denied service in many public establishments, forced to sit in the back of buses and give up their seats to whites, and disenfranchised by threats of violence when they attempted to vote. After the civil rights movement won battles over desegregation of public facilities and voting rights, blacks became a political force in the South and served as mayors of cities that had once denied them basic rights, such as Atlanta, Georgia, and Jackson, Mississippi. In 2009 Barack Obama took office as the first African-American president of the United States.

In addition to fighting for political and economic rights, social movements have changed cultural norms and practices. A striking example is provided by the lesbian, gay, bisexual, and transgender (LGBT) movement and its success in promoting marriage equality and acceptance of sexual diversity. Although changes have occurred rapidly in recent years, the movement engaged in decades of struggle prior to the recent victories and activists continue to do battle around the world. In Canada, a group calling itself the Association for Social Knowledge formed in Vancouver in 1964 to begin the long process of creating a positive gay identity at a time when gays and lesbians were denied basic rights such as employment and were often arrested simply for socializing together in bars and other public places. By 1971, the low-key approach of early activists gave way to a gay liberation movement that marched on Parliament Hill to demand the "freedom to love." Since the 1970s, LGBT groups have lobbied for inclusion in human rights codes, filed lawsuits to secure legal protections, and staged numerous "gay pride" parades and demonstrations. In 2005, after many years of equity-seeking work by the LGBT movement, same-sex marriage became legal throughout Canada. Over a dozen other countries have also recognized same-sex marriages in recent years.

In all of these examples, individuals banded together in collective efforts to create social change by presenting demands for justice and pressuring authorities to respond. Social movements are important vehicles for social and political change; participants have organized to protect the environment, oppose wars, resist colonization, and advocate for the rights of more and more groups, including workers, women, LGBT people, students, children, disabled people, senior citizens, and many racial and ethnic groups. Yet it is not always apparent how it is possible to bring together a variety of groups and individuals with varying interests and ideologies to form a cohesive movement capable of effecting real changes. Researchers who study social movements are confronted with numerous puzzles as they attempt to explain the growth and impact of movements.

Among the important problems that social movement scholars attempt to solve is the question of what sparks a movement and why particular movements originate when they do. Grievances about conditions such as poverty and government repression are clearly important, but they are not the only reasons that movements form at some times and not others. For example, Indigenous peoples in what is now Canada faced the injustices of colonization for hundreds of years before the emergence of nationwide protests in the late 1960s, which continue to shape contemporary politics. To explain the increased mobilization, as well as periods of demobilization, scholars have looked at factors such as federal policy shifts and the rise of organizations. Another problem is to explain why people take part in sometimes very risky collective actions. While it might seem obvious that participants are motivated by movement grievances and goals, most people who believe in causes are not active supporters of those causes. To explain why some people contribute to movements while others do not, movement theorists look at the role of factors such as social networks, ideology, and resources. Some movement organizations are more effective than others at attracting participants and formulating effective strategies. Thus, studies of social movements examine a wide range of issues such as how and when movements originate, how they attract and maintain support, how they present issues and formulate strategies and tactics, how they structure organizations, why they generate opposition and sometimes decline, and how and why they succeed or fail in achieving cultural and political changes. These key issues are relevant to activists and policymakers as well as to social scientists.

This book introduces students and other readers to the study of social movements by looking at some influential theories in the field, the issues they raise, and how they help to explain the mobilization and outcomes of social movements. We review major theories of social movements and collective action and identify important theoretical issues that we will explore in connection with a selection of substantive movements. We also discuss the cluster of protest movements that arose in many countries in the 1960s, creating strategies and changes that continue to influence collective action in the twenty-first century. Chapters on Indigenous peoples', women's, LGBT, environmental, and global justice movements analyze general issues in the study of social movements as they apply to each movement, including how these social movements originate, mobilize participants, and bring about social change. In this introductory chapter, we consider the concept of social movements and related ideas, and place the study of contemporary movements in historical context.

The Origins of the Social Movement

The social movement, as we know it today, is a relatively recent means of organizing for social change. Charles Tilly, who did extensive historical research on the origins of the social movement in the Western world, quotes from an account of a "movement" in 1682 in Narbonne, France, to make this point:

> [T]here was a little movement in Narbonne on the occasion of the collection of the *cosse* tax, which had been ordered by an act of the royal council. Many women gathered with the common people, and threw stones at the tax collectors, but the Consuls and the leading citizens hurried over and put a stop to the disorder. (Tilly, 1984: 297)

Although this seventeenth-century incident is referred to as a "little movement", it bears scant resemblance to what we think of today as a "social movement." The term *petit mouvement* was part of the vocabulary of the time, used to refer to "a localized collective action by ordinary people which the authorities considered necessary and proper to end by force" (Tilly, 1984: 298). Tilly points out that today we would not consider this type of action a **social movement** unless it were more enduring, part of a series of collective actions rather than one incident, and enacted by participants with common interests and a distinct identity, who had broader goals than stopping a particular tax. Moreover, the forms of protest have changed. Today, protesters would be unlikely to stone the target of their grievances, often the state or other established power holders, and instead would be more likely to take to the streets and protest. In Quebec, for example, students marched with other Quebecers banging pots and pans during the Maple Spring of 2012 to fight increases to university tuitions. Tilly uses the concept of a **repertoire of collective action** to get at the idea that limited forms of protest are familiar during a given time. Using the repertoire of tactics available to them, activists engage in what Tilly calls **claim-making performances** in interaction with targets. Repertoires and performances evolve over time "through incremental transformation in use" (Tilly, 2008: 13). When we compare long periods of history, we can see major changes in repertoires; our contemporary protest repertoire has changed dramatically since the women of Narbonne stoned their tax collectors.

Collective action in Western countries such as France and England (Tilly, 1986, 1995, 2004, 2008) was once localized and defensive. People got together within their communities to defend local interests, using protest forms drawn from local culture and typically directed at particular individuals. For example, the **charivari** was a traditional form of collective action directed towards individuals who had transgressed community norms, such as a married man who got a single woman pregnant. The guilty party would be subject to a noisy demonstration designed to humiliate him or her before the community. As historian Edward Shorter (1975: 219) describes, there were many variations of the charivari, based on local tradition:

> Sometimes the demonstration would consist of masked individuals circling somebody's house at night, screaming, beating on pans, and blowing cow horns (which the local butchers rented out). On other occasions the offender would be seized and marched through the streets, seated perhaps backwards on a donkey or forced to wear a placard describing his sins. Sometimes the youth would administer the charivari; on other occasions villagers of all ages and sexes would mix together.

Despite such variations, the charivari shared characteristics in common with other forms of protest in the traditional repertoire, which also included food riots, grain seizures, and land revolts (Tarrow, 2011: 41–46). All of these traditional forms of action were short in duration and local in scope. Even when a national issue such as taxation was involved, the targets of the protest were local authorities and the actions were particular to the local community (Tilly, 1995: 45). In contrast to this traditional repertoire, a new repertoire of collective action consisting of tactics such as large-scale demonstrations, strikes, and boycotts began to develop in Europe and North America in the late eighteenth century and became firmly established in the nineteenth century. The new repertoire was cosmopolitan rather than parochial, with protests often targeted at national rather than local authorities. The tactics of the new repertoire were "modular" (Tarrow, 2011), meaning that they could easily be transported to many locales and situations rather than being tied to local communities and rituals. For example, the boycott and the mass petition were tactics that could be aimed at any target with regard to any type of grievance. The nineteenth-century abolition movement was one of the first social movements to use these tactics, organizing a boycott of sugar grown with slave labour and sending petitions signed by large numbers of supporters to the British Parliament (Tarrow, 2011: 48–49).

The story of how this shift in repertoires came about is a complicated one (Tarrow, 2011; Tilly, 1995, 2004, 2008; Tilly and Wood, 2013), but it involved the expansion of nation-states and the spread of capitalism. With the development of national electoral politics, special-purpose associations formed to represent the interests of various groups, including dissident aristocrats and bourgeois activists who sometimes formed alliances with dissatisfied workers. These coalitions adopted new means of making claims, such as mass petitions and disciplined marches, to replace the often violent direct actions, such as food riots and grain seizures, which were central to the older repertoire and more likely to be repressed by authorities. With the spread of wage labour, workers gained independence from particular landlords and masters and they were freer to engage in political activities (Tilly and Wood, 2013: 27). The repertoire of collective action gradually changed and the social movement became part of the new repertoire.

Thus, the social movement emerged in a particular historical period as a result of large-scale social changes and political conditions. Although in recent years social media have broadened the repertoire of contention to include tactics such as flash mobs and clicktivism, social movements still select many tactics from the same repertoire that became established in the nineteenth century. Tilly notes, however, that the social movement and its repertoire are products of historical circumstances and could change as political conditions change. For example, insofar as centralized nation-states are replaced with transnational bodies, the national social movement may become a less effective form of political organization (Tilly and Wood, 2013: 15). Indeed, social movements have become increasingly transnational and new forms of action have emerged along with new communication technologies and processes of globalization (Bennet and Segerberg, 2013; Earl and Kimport, 2011).

Defining Social Movements

Most social movement scholars would agree that social movements "are collective efforts, of some duration and organization, using non-institutionalized methods to bring about social change" (Flacks, 2005: 5). Many would add that movements often use institutionalized methods, such as legislative lobbying, but would agree that they need to employ at least some non-institutionalized methods, such as demonstrations, to qualify as social movements. Beyond this general understanding, varying definitions of social movements lead to different emphases in the study of particular movements.

Research by Charles Tilly and others on the origins of the social movement has been influential in promoting a political view of social movements (McAdam et al., 2001). In this view, social movements are one form of **contentious politics**:

contentious in the sense that social movements involve collective making
of claims that, if realized, would conflict with someone else's interests, politics in the sense that governments of one sort or another figure somehow
in the claim making, whether as claimants, objects of claims, allies of the
objects, or monitors of the contention. (Tilly and Wood, 2013: 3–4)

According to Tilly, social movements—as they developed in the West
after 1750—came to consist of sustained **campaigns** that made collective
claims aimed at authorities. They typically created special-purpose associations or coalitions and engaged in tactics such as demonstrations, petition
drives, public statements, and meetings—*contentious performances* drawing
on the modern *social movement repertoire* (Tilly, 2008). Movement actors
attempt to represent themselves publicly as worthy, unified, numerous, and
committed (Tilly and Wood, 2013: 5). For example, demonstrators gathering on Parliament Hill to protest for an inquiry into murdered and missing
Indigenous women bring their children and grandmothers with them to
show worthiness, adopt similar slogans and use chants to show their unity,
mobilize large numbers to illustrate the size of their constituency, and appear
regardless of bad weather or other inconvenience to show their commitment.

Based on this contentious politics approach, Sidney Tarrow (2011: 9
[emphasis in original]) provides a succinct definition of social movements
as "*collective challenges, based on common purposes and social solidarities, in sustained interaction with elites, opponents, and authorities.*" Social movements are
sustained in that they consist of multiple campaigns or at least multiple episodes of collective action within a single campaign. Movement campaigns
consist of *interactions* among movement actors, their targets, the public, and
other relevant actors. The targets of movement claims are often government
authorities, but they may also be other types of authorities, such as business
owners or religious leaders (Tilly and Wood, 2013: 4). Certainly, not all
social movements target the state.

Nor are social movements the only form of contentious politics.
McAdam, Tarrow, and Tilly (2001) include in their definition of contentious politics various public and collective political struggles, such as revolutions, nationalism, and strikes, as well as social movements. They also
consider actions by established political actors within institutions as contentious politics, provided the action is episodic and departs from the everyday,
non-collective action that goes on within institutions. For example, Egale,
a national organization representing LGBT communities, has intervened in
Canadian courts and tribunals in 25 cases, almost half appearing before
the Supreme Court (Egale, 2014). Their research has been used by activists, other equity-seeking groups, mainstream political parties, and even
governments, and it was central to Canada's recognition of same sex marriage. McAdam et al. (2001: 7–8) distinguish between *contained contention*

by established political actors and *transgressive contention*, which involves at least some "newly self-identified political actors" and/or "innovative collective action" by at least some parties.

Although the distinction between social movements and other phenomena such as *political parties* and *interest groups* is not always sharp, movement scholars have generally regarded movements as *challengers* that are, at least in part, *outsiders* with regard to the established power structure (Gamson, 1990 [1975]; Tilly, 1978). Political parties and interest groups, in contrast, are *insiders* with at least some degree of access to government authorities and other elites. However, political insiders may engage in (usually) contained contention, and movements may become **professionalized** in the sense that they include fairly stable organizations that are headed by paid leaders and have memberships consisting largely of financial contributors, or "paper members," rather than activists (McCarthy and Zald, 1973). It may be difficult to distinguish between a professional movement organization and an established interest group. For example, large national environmental organizations, such as Greenpeace or the Sierra Club, are professionalized movement organizations often referred to as "Big Green" in reference to their relatively large staffs and budgets. Elizabeth May, the former director of the Sierra Club Canada, even became a Member of Parliament and leader of the Green party.

Some social movement theorists have distinguished between social movements and the organized entities that typically populate movements. John McCarthy and Mayer Zald (1977: 1217–18) define a social movement as "a set of opinions and beliefs in a population which represents preferences for changing some elements of the social structure and/or reward distribution of a society" and a **countermovement** as "a set of opinions and beliefs in a population opposed to a social movement." For example, laws governing abortion in Canada were struck down in 1988 because of activism by feminists and family planning advocates and because Dr Henry Morgentaler challenged the laws in the Supreme Court. A countermovement composed of opponents of abortion, including many Catholics and conservative Christians, tried to block their efforts and has since protested governments to legislate new laws prohibiting it. In response, groups such as FEMEN Canada have protested these groups to keep abortion available to Canadians.

In this view social movements are "preference structures," or sets of opinions, beliefs, and goals which may or may not be turned into collective action depending on pre-existing organization and on opportunities for and costs of expressing preferences. Movements supported by populations that are internally organized through communities or associations are most likely to generate organized structures (McCarthy and Zald, 1977; Oberschall, 1973). For example, the abortion rights movement built on women's movement organizations, while the anti-abortion movement was able to mobilize in part through churches. A **social movement organization (SMO)** is defined as "a complex, or formal, organization which identifies its goals with the preferences of a social movement or a countermovement and attempts to implement those goals" (McCarthy and Zald, 1977: 1218). Movements differ from one another in the extent to which they are organized by formal organizations and in the extent to which they trigger organized opposition or countermovements. The Canadian abortion rights movement was originally organized in part by the Canadian Abortion Rights Action League (CARAL), Canadians for Choice, and the Pro-Choice Action network, and was supported by the National Action Committee on the Status of Women (NAC) while the countermovement was mobilized by the Catholic Church, the Campaign Life Coalition, and REAL Women of Canada, among other organizations. McCarthy and Zald refer to the collection of organizations within a movement as a **social movement industry** and to all of these "industries" in a society as the **social movement sector**. Thus, the abortion rights movement industry consists of single issue groups such as CARAL and women's movement organizations such as the NAC. The social movement sector consists of the abortion rights movement industry, but also its countermovement industry, and the environmental movement industry, the LGBT movement industry, and so on.

McCarthy and Zald's definition of the social movement as a preference structure differs from most other definitions, including the contentious politics view of movements as collective challenges, in that McCarthy and Zald separate preferences for change from organized collective action. They argue that this approach has the advantage of recognizing that movements are "never fully mobilized" and that the size or intensity of preferences may not predict the rise and fall of the organized movement (McCarthy and Zald, 1977: 1219). Collective action may depend less on the grievances of unorganized groups than on social movement leaders who act as "entrepreneurs" in mobilizing—and perhaps even creating—preferences (McCarthy and Zald, 1973). In other words, grievances are often present in a population, but a movement may never form unless leaders take the initiative to make persuasive arguments and organize supporters. Moreover, McCarthy and Zald's approach leads us to focus on social movement organizations and the interactions of these organizations within the context of a particular social movement. Organizations have different structures which affect their strategies and longevity and they may co-operate or compete with one another. In some instances, organizational interests may interfere with the attainment of movement goals or preferences.

The distinction between a social movement and a social movement organization is important because major social movements typically include multiple organizations, and internal organizational dynamics and inter-organizational alliances are critical to movement strategies and outcomes.

For example, the environmental movement in North America includes organizations such as Greenpeace, the Sierra Club, the Nature Conservancy, the World Wildlife Fund, and Earth First!, to name only a few of the many active organizations. Some of these organizations are national or international ones, others are local or regional, and some are federated organizations with national, regional, and local affiliates. Organizations within movements have different ideologies and strategic approaches and may compete with one another for members and funding despite their common commitment to environmental protection.

We might expect the multiple organizations within movements to cooperate naturally with one another and pool their resources to attain common goals. While many groups do form effective alliances, coalitions of movement organizations are often difficult to form and maintain, particularly among those with different ideologies, structures, and strategic preferences. In some cases movement organizations compete with one another for members and funding despite sharing common goals. Thus, the conditions under which effective coalitions form are of great interest to social movement theorists. One finding is that movement organizations facing organized countermovements, which increase the urgency of cooperation, are most likely to form coalitions (Staggenborg, 1986). Movement–countermovement interactions, as well as interactions with the state, are an important topic for social movement research and often involve organizational dynamics (Meyer and Staggenborg, 1996; Zald and Useem, 1987).

At the same time that analyses of social movement organizations are critical to social movement theory, scholars have recognized that movements consist of more than politically motivated organizations with an explicit mandate to seek change in public policy. The notion of a **social movement community** captures the idea that movements consist of networks of individuals, cultural groups, alternative institutions, and institutional supporters as well as political movement organizations (Buechler, 1990; Staggenborg, 1998). Moreover, movements also consist of more than the public protest events emphasized by the contentious politics approach. Although the contentious politics approach recognizes that movements can target authorities other than the state, critics charge that movements such as those centred on religion or self-help tend to be neglected along with less visible forms of collective action, such as efforts to change institutions and create new forms of culture. Consequently, a number of theorists have called for broadening our conception of social movements.

Mayer Zald (2000) suggests that we should view **"ideologically structured action"** as movement activity. He argues that movement-related activity occurs within such organizations as political parties, government agencies, and religious institutions, and that families and schools are important in socializing movement supporters. In short, action shaped by movement ideology can be found in a variety of institutions and structures of everyday life. David Snow (2004) argues that movements can be conceived as "collective challenges to systems or structures of authority," including various types of organizations and institutions and also sets of cultural beliefs and understandings. Thus, movement activity occurs in a wide range of venues, through a variety of forms of collective action. Movements consist of informal networks as well as formal organizations, and they produce culture and collective identity as well as political campaigns (cf. Armstrong, 2002; Diani, 1992; Melucci, 1989, 1996; Polletta and Jasper, 2001; Rupp and Taylor, 1999).

The danger, as Tilly and Wood (2013: 10–11) point out, is that "one may see social movements everywhere." In their approach, social movements consist of sustained campaigns directed at authorities that use the social movement repertoire of tactics and create public displays of worthiness, unity, numbers, and commitment. Movements can be compared to other forms of contentious politics such as conflict over policy within institutions. This approach has the merit of keeping the definition of social movements tied to the historical origins of the social movement that Tilly has so carefully documented. Nevertheless, studies of contemporary social movements such as the women's movement show that we cannot completely understand the maintenance and outcomes of important social movements without looking broadly at their cultural, institutional, and political manifestations (Staggenborg and Taylor, 2005).

In sum, despite commonalities, varying definitions of social movements are associated with different research emphases. The contentious politics definition of the social movement—as a sustained challenge to elites or other opponents by shifting coalitions of collective actors through a series of public campaigns—points to the political nature of social movements and their role in putting issues on the public agenda and changing public policies. McCarthy and Zald's view of social movements as preference structures leads us to focus on how preferences get transformed into organized movements through the enterprise of leaders and the creation of different types of movement organizations. Conceptualizations of social movements as including ideologically structured action, social movement communities, and challenges to different types of institutional authorities all point to the multiple arenas in which movements operate. These different emphases are not necessarily incompatible, and their usefulness depends in part on the nature of the movement being studied.

Outline of the Book

The field of social movements is an exciting one that contains a healthy mix of interesting theoretical ideas and empirical studies of real social movements. The best way to introduce the field is to look at some important movements, using the tools of social movement theory. The book highlights a few contemporary movements, including Indigenous peoples' movements, the women's movement, the LGBT movement, the environmental movement, and global movements for social justice. Although these are all progressive movements, they have provoked opposition in the form of right-wing or conservative movements, which are countermovements, particularly in the cases of the women's, LGBT, and environmental movements. The selection of movements discussed in subsequent chapters is based on our expertise and interest, and we make no claim of providing a comprehensive survey of social movements. However, the book does attempt to equip readers with an understanding of the theoretical questions and issues involved in studying social movements, which can be applied to a wide variety of movements. The substantive chapters in this book provide examples of how several important movements have been analyzed by social movement theorists. Although much of the research has been on movements in the United States, the book draws on studies from Canada and other Western countries, with some attention to global developments.

Before delving into the specifics of particular movements, we discuss the theoretical approaches, and issues stemming from those perspectives, that guide social movement theorists. Chapter 2 provides a review of several major theoretical traditions in North America and Western Europe: collective behaviour theory, resource mobilization and political process perspectives, and new social movement theory. We note various attempts to synthesize ideas from these approaches, as well as efforts to go beyond them. Our goal is to familiarize readers with the ideas in these perspectives and to highlight the contributions as well as limitations of each. Theories about social movements are important because they direct researchers to different types of questions regarding movements. Chapter 3 elaborates on the general types of issues studied by social movement theorists, which come out of the theoretical perspectives and guide studies of substantive movements. Because of the importance of the mass media to the movements described in the book, a section of the chapter is devoted to the role media play in contemporary social movements.

In Chapter 4, the historical importance of the 1960s cycle of protest for contemporary social movements is examined. We describe the American civil rights movement, which had a worldwide impact on strategies of protest and political consciousness, and the New Left student and anti-war movements of the 1960s in North America and Western Europe. This discussion is important to subsequent chapters because the modern movements to be discussed were part of this cycle of contention or were strongly influenced by it. The 1960s **protest cycle** has also influenced subsequent generations of activists in more recent waves of protest.

In Chapter 5, we analyze the mobilization of Indigenous protest that gained momentum during the cycle of protest of the 1960s, and relate Canadian Indigenous protest to broader trends in Indigenous protest elsewhere in the world. We consider the importance of critical events, political opportunities, organization and resources, and collective identity in the mobilization of Canadian Indigenous peoples.

In Chapter 6, we focus on the key question of what has happened to the contemporary women's movement since the 1960s. We examine the origins of the contemporary movement, the range of feminist activities, and how the women's movement has survived and changed over time, including its development within institutions, other social movements, and cultural venues. We also look at the role of anti-feminist countermovements in challenging feminist goals and channelling movement activism. The chapter demonstrates and explains the continuity and growth of feminism through its different waves and the expansion of the global women's movement.

In Chapter 7, we discuss the origins and strategies of the contemporary LGBT movement and the role played by factors such as political opportunity, state repression, and countermovement campaigns. We examine a variety of movement approaches, including liberationist, equal rights, and queer politics, and the outcomes that have been achieved in Canada and other countries.

In Chapter 8, we take up the problem of maintaining a movement that can deal with serious and ongoing environmental problems over many years. We examine problems of winning and maintaining public interest and individual participation, combating countermovements, and creating effective organizations and strategies. After discussing recent debates on movement strategy, we look at the mass-media–focused efforts of Greenpeace, green lobbies and consumer boycotts, and grassroots direct-action campaigns.

In Chapter 9, we focus on the movement for global justice that came to public attention with the demonstrations against the World Trade Organization (WTO) meetings in Seattle in 1999. In examining the origins of this global movement, we discuss the importance of the Canadian anti–free trade movement in generating a model for cross-national movement organization. We discuss the strategic and organizational challenges facing the movement as it brings together local and international activists and organizations from a variety of different social movements and attempts to influence international labour, environmental, and human rights standards. We then discuss other recent movements for social and economic justice, including the Occupy movement.

Chapter 10 concludes by tying together themes from the previous chapters and laying out important challenges for social movements. It stresses the importance of social movements in bringing about social and political change.

Discussion Questions

1. Which definition of social movements is most useful for understanding contemporary movements such as the environmental movement?

2. How do different definitions of social movements focus our attention on different aspects of movements?

3. What are the major tactics within the contemporary repertoire of collective action? What explains the use of these tactics in our society? How are these tactics changing with new communications technologies?

Suggested Readings

McCarthy, John D., and Mayer N. Zald. 1977. "Resource Mobilization and Social Movements: A Partial Theory," *American Journal of Sociology* 82, 6: 1212–41. This is one of the seminal statements on resource mobilization theory.

Tarrow, Sidney. 2011. *Power in Movement: Social Movements and Contentious Politics*, Revised and Updated Third Edition. Cambridge: Cambridge University Press. This book provides an important synthesis of theoretical and substantive themes in the field.

Tilly, Charles and Lesley J. Wood. 2013. *Social Movements, 1768–2012*, 3rd ed. Boulder, CO: Paradigm Publishers. This book is a very good summary of Tilly's extensive historical work on social movements.

2 Theories of Social Movements and Collective Action

Several major theoretical approaches have influenced the thinking of social movement scholars in Europe and North America. These theoretical approaches are important as perspectives that guide students of social movements to focus on particular issues, questions, and methods of inquiry. Often, researchers borrow from different theoretical approaches in carrying out their studies and in recent years theorists have attempted to synthesize the major approaches (Fligstein and McAdam, 2012; 2011; McAdam, Tarrow, and Tilly, 2001; Tilly and Tarrow, 2006). Few scholars in the study of social movements have aimed to build universal theories that attempt to make general statements about movements across time and place. Rather, researchers have generally recognized the importance of historical context and cultural differences, at the same time building a body of ideas about how movements operate within particular circumstances. Before the 1980s, European and North American scholars developed analytical approaches for the most part independently of one another, with "new social movement theory" originating in Europe and "collective behaviour" and "resource mobilization" theories coming mostly from the United States. Many cross-national collaborations and influences between Europeans and North Americans have since resulted in extensions and integrations of these theories.

This chapter begins with overviews of collective behaviour theory, resource mobilization and political process theories, and new social movement theory, showing how each of these approaches raises different types of questions and points to different ways of describing and analyzing social movements. After summarizing these major theoretical approaches, we look at efforts to fill gaps in these theories, integrate approaches, and create new ones. In Chapter 3, we discuss further some of the important issues raised by the theories outlined below.

Collective Behaviour Theory

A number of different perspectives are included in the category of **collective behaviour theory**, sometimes referred to as the classical model of social movements. Collective behaviour theories have also been labelled *strain* or *breakdown theories* because they typically posit that collective behaviour comes about during a period of social disruption, when grievances are deeply felt, rather than being a standard part of the political process (Jenkins, 1981; Marx and Wood, 1975; McAdam, 1999 [1982]; McPhail, 2006; Morris and Herring, 1987). Collective behaviour theorists have studied a wide variety of phenomena, including crowds, panics, mobs, riots, crazes, fads, religious cults and revivals, social movements, and revolutions. The study of crowds dates back to the late nineteenth century, when European theorists such as Gustave Le Bon (1895) tried to explain crowd behaviour by analyzing the psychology of the collective or large gathering. Le Bon emphasized the irrationality and abnormality of crowds, and his work has often been invoked by scholars criticizing the supposed tendency of collective behaviour theory to treat social movement participants as irrational and pathological. Some, such as Crossley (2002: 11), however, argue that such a portrayal of the perspective is a "gruesome caricature." Most collective behaviour theorists in fact reject the view that collective behaviour is irrational, although many are concerned with the psychological states of participants and the spontaneous dynamics of collective actions outside established structures.

In general, collective behaviour theories share several assumptions (Morris and Herring, 1987: 145). First, they see collective behaviour as existing outside of institutionalized structures, though some theorists note the linkages between institutional and non-institutional actions. Various forms of collective behaviour are connected insofar as they are all unstructured situations unbound by established norms. Second, collective behaviour theorists argue that social movements and other forms of collective behaviour arise as a result of some type of structural or cultural breakdown or strain such as a natural disaster, rapid social change, or dramatic event. Third, collective behaviour theorists assign an important role to the shared beliefs of participants in analyzing the emergence of social movements and other forms of collective behaviour. Although pre-existing organization and strategy are typically mentioned by collective behaviour theorists, they are not a major focus, whereas the psychological states of participants and emergent ideologies and forms of organization receive much attention. Beyond these similarities, there are major differences among collective behaviour approaches.

The Chicago School Approach to Collective Behaviour

The Chicago School approach to collective behaviour was initiated in the 1920s by Robert Park and Ernest Burgess (1921) and was developed by a number of other sociologists associated with the symbolic interactionist approach at the University of Chicago, including Herbert Blumer (1951), Ralph Turner and Lewis Killian (1957, 1972, 1987), and Kurt and Gladys Lang (1961). **Symbolic interactionism** is a social psychological theory that focuses on how actors construct meanings through social interaction. According to the Chicago School perspective, collective behaviour develops in situations where established systems of meaning and sources of information have broken down, forcing participants to construct new meanings to guide their behaviour (Morris and Herring, 1987: 147). Collective behaviour theorists are concerned with how participants in social movements manage to act collectively, creating goals, new organizational structures, and new culture. Turner and Killian emphasize the role of the "emergent norm" as a shared view of reality that justifies and co-ordinates collective behaviour, which McPhail (2006) calls a "feedback loop." In the case of social movements, which are complex and sustained forms of collective behaviour, emergent norms may become "highly elaborated ideologies such as the environmentalist's view of the consequences of ecological imbalance and the Marxist's view of class struggle" (Turner and Killian, 1987: 8). In emphasizing emergent norms, Turner and Killian recognize that not all grievances translate into collective behaviour; they have to be framed in such a way as to create feelings of injustice or outrage that motivate action (Pinard, 2011: 8–10). For example, environmentalists may be motivated by shared outrage that the planet is being destroyed by fossil fuel industries, but protests in the streets in response are relatively infrequent.

Thus, Chicago School collective behaviour theorists focus on the emergence of social movements and the creation of new forms of meaning, activity, and organization. Collective behaviour is a means of bringing about social change, and emergent forms of social order develop through the interactions of individuals in social movements. Ideology plays an important role in highlighting injustices and guiding collective behaviour, but the beliefs that govern this behaviour are not fixed; systems of belief emerge and develop as social movement actors interact with one another, the public, opponents, and authorities. Emergent norms may develop in response to a precipitating event or some type of extraordinary condition as individuals within pre-existing or new groups interact with one another and try out forms of action, revising their ideas and actions in response to changing events and opportunities (Turner and Killian, 1987: 10).

Smelser's Theory of Collective Behaviour

In his influential book *Theory of Collective Behavior* (1962), Neil Smelser presents a model consisting of six determinants. The model is "value added" in that each determinant or social condition adds value to the explanation; the conditions operate within the context of one another and together explain collective behaviour. First, conditions of *structural conduciveness* permit or encourage certain types of collective behaviour. For example, panics occur in money markets, rather than in financial systems where property is tied to kinship and cannot be easily transferred (Smelser, 1962: 15). Second, conditions of *structural strain* create real or anticipated deprivation; this strain, such as the threat of economic deprivation, combines with the condition of conduciveness. Third, the *growth and spread of a generalized belief* makes the situation meaningful to potential participants in collective behaviour; the generalized belief identifies the source and nature of the strain and suggests possible responses. Fourth, *precipitating factors*, such as a dramatic event, give the generalized beliefs a concrete target for collective action. For example, an incident of police brutality might provoke a race riot when it occurs in the context of conduciveness, strain, and a generalized belief (ibid., 17). Fifth, *mobilization for action* must occur, and Smelser notes that leadership is particularly important in mobilizing participants. Sixth, *social control* may act to prevent the collective behaviour, perhaps by minimizing strains, or to limit the scope of the collective behaviour. The potential or actual episode of collective behaviour will be affected by the actions of police, the courts, the press, community leaders, and other agents of social control.

Theorists have found the idea of a value-added model useful, and a number of studies have shown the factors identified by Smelser to be important in predicting collective action. However, scholars have also raised a number of criticisms. Smelser's theory, along with other breakdown theories, has been criticized for relying too heavily on structural strains to explain social movements. Critics have argued that no clear criteria exist for identifying strain in a society; once a social movement or other form of collective behaviour occurs, it is always possible to find some type of strain, making the argument tautological (Useem, 1975: 9; Wilson, 1973: 35). Moreover, the theory seems to assume that societies are normally stable and that strains, and the social movements that accompany them, are unusual. In fact, strains may be a fairly constant feature of societies, and the rise of movements may be better explained by factors such as political opportunities, resources, and organization. Critics have also objected to Smelser's characterization of generalized beliefs as "short-circuited" in the sense of bypassing normal routines and controls and "akin to magical beliefs" insofar as expectations of the consequences of collective action may be unrealistic (Smelser, 1962: 8). Smelser and other collective behaviour theorists have often been lumped with Le Bon and accused of treating participants in collective behaviour as "irrational." However, collective behaviour theorists have vehemently denied this charge, arguing that their approaches do not assume irrationality on the part of movement participants (Killian, 1994; Smelser, 1970; Turner, 1981).

Mass Society Theory

One version of collective behaviour theory, **mass society theory**, views collective behaviour as an extreme response to social isolation. Mass society theory takes off from the Durkheimian notion that social stability is maintained by the existence of common values that are transmitted and sustained through various social institutions. A "mass society" is one in which there are few secondary or intermediate groups, such as religious groups or community organizations, to bind people together and keep them attached to the mainstream society. In *The Politics of Mass Society*, William Kornhauser (1959) argued that social changes, such as rapid industrialization and urbanization or economic depressions, uproot people from their normal associations, as in the case of new immigrants to cities or unemployed workers. Consequently, individuals become isolated from social and political institutions. This creates social "atomization" and feelings of "alienation and anxiety" that make people susceptible to recruitment by social movements such as the German Nazi movement. In a popular version of mass society theory, Eric Hoffer (1951) argued in *The True Believer* that alienated, fanatical, and irrational individuals participate in social movements as a means of finding an identity and sense of belonging in a rapidly changing society.

A large body of empirical research has challenged mass society theory, showing that the theory is essentially wrong (Jenkins, 1981: 92–3). In fact, it is not isolated individuals who are most likely to be drawn into social movements, but just the opposite. Research shows that individuals who are tied into social networks, and who participate in organizations, are most likely to be recruited into social movements. Whereas mass society theorists viewed organizations as playing a conservative role in keeping individuals from participating in collective action, they failed to appreciate the role of pre-existing organizations in mobilizing participants for social movements (Morris and Herring, 1987: 155). For example, although many people attribute the famous Montgomery bus boycott to the spontaneous actions of a lone person, Rosa Parks, who refused to sit at the back of a bus, the movement was actually backed by African American churches and organizations that provided a pre-existing organizational base through which the civil rights movement mobilized local communities, refocusing the cultural content of the churches on movement messages (Morris, 1984: 96–97).

Relative Deprivation Theory

Relative deprivation theory is based on the observation made by Alexis de Tocqueville and others that people often rebel when things are improving; it is not the most deprived groups that engage in collective action, but those who seem to be improving their positions or who are among the best off within an aggrieved group. When conditions start to improve, expectations rise, but when the rate of improvement does not match expectations, people feel deprived. For example, Freeman (1975) argues that support for the American women's movement increased as women gained access to education but did not achieve commensurate access to high-paying occupations.

Deprivation is *relative* because people feel dissatisfied with their situations relative to what they think they deserve, and they assess what they deserve by comparing their progress to that of other groups. Thus, college-educated women might compare themselves to men of the same educational levels in assessing their occupational satisfaction. Social changes, such as large-scale economic shifts, generate feelings of relative deprivation. In this situation, people's expectations rise as they experience change, and then they are frustrated by the gap between their expectations and their actual situations. When people become angry and frustrated, according to relative deprivation theory, they rebel.

Relative deprivation theories were popular in the 1960s and 1970s (e.g., Davies, 1962, 1971; Gurr, 1970), but they have since been strongly criticized on a number of grounds (Gurney and Tierney, 1982; Jenkins, 1981). One difficulty is that relative deprivation studies typically infer psychological states of relative deprivation from objective indicators such as unemployment rates. Studies designed to test the theory have found little evidence that such objective measures of relative deprivation are good predictors of various types of rebellions; instead, factors such as organizational capacities and governmental sanctions are better predictors of collective action (Jenkins, 1981: 100–1). Although feelings of relative deprivation may be present, they are not likely to generate collective action in the absence of other factors such as resources and organization. Moreover, feelings of relative deprivation may be generated through participation in a movement, rather than being a precondition for the movement (ibid., 103). For example, women who worked in the New Left began to feel deprived relative to their male comrades, who occupied the most important roles in the movement and ignored women's complaints (Freeman, 1975: 57–62).

Resource Mobilization and Political Process Theories

In the 1970s, the focus of North American social movement research began to shift away from the concerns of collective behaviour theory to those raised by newly emerging **resource mobilization** and **political process** approaches (Gamson, 1990; [1975]; McAdam, 1999; McCarthy and Zald, 1973, 1977; Oberschall, 1973; Tilly, 1978). These new models of social movements and collective action resulted in part from the experiences of social movement theorists with movements of the 1960s and their criticisms of classical collective behaviour theories for inadequacies in explaining the new wave of protest. Although the criticisms did not apply equally to all versions of collective behaviour theory, they helped to shape the new perspectives, which departed from past theories in important ways (Jenkins, 1983). First, collective behaviour theory explanations for the rise of social movements and collective action were considered wrong or inadequate. Mass society theory, as we have seen, was not supported by empirical studies, and resource mobilization theorists argued that socially connected people, rather than social isolates, are most likely to be mobilized for collective action. Strain theories also failed to explain the rise of social movements insofar as neither large-scale strains in social systems nor individual discontents lead directly to collective action. The extent of movement mobilization and participation in a population cannot be predicted by the amount of frustration or suffering experienced by people. Second, resource mobilization and political process theorists rejected what they perceived as a sharp disjuncture in collective behaviour theory between "normal" or routine actions and collective action. The newer perspectives emphasized the continuities between collective actions and institutionalized actions, as social movements were seen as a continuation of the political process, albeit by disorderly means (Gamson, 1990: 139). Whereas collective behaviour theories, by emphasizing the motivations of individuals, focused on social movements as psychological phenomena, the newer perspectives treated social movements as political phenomena (McAdam, 1999: 11–19). Individual participants were seen as rational actors pursuing their interests, and it was argued that movements arise out of pre-existing organization, engaging in both institutionalized and non-institutionalized forms of action.

Resource Mobilization Theory

Early resource mobilization theorists argued that strains or grievances can nearly always be found; the mobilization of social movements requires resources, organization, and opportunities for collective action. As the label "resource mobilization" suggests, **resources** are seen as central to successful collective action in this approach, and a wide variety of studies demonstrate linkages between resource availability and collective action (Edwards and McCarthy, 2004). Resources include both *tangible* assets, such as funding, and *intangible* assets, such as the commitment of participants (Freeman, 1979). Edwards and McCarthy (2004: 125–8) identify various types of resources used and created by social movements: *moral resources*, such as legitimacy; *cultural resources*, including tactical repertoires and strategic know-how; *social-organizational resources*, including movement infrastructures, networks, and organizational structures; *human resources*, such as the labour and experience of activists; and *material resources*, such as money and office space.

In their seminal articles advancing an entrepreneurial-organizational version of the theory, McCarthy and Zald (1973, 1977) argue that **movement entrepreneurs** play an important role in defining movement issues by drawing on public sentiments and increasing public demand for change. While stressing the importance of resources such as skills, money, and time for movement mobilization, they note that resources do not necessarily come from **beneficiary constituents**, who are members of the aggrieved groups that stand to gain from the successes of a movement; rather, they may come from **conscience constituents**, who contribute to movements but do not personally benefit from their achievements (McCarthy and Zald, 1977: 1221–2). In some instances, the ability to mobilize conscience constituents determines movement effectiveness. For example, the periods of the most widespread and successful Canadian Indigenous mobilization occurred when First Nations were able to link their mobilization to national organizations as well as gain the support of non-Indigenous organizations and peoples (Ramos, 2006; 2008). Other researchers, however, emphasize the importance of internal resources for oppressed groups. In the case of the American civil rights movement, Morris (1984) found that black churches and other community institutions provided resources that were critical to movement success.

Social movement organizations and their leaders are typically important in mobilizing resources for movements, whether from beneficiary or conscience constituents. Resource mobilization theorists have called attention to the varying structures of social movement organizations that influence their longevity and strategic choices. Studies have suggested that organizations with more formalized or bureaucratic structures are better able to sustain a movement over time, whereas informal organizations are better at innovating tactics and taking quick action in response to events (Gamson, 1990; Staggenborg, 1988, 1989). For example, the environmental movement includes a wide variety of organizations, which have different types of structures and engage in different strategies and tactics. Loosely structured and participatory groups such as Earth First! tend to attract activists who are willing to take risks and engage in direct actions; such groups have organized blockades to prevent logging and have engaged in other acts of civil disobedience to protect the environment. In contrast, bureaucratic organizations such as the Sierra Club or David Suzuki Foundation are more involved in lobbying governments and are better able to raise funds to maintain a large organization with paid staff.

Resource mobilization theorists have identified various types of **mobilizing structures**, which are used to organize participants in social movements. These include political movement organizations, but also formal and informal networks, cultural groups, and other organizational vehicles that movements use to recruit participants and organize action campaigns (McAdam et al., 1996: 3). Della Porta, Andretta, Mosca, and Reiter (2006) show that the global justice movement is largely shaped by a new structure of mobilization, the alternate forum or mock summit, which parallel international meetings such as the G8 or European Social Forum. This structure allows activists to articulate a globalization from below, one that is more socially just. Others examining the new tactics related to the Arab Spring argue that social media promote rhizomic structures with the appearance of no central plan but a core network that keeps information and mobilization flowing (Castells, 2012).

Political Process Theory

Political process theory developed as an approach that both builds on resource mobilization theory and attempts to correct deficiencies in the earlier approach. While resource mobilization theory emphasizes the importance of elite support for social movements such as foundation funding, it downplays the role of an aggrieved mass base (McAdam, 1999: 25–9). In his influential study of the civil rights movement, McAdam (1999) identifies three types of factors that are critical to the mobilization of social movements: the degree of organization in an aggrieved community, their level of consciousness or "cognitive liberation," and the "structure of political opportunities." All of these factors are influenced by larger socio-economic processes, such as the decline of cotton as a cash crop and the movement of blacks from rural to urban areas, which strengthened black churches and black colleges as organizational bases of the civil rights movement.

The political process approach emphasizes the interactions of social movement actors with the state and the role of political opportunities in the mobilization and outcomes of social movements. Political process theorists argue that social movements are most likely to emerge when potential collective actors perceive that conditions are favourable. The concept of **political opportunity** refers generally to features of the political environment that influence movement emergence and success, but specific definitions of political opportunity differ considerably (Meyer, 2004). Sidney Tarrow's (2011: 164–7) elaboration of the elements of political opportunity is perhaps the most widely employed schema. He conceives of political opportunity as including the extent of openness in the polity, shifts in political alignments, divisions among elites, and the availability of influential allies. When opportunities expand generally, a variety of movements may mobilize, resulting in a **cycle of contention**, which is "a phase of heightened conflict across the social system" (Tarrow, 2011: 199). For example, during the 1960s a large number of protest movements mobilized in Europe and North America, including the civil rights movement, Indigenous peoples' movements, the women's movement, the LGBT movement, the environmental movement, and the New Left. Moreover, movements are not only influenced by political opportunities; they can also create opportunities for themselves and other movements. Tarrow suggests that movements that are "early risers" in a protest cycle may open up opportunities for later movements by demonstrating that targets are vulnerable to collective action.

In addition to affecting the emergence of social movements, political opportunities may alter the strategies and outcomes of protest. However, opportunities for mobilization and opportunities to effect change are sometimes different (Meyer, 2004: 136–7). Social movement theorists have recognized that *threats* are as likely as opportunities to mobilize activists by creating feelings of outrage and urgency. It may be more difficult to mobilize participants when authorities or other elites are sympathetic to movement goals because supporters may feel that there is no need for collective action. When threats arise or negative outcomes occur, there may be little opportunity for effecting change but great opportunity for mobilization as movement supporters become alarmed by unfavourable changes. When a countermovement mobilizes to oppose movement goals, movement supporters are likely to respond with heightened activity. For example, the rise of the masculinism movement in Quebec in reaction to feminists securing greater rights and protections for women led to the targeting of radical feminists and disputes over the funding of women's groups. This in turn obliged the feminist movement in Quebec to mobilize in defence of hard-fought victories, resulting in greater solidarity among feminists (Blais and Dupuis-Déri, 2012).

A Synthetic Approach

By the 1980s and 1990s, resource mobilization and political process approaches dominated North American social movement theory. The two approaches were sometimes treated as distinct models (McAdam, 1999) and sometimes as two variants of resource mobilization theory, with a political process version of resource mobilization theory associated with theorists such as William Gamson, Anthony Oberschall, and Charles Tilly and an entrepreneurial-organizational version of resource mobilization theory formulated by John McCarthy and Mayer Zald (McCarthy and Zald, 2002; Perrow, 1979). Increasingly, however, resource mobilization and political process approaches could be seen as part of one evolving perspective, with many of the same theorists contributing to each and attempting to synthesize the model (McAdam et al., 1988, 1996). Key elements of the synthetic approach became so essential to social movement studies that McAdam, Tarrow, and Tilly (2001) went so far as to refer to the synthesis as the "classical social movement agenda."

The synthetic resource mobilization/political process model views social movements as political entities aiming to create social change. Scholars have analyzed various features of the movement environment and of movement organizations and strategies that influence the mobilization and outcomes of collective action. The approach initially downplayed grievances and ideology, as these were thought to be overemphasized by collective behaviour theorists, who focused on individual discontent as the driving force behind collective action. Later theorists sympathetic to resource mobilization/political process theory developed the concept of **collective action frames** as a

way of capturing the importance of meanings and ideas in stimulating protest (Benford and Snow, 2000). Collective action frames are interpretations
of issues and events that inspire and legitimate collective action, and *framing*
is an important activity of movement leaders and organizations. The **framing perspective** emphasizes the role of movements in constructing cultural
meanings, as movement leaders and organizations frame issues in particular
ways to identify injustices, attribute blame, propose solutions, and motivate collective action. Cogent framing is critical to movement expansion; for
example, Occupy Wall Street's "We are the 99%" proved to be an effective
frame to which many bystanders responded and which brought discussion of
inequality to the forefront of North American debates. In what is now a large
literature on collective action frames, movement theorists have analyzed the
role of framing in a variety of movement processes. Snow and Benford (1992)
distinguish between **master frames**, which are generic types of frames
available for use by a number of different social movements, and movement-
specific collective action frames, which can be derived from master frames.
They argue that the availability of an innovative master frame helps to
explain the emergence of a protest cycle consisting of a number of different
social movements. For example, they suggest that the "rights frame" was a
master frame used by the civil rights movement and adapted by a number of
other movements such as the women's movement and the gay rights movement in the protest cycle of the 1960s. Dominique Clément (2008) shows
that the human rights frame largely contributed to a rights-based state in
Canada, cemented in the country's Constitution. In addition to their role in
the growth of a protest cycle, master frames can be used to bring different
movements together in coalitions. Gerhards and Rucht (1992) analyze the
ways in which organizers of multi-movement campaigns extended master
frames dealing with peace and globalization to address the concerns of a
variety of different movement activists, such as feminists, environmentalists,
and union members. In a study of cross-movement activism in Vancouver,
Carroll and Ratner (1996) found that the use of a master frame stressing the
"political-economy account of injustice" brought together activists from the
labour, peace, and feminist movements.

Opposing movements often compete with one another to develop the
most convincing frames. In the English Canadian women's movement,
for example, the frame of "womanhood" as challenging heteronormative
and middle class definitions versus the more traditional conceptualiza-
tion was key to struggles between NAC and REAL in their attempts to vie
for potential supporters and to alter public opinion (Bashevkin, 1998). In
addition to framing competitions between movements and countermovements, *frame disputes* often take place within social movements (Benford,
1993). For example, divergent conceptualizations of environmental justice
are employed by radical and mainstream environmental groups. Disputes

over frames are common because social movements are not unified actors, but typically consist of many different types of groups and individuals with varying ideological and strategic perspectives. Framing disputes may occur either within or between movement organizations, and their consequences may include the decline of some types of movement organizations, the depletion of resources that could have been used to accomplish goals, factionalism, and lack of cohesiveness in a movement (ibid., 694–7). Although the impacts of frames are often difficult to assess, movements that succeed in creating persuasive and coherent frames appear better able to attract movement participants, form coalitions, win public approval and media attention, and influence authorities. Moreover, effective frames may help movements to overcome a lack of political opportunities (Polletta and Ho, 2006).

The concepts of *political opportunities*, *mobilizing structures*, and *cultural framing* became the core elements of North American social movement theory in the 1990s (McAdam et al., 1996). Attention to political opportunities reflected the state-centred approach of political process theory, and conceptions of mobilizing structures drew on the entrepreneurial-organizational version of resource mobilization theory. The concept of framing provided a means for resource mobilization theorists to bring ideas and cultural elements into social movement theory, but the strategic approach to framing did not satisfy critics who argued for a broader approach to culture and ideology. Consequently, there was a "cultural turn" in social movement theory as scholars began to examine a variety of cultural processes. **Discourse analysis** became important as theorists looked at questions such as how actors construct frames and discursive strategies using the genres available in the contexts where framing occurs (Steinberg, 1998: 856). Expanding on the concept of political opportunities, Ferree et al. (2002) use the concept of a **discursive opportunity structure** to examine the factors, such as cultural context and mass media norms, that shape movement discourse in different countries. Some, such as Rholinger (2007), recognize that such structures create fields of discourse that represent the spaces and issues that are packaged into frames. More broadly, a number of movement theorists have proposed the notion of a **cultural opportunity structure** or "cultural opportunities" to refer to elements of cultural environments, such as ideologies, that facilitate and constrain collective action along with political opportunities (McAdam, 1994; Noonan, 1995). This cultural turn in North American social movement theory has been influenced by European new social movement theories, which emphasize symbolic activities in cultural spheres as well as instrumental actions directed at the state (Buechler, 1995: 442).

New Social Movement Theory and Collective Identity

In Europe, the approach known as **new social movement theory** developed independently of North American theories, emphasizing the new types of social movements that emerged in "post-industrial" or "advanced capitalist" society, including the peace, environmental, gay and lesbian, student, and women's movements. New social movement theorists argue that these movements differ in structure, type of constituents, and ideology from the "old" movements of industrial society, notably the labour movement. Among their common characteristics, new social movements rely on a range of networks and informal, participatory structures rather than on centralized organizations; they are concerned with the cultural as well as the political sphere; they appeal to many diverse participants as opposed to a limited number of constituents motivated largely by economic interests; they involve the construction of collective identities; and they focus on a broad range of values related to quality of life (Buechler, 2011: 159–62). As is the case with collective behaviour and resource mobilization perspectives, a number of different views fall under the category of new social movement theory (Buechler, 1995, 2011; Pichardo, 1997). Some theorists have been concerned with how large-scale socio-economic trends are related to the emergence of new social movements, while others have focused on changes in the sites of conflict and nature of civil society in an "information society."

Scholars concerned with the effects of modernization argue that new movements mobilized because there are new grievances in a post-industrial society, resulting in new values, new forms of action, and new constituencies (Klandermans, 1986: 21). For example, German theorist Jürgen Habermas (1984, 1987) draws attention to the new goals and demands associated with movements in post-industrial societies. He argues that new social movements are concerned with defence of the "lifeworld," that is, the sphere of life not governed by instrumental, economic concerns but where real debate and communication create normative consensus. Because political and economic institutions are interfering in this realm, new movements have arisen to defend against bureaucratic and economic intrusions and to raise issues related to quality of life, democratic participation, and identity. Although economic concerns remain important in new social movement theory, the nature of the economic concerns has changed and new concerns have been added. For example, new international movements have emerged in an era of global capitalism with new kinds of grievances such as the effects of world trade and environmental degradation. "Post-materialist" values, focusing on quality-of-life issues, are central to new social movements (Inglehart, 1990).

Scholars who focus on the new sites of conflict that accompany large-scale transformations stress the various processes involved in the creation and ongoing construction of social movements. Manuel Castells focuses on the ways in which urban space has been transformed by capitalist dynamics such as commodification and consumerism; urban social movements arise to contest the use of urban space and to fight for goals such as state provision of public goods and community self-management (Buechler, 2011: 162–3). He also recognizes that in contemporary society communication power and information politics are key tools in contesting power because of the rise of the Internet and what he calls and increasingly "networked" society (Castells, 2012).

One key process emphasized by new social movement theorists is the creation of **collective identity**. This refers to the sense of shared experiences and values that connects individuals to movements and gives participants a sense of "collective agency," or the feeling that they can effect change through collective action (Snow, 2001). Castells emphasizes cultural identity in resisting bureaucratization and creating genuine community in urban settings (Buechler, 2011: 163). Alberto Melucci (1989, 1996) focuses on how collective identities are continually constructed by small groups in the "submerged networks" of everyday life. He sees social movements not as collections of relatively stable movement organizations or as unified actors, but as fluid networks that can erupt into collective action from time to time. To understand how social movements are constructed, we need to look at the formation and maintenance of the cognitive frameworks and social relationships that form the basis of collective action (Melucci, 1988: 331). Before a movement becomes visible, there is a period of "latency" when a new collective identity is emerging. For example, in North America women began to develop a feminist identity within civil rights and New Left student and peace movement networks (Mueller, 1994). Once a movement is underway, the "collective" is continually constructed, and failure to maintain solidarity may lead to tensions in the movement and a decline in collective action (Melucci, 1988: 333). In the case of the women's movement, different organizations and networks formed around various formulations of movement identity (Mueller, 1994: 247–8). As relationships are formed within the submerged networks of new social movements and new collective identities are constructed, activists produce new cultural models and symbolic challenges. For new social movement theorists, these cultural innovations are a key contribution of social movements to social change.

New social movement theory's focus on culture and collective identity has been influential in redirecting North American movement theory. A number of scholars attempting to fill in gaps in resource mobilization and political process approaches have adopted Melucci's (1988: 343) view of collective identity as a process that involves the formulation of cognitive frameworks, the activation of relationships among actors, and the investment of emotions. Recent studies have focused on collective identity to explain how interests get defined and movements emerge, how people are motivated to participate in collective action, how strategic choices are made, and what cultural impacts movements have (Polletta and Jasper, 2001: 284). Moreover, theorists interested in culture and collective identity also began to emphasize the role of emotions in protest, which helps to explain such problems as why individuals participate, how collective identity is created, and why movements continue or decline (Goodwin et al., 2001; Jasper, 1998). For example, Langman (2013) analyzes the Occupy movement as a new social movement that arose in response to a crisis of capitalism and created strong emotions, a collective identity, and a moral vision of a new type of society. Castells (2011) also notes the feelings of anger and indignation that fuelled the Occupy movement.

Along with its influence, however, new social movement theory generated much debate among movement theorists. In particular, scholars questioned how "new" the movements in post-industrial societies really are with regard to the forms of collective action employed, organizational structures created, and issues addressed. Charles Tilly (1988) argues that, from a historical perspective, recent social movements such as the environmental movement and the women's movement basically employ the same repertoire of actions as nineteenth-century movements, including forming associations, demonstrating, and petitioning. In response to the claim of new social movement theorists that new social movements are loosely structured, Dieter Rucht (1988) shows that in fact movements such as the environmental movement contain a mix of different organizational forms, including both bureaucratic organizations and grassroots collectives. And, disputing the idea that concerns with identity are new, Craig Calhoun (1993) shows that nineteenth-century social movements such as the labour movement were also concerned with issues of identity as, for example, they mobilized workers with different ethnic and regional backgrounds. Carroll and Ratner (1995) note both the historical importance of collective identity to labour movements and the need for contemporary unions to alter bureaucratic forms of organization and reconstruct collective identities in order to survive large-scale economic globalization and to attract workers such as women and visible minorities. In their research on labour organizations in Vancouver, they find that labour activists were involved in cross-movement coalitions, open to "cultural politics" such as feminist music and gay pride events, and sensitive to the concerns of a variety of different groups.

Thus, the distinction between "old" and "new" social movements may be difficult to defend on historical grounds of collective identity and organizational preferences. Nevertheless, new social movement theory's focus on collective identity and organizational preferences has been valuable in directing attention to some central theoretical issues such as the connection between large-scale features of society and social movements and the importance of culture, identity, and everyday life in the mobilization and outcomes of social movements.

New Directions in Social Movement Theory

Recent challenges to social movement theory come from different directions, yet voice surprisingly similar concerns. Some critics of the political process approach have argued that the theory is overly structural, focusing on the relatively stable **"political opportunity structure"** that influences movement mobilization and outcomes (Goodwin and Jasper, 1999). According to these critics, the structural focus neglects the agency of movement activists, who respond to opportunities and in some cases create them, as well as cultural elements of movements and their environments. Social networks, for example, are treated as structures that mobilize participants, but the ideas and emotions transmitted through networks are often overlooked. Culture is subsumed under framing activities, while a broader understanding of how culture constrains and facilitates collective action is underdeveloped.

McAdam, Tarrow, and Tilly (2001) argue that the political process model, which they helped to develop, is too static, failing to capture the dynamic interactions of contentious politics. That is, the model identifies key variables, such as political opportunities, but doesn't provide a way to examine the processes involved in collective action. For example, how do political opportunities become visible to potential challengers and perceived as an opportunity? McAdam et al. argue for a new approach that will uncover the underlying mechanisms and processes of change. While political process theory works best in analyzing relatively unified movements in democratic polities, their dynamic contentious politics approach is developed by comparing different types of contentious politics—movements, revolutions, strike waves, nationalism, and so forth—in a wide range of settings. To create a more dynamic model of contentious politics, McAdam et al. argue that opportunities and threats should be treated not as objective structures but as "subject to attribution," so that the perceptions of activists are important. Mobilizing structures should not be treated simply as pre-existing organizational sites but as structures that are actively appropriated by collective actors. Framing, similarly, is not just a strategic tool, but involves "the interactive construction of disputes among challengers, their opponents, elements of the state, third parties, and the media." Collective action involves interaction, and mobilization "occurs throughout an episode of contention" (ibid., 43–5). McAdam et al. aim to understand how collective actors attribute threats and opportunities, appropriate mobilizing structures, construct frames and meanings, and innovate collective action tactics.

In short, several of the major developers of political process theory agree with their critics that a more social constructionist approach to social movements and collective action is needed to focus on the perceptions and strategies of activists (Kurzman, 2004). Or, as Oliver et al. (2003) note, "there is a growing appreciation for the need to integrate structural political theories of movements with constructivist theories rooted in social psychology and cultural sociology." Klandermans (1997) discusses the interaction of structural factors, such as social networks, with social psychological factors, such as cognitive information processing, in the process of recruitment to social movements. Buechler (2000, 2002) proposes a "structural approach to social movements" that recognizes the interrelationships of large-scale patterns and human agency. Polletta (1997, 2004) argues that social movement theorists have erred in treating culture and structure as distinct entities, tending to equate culture with agency and structure with politics. In reality, culture, defined as "the symbolic dimensions of all structures, institutions, and practices" (Polletta, 2004: 100), constrains as well as enables collective action, and political opportunities have cultural dimensions.

Conclusion

Theorists of social movements and collective action continue to grapple with how best to integrate culture and politics, emotions and interests, macro-level changes and micro-level interactions. Ultimately, theories are important insofar as they help us to understand the rise, development, and decline of social movements and to investigate key issues in the study of collective action. Despite efforts at synthesis, distinct theories focus on different aspects of social movements and lead to different research questions. Table 2.1 outlines the differing views on origins, focuses, and outcomes of the major theoretical approaches to understanding social movements. Collective behaviour theories are important in pointing to the grievances and breakdowns in routine that may result from critical events and social changes and the importance of ideologies in mobilizing activists around these grievances. They tend to see protest as occurring outside the normal political process and as resulting in new forms of organization and new social understandings. Resource mobilization and political process theories focus much more on the role of pre-existing organizational structures, resources, and political opportunities in explaining the origins of movements, and they focus on the mobilizing structures, framing efforts, and opportunities that affect the maintenance and outcomes of movements. In this approach, social movements are an ordinary part of the political process, although they tend to employ disorderly protest rather than the established practices of insiders with routine access to the political system. In the new social movement approach, theorists emphasize both how large-scale changes affect the organization and goals of movements and how movements create new cultural forms and identities and develop ideas and strategies within the structures of contemporary society. Their approach leads to an emphasis on the ongoing creation of movement identities and movement cultures that sustain social movements and allow for periodic protests.

Table 2.1 Major Theories of Social Movements

Theoretical Perspective	Origins of Movements	Important Features and Focuses	Key Outcomes of Movements
Collective Behaviour	Social disruptions, strains, grievances; precipitating events	Social psychology of protest; emergent organization and norms; protest outside institutional structures	New meanings and forms of organization
Resource Mobilization and Political Process	Pre-existing organization; resources; political opportunities and threats; master frames	Connections between social movements and political process; mobilizing structures; framing strategies; institutional and non-institutional forms of action	New resources, organizations, and frames; cultural and political changes
New Social Movement	Large-scale changes; everyday networks and organizational structures; new types of grievances	Collective identity; submerged networks; new types of structures, constituents, and ideologies	New types of values, identities, and organizations; cultural innovations

These major theories of social movements all contribute to the formulation of research questions by social movement scholars. In investigating different issues related to theoretical approaches, scholars add to a growing body of knowledge about the mechanisms and processes underlying movement mobilization and outcomes. In the following chapter, we identify some of the important issues that scholars have examined in studying various social movements and elaborate on some of the themes touched upon in describing the major theoretical approaches.

Discussion Questions

1. How might a theory of social movements influence how a movement is studied and analyzed?

2. What different questions about movements and ways of analyzing them are raised by collective behaviour, resource mobilization/political process, and new social movement theories?

3. How are large-scale social changes important to each of the major theories of social movements?

Suggested Readings

Buechler, Steven M. 2011. *Understanding Social Movements: Theories from the Classical Era to the Present*. Boulder, CO: Paradigm Publishers. This is a very readable discussion of major theories of social movements and changes over time in theoretical approaches.

Jenkins, J. Craig. 1981. "Sociopolitical Movements," in S.L. Long, ed., *Handbook of Political Behavior*, vol. 4. New York: Plenum Publishers, 81–154. This is a very good review essay detailing theoretical approaches to social movements.

Nash, Kate and Alan Scott, eds. 2001. *Blackwell Companion to Political Sociology*. Malden, MA: Blackwell. An encyclopaedia of North American political sociology, this book is a one-stop resource that covers the main debates and innovations in this area of sociology.

3

Issues in the Study of Social Movements and Collective Action

Theories such as those reviewed in the previous chapter aim to explain the origins, growth and decline, and consequences of social movements and collective action. In this chapter, we identify key issues and elaborate on theoretical ideas about these concerns, drawing on the major theories of collective action. The issues explored by social movement scholars range from macro-level questions about large-scale structural changes to meso-level organizational dynamics and micro-level questions about individual decisions and interactions. Table 3.1 lists the kinds of questions that are asked at each of these levels of research. One of the challenges for theorists is to connect these levels of analysis in their explanations of social movements and collective action. The various issues to be covered are interrelated, and the following discussion is organized around the central categories of movement emergence, maintenance and decline, and outcomes. Under each of these broad headings, more specific problems are discussed. A separate discussion of social movements and mass media is also included because this topic is particularly relevant to several subsequent chapters dealing with specific movements. Following discussion of these substantive topics, we provide a short discussion of some of the methods used to study issues in social movement research.

Movement Emergence: Mobilization and Recruitment

Movements typically do not emerge suddenly, and new movements are often linked to previous ones. **Mobilization** is the process whereby a group that shares grievances or interests gains collective control over resources (Tilly, 1978: 54). The **recruitment** of individuals to movements is part of the broader process of mobilization, involving the commitment of individual resources, such as time, money, and skills, to a cause. Mobilization and recruitment are ongoing processes rather than one-time events, as groups challenging the social and political status quo need to continually maintain control over resources and keep individuals involved following their initial

Table 3.1 Key Issues in the Study of Social Movements

Macro (Large-Scale) Level

- How large-scale changes and events alter resources and organizational structures and create grievances that stimulate collective action
- How cultural and political opportunities facilitate the emergence of social movements
- How cycles of contention arise and spread
- How master frames originate and diffuse into a culture
- How changing political, cultural, and economic conditions affect the ongoing strategies and growth, maintenance, and decline of a social movement
- How social movements contribute to large-scale cultural and political changes that affect subsequent collective action
- How countermovements emerge in response to social movements

Meso (Organizational) Level

- What resources are available to groups and what organizational structures tie group members together prior to movement emergence
- How leaders use mobilizing structures, master frames, and cultural and material resources to organize movements
- How leaders and movement organizations frame injustices and recognize opportunities for collective action
- How collective identities are developed within structures of everyday life
- How the organizational structures of movement organizations affect maintenance and strategies
- How collective campaigns are mobilized and how they affect subsequent movement organization and collective action
- How coalitions are formed and maintained within and across social movements
- What are the impacts of interactions of movement organizations with other organizations, such as countermovement groups, established interest groups and institutions, government agencies, and mass media?

Micro (Individual) Level

- How social networks lead individuals to movement organizations
- How individuals come to believe that collective action is necessary and effective
- How outrage and other emotions are generated to motivate participation
- How individuals decide that the benefits of collective action are worth the costs
- How individuals take on collective identities and feel solidarity with a group
- Why individuals sustain or terminate their participation in social movements
- How individuals are affected by their participation in social movements

recruitment. We begin by looking at major factors in the mobilization of a social movement and then turn to the issue of individual recruitment and participation.

Influences on Mobilization

A number of factors are involved in mobilization, including large-scale socio-economic and political changes, opportunities and threats, critical events, pre-existing or emergent organization, leadership, resources, and frames. Collective behaviour, political process, and new social movement theorists have all pointed to the importance of large-scale social changes in stimulating social movements. Urbanization, for example, creates social problems, such as poor housing conditions, that lead to grievances among particular groups. Grievances do not automatically lead to mobilization and, as resource mobilization theorists have argued, some grievances are relatively constant over time. However, many grievances, such as unemployment rates, do vary over time and may be the triggers for movement mobilization and individual participation (Pinard, 2011: chapter 2). Large-scale changes affect grievances and they can also alter the organization and resources of groups. Leaders can organize participants through pre-existing structures as well as new movement organizations, using the cultural and material resources associated with them. In the case of the American civil rights movement, socio-economic and political changes were important to the rise of the movement. The decline of cotton as a cash crop in the United States created favourable conditions for the emergence of a civil rights movement (McAdam, 1999: 77), including the migration of many southern blacks to cities, where they were concentrated in black neighbourhoods and could support indigenous institutions. Urban black churches, for example, had far more members and better finances than rural ones, allowing them to support the ministers who became leaders of the Southern civil rights movement (Morris, 1984).

Both the resources controlled by a group and the extent of organization among members of a group or collectivity prior to movement mobilization are important factors. If individuals already share membership in some of the same organizations, they have a pre-existing communications network, resources, and leaders that can be mobilized; in some cases, blocs of people are recruited rapidly through pre-existing organizations (Oberschall, 1973: 125). Numerous studies find that social networks help to recruit individuals into social movements. Leadership is also important, either in the form of indigenous leaders or movement entrepreneurs who define issues and create movement organizations (McCarthy and Zald, 1973, 1977). While changing levels of deprivation may create grievances that fuel movements (Pinard, 2011), leaders sometimes frame issues in ways that stoke discontent. McCarthy and Zald suggest that entrepreneurs may even be able to mobilize movements in the absence of pre-existing grievances. Where grievances are long-standing and pre-existing organization exists, this type of entrepreneurial leadership is less likely to matter (Jenkins, 1981: 121), but leaders remain important in framing injustices and recognizing opportunities for collective action (Morris and Staggenborg, 2004).

Political process theorists suggest that political opportunities or threats lead to the emergence of a social movement. As Sidney Tarrow argues,

[c]ontention increases when people gain access to external resources that convince them that they can end injustices and find opportunities in which

to use these resources. It also increases when they are threatened by costs, which outrage their interests, their values, or their sense of justice, but they still see a chance to succeed. When institutional access opens, rifts appear within elites, allies become available, and state capacity for repression declines, challengers see opportunities to advance their claims. When these are combined with high levels of threat but declining capacity for repression, such opportunities produce episodes of contentious politics, sometimes producing changes in regimes (2011:160).

In this view, people are more likely to engage in collective action when they think they have a chance of succeeding. In other words, hope, as well as outrage, is an important motivation for collective action (Castells, 2012). Moreover, social movement activists create opportunities by demonstrating the effectiveness of protest, in some cases spurring a cycle of protest.

Even when political opportunities exist, potential collective actors do not always take advantage of them. Framing by leaders and organizations is important in diagnosing problems and suggesting collective solutions. Collective action frames translate grievances into broader movement claims, and they help to create a sense of injustice and a feeling that something can be done about the injustice. In addition to helping people understand issues, framing helps to create the emotional energy that makes individuals willing to participate in collective action. For example, movements might draw on sources such as nationalism and religion to appeal to potential movement participants (Tarrow, 2011: 153). Frames point to collective solutions and encourage people to adopt a collective identity associated with a movement, which involves a shared sense of being part of a group and a feeling of "collective agency" that invites collective action (Snow, 2001: 2213). Movements that frame issues in a way that resonates with the existing culture can sometimes mobilize support even in the absence of political opportunities. In a comparative analysis of same-sex marriage in landmark legal cases in Canada and the United States, Miriam Smith (2007) shows that, although the two countries have very different political opportunities and legislation, the movements in both countries share a common human rights frame. The differences in success of movements in the two countries are connected to their political structures and broader cultural attitudes. In Canada rights were protected by the Charter of Rights and Freedoms and human rights legislation and were seen as linked to the country's self-definition as progressive, whereas in the United States similar federal level legislation was lacking, and this sparked a counter-mobilization by the Christian Right. Despite differences in opportunities and outcomes, the frames used to mobilize supporters and advocate for equality were similar in both countries.

Such studies suggest that mobilization is a complicated process, involving meso-level collective action framing and micro-level perceptions as well as large-scale opportunities and changes. The case of the LGBT movement, discussed in Chapter 7, provides a particularly interesting example of the relationship between large-scale changes and strategic actions; even in the absence of political opportunity, activists used the master "rights" frame to raise the consciousness of constituents and build movement support, allowing the movement to take advantage of subsequent political opportunities.

Individual Recruitment and Participation

If movements need activists to mobilize, what makes individuals willing to commit their time, money, and skills to a social movement? The answer to this question may seem obvious in that participants typically share the movement's goals and want it to succeed. Yet not all **adherents** to a cause, defined as those who believe in the cause and want to see movement goals achieved, become **constituents**, defined as supporters who contribute resources to a movement (McCarthy and Zald, 1977: 1221). Collective behaviour theories stress the importance of grievances and individual discontent in generating collective action, but not everyone who is aggrieved, upset, or even outraged about a problem becomes an activist. There are many more adherents of social movements than there are constituents. For example, as we will see in Chapter 8, many people support environmental measures, but few of them contribute to environmental organizations.

One important argument for why this is the case comes from **rational choice theory**, which focuses on the costs and benefits of collective action for individuals. According to this theory, many latent groups have grievances, but few of them mobilize because the costs for the individual typically outweigh the benefits of participation. The problem of getting individuals to participate in social movements or other collective action is known as the **free rider problem**. Economist Mancur Olson (1965) argues that rational individuals will be free riders because the goal of collective action is a **collective good,** such as clean air or water, which the individual will receive regardless of whether or not he or she works to achieve it. Members of a latent group, such as women, may have a common interest in obtaining a collective good, such as pay equity, but they do not have a common interest in paying the cost of obtaining the collective good. Because the contribution of any one individual typically makes no difference to the outcome of the collective action, and because the collective good will be received—or not received—regardless of personal participation in efforts to secure it, the rational individual will be a "free rider" and allow others to pay the cost of obtaining the collective good. Olson argues that rational actors will participate voluntarily in collective action only under two conditions: (1) if they are offered **selective incentives**, which are benefits available exclusively to those who participate in collective action, or (2) if they are in a *small group situation,* where an individual might be motivated to pay the entire cost of obtaining the collective good or where his or her contribution might make a significant difference. Otherwise, individuals will be free riders unless forced into participation through coercion.

This logic presented an important challenge to social movement scholars, who responded with various explanations of how the free rider problem might be overcome. Whereas Olson focused on **material incentives,** other theorists have broadened the notion of selective incentives to include less tangible rewards for participation in collective incentives such as **solidary incentives,** which come from associating with a group, and **purposive incentives,** which come from the sense of satisfaction at having contributed to the attainment of a worthwhile cause (Wilson, 1973). McAdam and Friedman (1992) argue that collective identity can act as a selective incentive, as when people participate in movements because they want to share in an identity (e.g., environmentalist) available only to movement activists.

Rather than broadening the definition of selective incentives, other theorists have addressed the free rider problem by arguing that recruitment is affected not just by individual motivations, but by organizational arrangements and structures such as social networks. McCarthy and Zald (1973, 1977) argue that the free rider problem may be less salient for modern social movements because many are becoming professionalized. That is, many movements have paid leaders who work full time for movement organizations, and they often attract conscience constituents rather than beneficiaries. In the environmental movement, for example, many large organizations have paid staff and members who join by sending in financial contributions rather than by actively participating. When movements rely mainly on paid staff, along with financial contributions from "paper members," participation from large masses of people is less critical. Particularly in the age of the Internet, movements frequently ask large numbers of people to participate in very low-cost actions. For example, many movements today engage in "e-tactics" such as online petitioning (Earl and Kimport, 2011: 8–10). Owing to the low-risk commitments required of conscience constituents, many of whom have discretionary income available, the free rider problem is not particularly important.

However, not all movements involve low-risk activism and many still require participation from sizable numbers of people. Even movements that employ Internet technologies often engage in "e-mobilization," which "uses online tools to bring people into the streets for face-to-face protests" (Earl and Kimport, 2011: 5). Many social movements, including the civil rights, animal rights, anti-abortion, grassroots environmental, global justice, and Indigenous movements have required high-risk activism. In the contemporary context all of them also use the Internet and social media to mobilize online and offline. In 2011, for instance, large numbers of activists risked their lives in movements that were met with varying degrees of violence from the state, including the Arab uprisings and massive Spanish demonstrations, which helped to inspire the Occupy Wall Street protests (Castells, 2012). In each of these cases the Internet and social media played important roles in facilitating protest and framing the events.

Theorists emphasize the importance of different types of organizational bonds and social ties in recruiting activists to movements. When members of an aggrieved group are tied together by structural factors that generate group solidarity, individuals are more likely to participate in group actions (Fireman and Gamson, 1979). For example, a person who has friends in a group, or who participates in the same social clubs or other organizations with members of a group, is more likely to respond to a call to collective action by the group than someone who lacks such ties. Some individuals, such as visible minorities, may have "no exit" from a group, insofar as they are identified and treated as group members whether they like it or not (ibid., 22). If an individual is closely tied to a group of people engaging in collective action, he or she has a big stake in the group's fate and may find it hard not to participate when everyone else is involved. When collective action is urgent, the person is likely to contribute his or her share even if the impact of that share is not noticeable. Critics of rational choice theory note that decisions about participation in collective action are made not by isolated individuals but by people in group contexts, such as local communities and friendship networks (Klandermans, 1997; Marwell and Oliver, 1993). Recent studies of online activism suggest that face-to-face communities are less important for some forms of protest and that new mediums sustain networks (Bennett and Segerberg, 2013; Earl and Kimport, 2011).

McAdam, McCarthy, and Zald (1988: 707–9) identify several types of structural factors that increase the likelihood of activism. First, studies suggest that *prior contact with a movement member* makes an individual more likely to become an activist. Often, individuals are asked to come along to a meeting or activity with a friend, and this contact then leads to further involvement. Based on a study of recruitment to religious movements, Snow, Zurcher, and Ekland-Olson (1980) argue that social networks are in fact more important than ideological motivations for participation; often, individuals become involved through networks and take on movement beliefs after their initial exposure to a group, through interaction with members. Second, *membership in organizations* makes people more likely to become movement activists insofar as their organizational memberships give them access to information and make them targets of movement recruitment efforts within organizations. Third, a *history of prior activism* increases the likelihood that individuals will participate in subsequent movements. People gain organizing skills that are transferable from one movement to another, and subsequent activism is a way of retaining one's identity as an activist. Finally, *biographical availability* makes individuals more likely to be recruited to social movements. Individuals who have responsibilities such as young children and demanding jobs are likely to be less available for participation than people with flexible work schedules and fewer domestic responsibilities. Based on case studies of religious movements, Snow, Zurcher, and Ekland-Olson (1980) propose a similar concept of *structural availability* to explain the recruitment of some individuals from the streets rather than through social networks. They argue that these individuals were structurally available insofar as they lacked commitments that would prevent their participation. Thus, network ties to activists can draw individuals into movement participation, and a lack of competing ties can also free people to participate.

Social movement theorists recognize that participation in social movements is a process rather than a one-time event. Klandermans and Oegema (1987) distinguish several steps in the process: taking on the attitudes and goals of the movement, becoming a target of movement recruitment attempts, becoming motivated to participate, and overcoming barriers to participation. Beyerlein and Hipp (2006) find that biographical *un*availability, such as having young children, prevents many people from becoming willing to protest, thereby preventing them from getting to the stage of actual participation. In addition to there being several steps in the process of participation, individuals who become participants exhibit a variety of patterns in their participation after their initial recruitment. In a longitudinal study of movement participation, Corrigall-Brown (2012) finds that, while some people become life-long activists and some disengage after one incident of participation, many people participate in movements off and on at different points in their lives. Factors such as ideology, resources, and biographical availability vary in their impact over the life course, affecting trajectories of participation. For example, marriage makes people more likely to disengage from participation, but individuals who are divorced or widowed frequently return to movement participation (Corrigall-Brown, 2012: 56).

Movement Maintenance, Growth, and Decline

Social movements, by definition, endure over some length of time, interacting with the broader public, mass media, supporters and opponents, authorities, and other targets. Once initial mobilization occurs, movements have to be maintained and they may either grow in strength or decline. The commitments of individual participants need to be retained and new supporters must be recruited. As resource mobilization theorists have emphasized, social movement organizations are central to this process. Movement organizations and coalitions of organizations are typically the main organizers of movement campaigns, which are important to the growth of movements and their ability to bring about change. However, movements are not stable and unified entities. They consist of shifting coalitions of actors and, for long-lived movements, there may be periods without a great deal of visible collective action. Movements are maintained not only by formalized organizations but by the more informal networks and cultural groups within social movement communities that keep people with a common collective identity tied together even during times when there is not much movement action going on. Movements can also endure within institutions, other social movements, political parties, and various other venues where ideologically structured action occurs.

The following discussion begins with movement organizations and the characteristics that help them to survive and generate collective action. We then consider collective action strategies and campaigns, and their importance to movement growth and decline. Finally, we examine other types of structures through which movements grow and sustain themselves.

Social Movement Organizations

Social movement organizations (SMOs) play an important role in mobilizing participants for collective action in most modern social movements. One important question is how the structures of these organizations affect their longevity and effectiveness. Scholars have identified some key dimensions on which SMOs vary, including the extent of **bureaucratization** or **formalization** in the organization and the extent of **centralization** (Gamson, 1990). Organizations that are more formalized or bureaucratic have established procedures for decision-making, a developed division of labour, explicit criteria for membership, and rules governing subunits such as standing committees or chapters. More informal SMOs have fewer established procedures, rules, and membership requirements and a less developed division of labour. Decisions in informal organizations are likely to be made on an ad hoc basis and organizational structures are frequently adjusted. Centralized SMOs have "a single centre of power" whereas power is dispersed in decentralized organizations (ibid., 93). Although formalization and centralization tend to go together, it is possible to have decentralized formal SMOs and centralized informal SMOs.

These differences are important because they affect organizational maintenance, goals, and strategies. Some theorists have argued that formalization leads to a focus on organizational maintenance at the expense of protest, resulting in a decline of insurgency. In their classic study, *Poor People's Movements*, Piven and Cloward (1977) look at how movements of relatively disadvantaged people, such as unemployed workers and welfare activists, mobilize in response to opportunities but fail to keep their movements alive. They argue that poor people's movements can succeed only by engaging in disruptive tactics under extraordinary conditions, such as the Great Depression or the turbulence of the 1960s. During such times, poor people, who are ordinarily caught up in the struggle to survive and lacking in resources for collective action, are often compelled to take action. Organizers have often tried to sustain poor people's movements by building large-scale organizations, but Piven and Cloward contend that such efforts are doomed to fail. By focusing on building organizations rather than engaging in mass insurgency that will force elites to make concessions, they argue, leaders will squander the period of opportunity, which is always limited. Canadian Indigenous communities have faced such tensions in efforts to resist colonization. Radical actions such as blockades or armed standoffs have been effective in triggering government reaction such as formation of the Royal Commission on Aboriginal Peoples in the wake of the 1990 Oka Crisis; they have also been successful in pressuring governments to negotiate land claims settlements, as seen in the Ipperwash case, as well as raising broader support and awareness, as seen more recently with the Elsipogtog anti-fracking protests in 2013. Leaders of national Aboriginal organizations, however, usually prefer less disruptive tactics. This has led some, such as Taiaiake Alfred (1999), to claim they have been co-opted and are thus ineffective in fighting ongoing colonization. Although radical movements are inevitably short-lived, Piven and Cloward advocate gaining as much as possible from militancy during extraordinary times rather than building organizations.

Other scholars, writing about other types of groups, point to the benefits of bureaucratization in keeping organizations ready to pursue emerging opportunities and of centralization in preventing internal conflict and factionalism (Gamson, 1990; Staggenborg, 1988). Rupp and Taylor (1987) document the role of the centralized National Women's Party (NWP) in keeping the American women's movement alive during the "doldrums" between the passage of women's suffrage in 1920 and the rebirth of the women's movement in the 1960s. The NWP became a rather exclusive organization of highly committed women with close personal ties who shared the experience of participating in the suffrage movement and maintained a close community. Taylor (1989) shows how such a centralized, "elite-sustained" organizational structure can keep a movement in **"abeyance"** during a slow period when there is little collective action and it is difficult to recruit new members. Rodgers and Knight (2011) caution that the recent absence of a national women's organization in Canada left provincial and local organizations with the task of advocating for women's issues. They argue that the movement is in a period of reconceptualising feminism and that communities are maintaining activist networks and developing new strategies.

With regard to strategies and tactics, studies suggest that more centralized and formalized structures are associated with the use of institutionalized tactics, such as legislative lobbying, while decentralized and informal structures promote tactical innovation and direct action (Freeman, 1975, 1979; Gerlach and Hine, 1970; Staggenborg, 1988, 1989). Movements such as the environmental movement succeed and endure in part because they include a variety of organizational structures with different capacities. In Canada, for example, national environmental organizations, such as the Canadian Wildlife Federation, lobby government officials and provide information to the public collected by their professional staffs, while grassroots organizations engage in direct-action tactics such as blockades of roads and "tree-sits" to prevent logging and create media attention for the movement.

One of the important problems that SMOs face is how to encourage participation while avoiding internal conflict. Leadership is important to this problem insofar as movement leaders inspire commitment, devise strategies, shape organizational structures, and provide opportunities for activists to participate in decision-making processes. Leaders interact with potential participants and "offer frames, tactics and organizational vehicles that allow participants to construct a collective identity and participate in collective action at various levels" (Morris and Staggenborg, 2004: 180). When individuals have an opportunity to contribute meaningfully to organizational decisions about strategies and goals, they tend to develop greater solidarity and commitment to the SMO. Yet, there are often conflicts over who has authority in movement organizations and what structures allow for genuine participation.

Movements such as the New Left, women's, and social justice movements tried to develop forms of "participatory democracy" whereby activists are closely involved in organizational decision making. At its worst, this type of structure can degenerate into what Jo Freeman (1972) describes as the "tyranny of structurelessness." The lack of clear leadership led to confusion within the Occupy and Idle No More movements over the goals they wished to achieve and who had authority to speak on their behalf. Groups that shun "structure," Freeman shows, may nevertheless end up with exclusive informal structures and unaccountable leaders. At its best, however, participatory democracy is a process that helps to build movements by involving participants and developing their political skills, creating solidarity, and encouraging the development of new tactics. In a study of several American movements, including the civil rights movement, the New Left, and the women's movement, Francesca Polletta (2002) found that participatory democracy was beneficial in developing strategy insofar as activists learned to engage in discourse that allowed them to consider different options carefully. Active participation required individuals to take "ownership" of decisions reached collectively.

Research by Polletta and others suggests that successful movement organizations have structures that enable them to develop accountable and diverse leadership and to formulate effective strategies. However, they can also be constraining. As Jeffrey Cormier (2005) shows in his analysis of the Canadianization movement during the 1960s and 1970s, organizational form is influential in the kinds of strategies adopted by movements. The movement consisted of professors and professional organizations seeking to increase the number of Canadian-born and -trained scholars in the academy. At the time, Canadian universities were expanding and many of the new positions were being filled by Americans leading many to worry about the "Americanization" of higher education. Cormier identified two organizational forms that drove the movement. One was led by outspoken academic leaders loosely tied to supporters and the other was a professional association, the Canadian Sociology and Anthropology Association. The organization with high-profile leaders was able to broadly define the movement and was more nimble, but less accountable, whereas the professional association was more constraining because of its use of committees and other bureaucratic forms that defined its leaders' roles and ability to act politically. The professional association legitimized Canadianization but was constrained in its framing of the issue.

Thus, one of the most important problems for social movements is the creation of organizations that are able to minimize internal conflict and develop effective strategies. SMOs are not the only structures within social movements, and increased use of Internet technologies makes it possible to organize without formal organizations (Earl and Kimport, 2011: 107–20). Nevertheless, movement organizations remain important to contemporary social movements, and activists often work through SMOs to direct social movement campaigns. These strategic campaigns are critical not only for achieving movement goals but also for the growth and maintenance of social movements.

Movement Strategies and Campaigns

Social movements are loose and changing coalitions of groups and individuals that interact with opponents, bystanders, and targets through collective action. Movement activists have at their disposal a variety of strategies and tactics within the repertoire familiar at the time. The modern repertoire of collective action includes demonstrations, public meetings, petitions, and press statements, and activists often display "symbols of personal affiliation" and form "specialized associations devoted to pursuit of a cause" (Tilly, 2008: 72). Many movements engage in a mix of direct-action tactics, which bypass established avenues of influence, and institutionalized tactics such as lobbying, which use established channels. Activists engage in "contentious performances," which are often part of movement campaigns (Tilly, 2008).

Marwell and Oliver (1984: 12) define the **collective campaign** as "an aggregate of collective events or activities that appear to be oriented toward some relatively specific goal or good, and that occur within some proximity in space and time." Social movements typically consist of a series of collective campaigns, which extend beyond single events and are aimed at government officials or other authorities (Tilly and Wood, 2013: 4). A campaign at one period of time may alter the conditions for subsequent campaigns by changing political opportunities, creating new networks, and providing models of contentious performances (Tilly, 2008). Through strategic campaigns, movement participants engage in dynamic interactions with authorities and third-party opponents and supporters; as these actors respond to movement strategies, movement actors in turn alter their strategies and organizational structures. The women's movement, for example, developed vehicles for new strategies, such as participation in electoral politics, in response to anti-feminist countermovements and unreceptive governments (see Chapter 6).

During movement campaigns, various types of interactions affect mobilization, strategies, and outcomes. These include interactions with allies, countermovements and other opponents, and mass media as well as government officials and other authorities. Scholars have conceived of movement organizations as operating within a **multi-organizational field**, which includes, in addition to SMOs, a variety of other types of organizations that might either oppose or support the movement (Curtis and Zurcher, 1973; Klandermans, 1992). By thinking about movements in this way, we can study the various types of interactions between movement organizations and other types of organizations in a broader field of action. Movement actors change the fields in which they are embedded, and they are also constrained by other actors in those fields (see Fligstein and McAdam, 2012). Within and across movements, participants may form coalitions and engage in cooperative actions, compete with one another, or come into conflict with one another. Similarly, movements engage in a variety of different types of exchanges with non-movement adversaries, mediators, and audiences (Rucht, 2004). As the frequent targets of protest, government authorities or other elites may facilitate or repress protest campaigns through a variety of means. Movement leaders and organizations adjust their strategies and tactics as they respond to opponents and targets and as they form coalitions or compete with other movement activists and organizations.

The *policing of protest* is a key aspect of state response to movement campaigns. Police handling of protests is more or less repressive or tolerant under different types of governments and in response to different types of collective action, and trends in the policing of protest have important impacts on collective action, in some cases reducing disruption and visibility (della Porta and Fillieule, 2004). Studies of policing in Western democracies have traced several trends in the nature of policing that affect the strategies and outcomes of social movements. During the 1960s, police used an "escalated force" style characterized by "ever-increasing amounts of force to disperse protesters and break up demonstrations," whereas the period from the mid-1970s to the late-1990s was one of "negotiated management" in which police and protesters reached agreements "limiting the scale and scope of demonstrations, but not preventing them from happening" (Gillham and Noakes, 2007: 342). After the Seattle demonstrations of 1999, however, policing styles began to change again. The negotiated management approach has been replaced in some cases by a "dual model" of protest policing which uses a soft approach to predictable protests and encourages protest zones, but uses militarized policing and riot control strategies for more radical protests (Wood 2015). Activists in the global justice movement (see Chapter 9) have made numerous strategic adjustments in response to the policing of large demonstrations at the sites of international meetings.

Movement campaigns may occur in response to **critical events**, and campaigns also generate such events. Critical events focus the attention of movement supporters, members of the public, and authorities on particular issues, creating threats and opportunities that affect movement mobilization and outcomes. There are various types of critical events, including large-scale socio-economic and political events, natural disasters and epidemics, accidents, policy outcomes, face-to-face encounters between movement actors and authorities or other parties, and strategic initiatives of movements, such as demonstrations (Staggenborg, 1993). Some types of critical events are completely outside of movement control, while others are orchestrated by movements. However, even when movements do not control the occurrence of an event, they may be in a position to make use of critical events. Depending on their organizational capacities, movements may be able to plan campaigns that take advantage of unforeseen events. For instance, mobilization takes place against environmental harms caused by human-made disasters such as the 2010 BP Oil Spill in the Gulf of Mexico (Hoffbauer and Ramos 2014). During campaigns, movements may be able to create events, such as dramatic confrontations with police, to call attention to movement issues and spread movement frames. In the case of Indigenous protest in Canada (see Chapter 5), the impact of some critical events, such as the "Indian Summer" of 1990, influenced subsequent mobilization and protest.

Movements thrive when participants are engaged in collective campaigns, which allow them to mobilize previously inactive movement supporters and strengthen the commitments of activists to a movement community (Downton and Wehr, 1991). During a campaign, there are more ways for activists to become involved and more opportunities for participants to take leadership roles. Collective identities often undergo expansion during campaigns, incorporating the concerns of new actors, and individuals typically become more identified with the movement as they participate in its campaigns. During the 2000 World March of Women, for example, activists from community organizations and unions in Montreal became active in the women's movement through their participation in the campaign, and many local participants came to identify with global feminism (Staggenborg and Lecomte, 2009). Movements that are no longer capable of mobilizing public campaigns, or that have difficulty devising campaigns appropriate for achieving movement goals, are likely to have a hard time maintaining themselves.

McAdam (1983) demonstrates the importance of particular campaigns in the growth of the American civil rights movement. He shows that peaks in movement activity occurred with tactical innovations, which were then countered by opponents, creating the need for new tactics. Bus boycotts sparked movement growth in the 1950s, resulting in some victories but also some effective counter-tactics that limited continued use of the tactic. Next, the movement experienced dramatic growth with the sit-ins of 1960. After mass arrests helped to diffuse the campaign, movement activity declined until the freedom rides of 1961 revived the movement. When that campaign was neutralized by government action, community-wide protests again revived the movement in southern cities such as Albany, Georgia and Birmingham and Selma, Alabama. After these campaigns, which resulted in many victories in desegregating public facilities, the movement faltered in devising non-violent tactics to address more entrenched and systemic problems of economic inequality. The urban riots of 1966–68 in northern US cities spurred calls for economic reforms, but the civil rights movement found it very difficult to devise campaigns to address issues of race and poverty, leading to a decline in the civil rights movement in the late 1960s.

Other studies also point to the importance of collective campaigns in expanding movements. Lofland (1979) shows how a religious movement achieved "white-hot mobilization" in part by devising campaigns and public events that involved participants and created excitement about the movement. Kleidman (1993) demonstrates how the American peace movement ebbed and flowed in the twentieth century with several major campaigns that created peaks in the movement. Voss and Sherman (2000) show how some labour unions revitalized in recent years through innovative campaigns that encouraged member participation. Often, movements expand during such campaigns through coalition building, as coalitions of organizations within movements and coalitions across movements often are needed to wage extensive campaigns. Particularly when cross-movement coalitions are involved, master frames are critical in providing a common language that can be used to address the concerns of a variety of groups (Carroll and Ratner, 1996; Gerhards and Rucht, 1992; Van Dyke, 2003). In the case of the global justice movement, for example, we will see how a master frame focusing on the consequences of neoliberal economic policies helped to unite feminists, environmentalists, labour union members, and other activists.

In some instances, countermovement campaigns generate new movement strategies and new rounds of collective action. Movements and countermovements often respond to one another, and successful action by one side frequently spurs new activity by its opposition. For example, when Canadian abortion rights activist Henry Morgentaler opened an abortion clinic in

Toronto in 1983, anti-abortion activists launched an intensive campaign of daily protests against the clinic, and abortion rights supporters responded by organizing demonstrations to protect the clinic (Cuneo, 1989). When the militant anti-abortion group Operation Rescue mounted major protests against abortion clinics in the United States and Canada in the late 1980s and early 1990s, the campaign stimulated a great deal of mobilization by abortion rights groups in response. While countermovements oppose movement goals, they also help to fuel movement campaigns, as we will see in the cases of the women's movement and the LGBT movement. In federal systems such as the United States and Canada, there are numerous venues in which opposing movements can spar; when one side chooses a particular battleground such as the courts or legislatures, the other side may feel compelled to follow suit (Meyer and Staggenborg, 1996, 1998).

As battles over deeply felt issues such as abortion and LGBT rights show vividly, emotions as well as organization and strategic planning are central to movement campaigns. Recognizing that analyses of resource mobilization and political processes are inadequate without an understanding of how strong feelings fuel movements, recent scholarship has examined the impact of emotions on the mobilization, strategies, and outcomes of movements (Goodwin et al., 2001). Emotions are connected to the larger cultural context, and movement leaders often need to manage emotions in ways that are culturally acceptable and that appeal to the public. In a study of victims' rights groups in Canada in the early 1980s, Stanbridge and Kenney (2009) examine the ways in which victim-advocate groups managed and framed the grief and anger of crime victims and appealed for public support. While victims were attracted to advocacy groups as places where they could freely express their grief (e.g., at the murder of a family member), advocacy groups were mindful of cultural "feeling rules" that prevented too much public expression of grief. In appealing to the public, victims expressed emotion, which helped to create sympathy, but they also used frames that won public support, such as "justice and fairness, not revenge" (ibid., 490).

Emotions and their cultural contexts affect the types of organizations and campaigns that emerge in different time periods. Deborah Gould (2009) argues in her study of the AIDS activist organization AIDS Coalition to Unleash Power (ACT UP) that emotions shared by gay men and lesbians changed the nature of AIDS activism over time. In the early years of the epidemic (1981–86), feelings such as gay shame and fear of rejection existed alongside feelings such as gay pride. These feelings, which were not necessarily acknowledged, influenced gay communities to respond to the AIDS crisis with strategies, such as the provision of services for people with AIDS, that demonstrated the "respectability" of gay people (Gould, 2009: 85). By the time ACT UP was formed in 1987, the "emotional habitus" or "prevailing ways of feeling and emoting" in lesbian and gay communities had shifted (ibid., 10), and anger fuelled a new militancy, resulting in the use of confrontational direct-action tactics by AIDS activists.

Organizational structures, critical events, and emotions all influence the collective action that is central to social movements. Movements survive and grow through their ability to generate action campaigns. As collective campaigns ebb, movements contract in size and become less publicly visible. Although no movement can sustain non-stop public campaigns, long-lived movements do not completely disappear between campaigns; they typically remain alive in less visible venues.

Movements within Institutions, Other Social Movements, and Culture

Beyond the visible faces of movements in political organizations and public campaigns, movements survive and grow in numerous other settings, including institutions, other social movements, and cultural groups and activities. A number of studies have examined movements within institutions as forms of ideologically structured action that expand movements and secure new advantages (Zald, 2000). For example, the women's movement helped to establish women's studies programs and feminist student organizations that fought for women's equality inside and outside universities (Staggenborg, 2010). In Canada the lines between social movements and dominant political institutions are often blurred (Ramos and Rodgers 2015). For example, the national women's movement organization, NAC, organized out of the Royal Commission on the Status of Women (see Chapter 6) and Egale successfully influenced policy decisions and intervened in court cases (see Chapter 7). In general, state funding of civil society and social movement organizations in Canada has been widespread (Pal, 1993). Some claim that public demonstrations have become so common that they are "a routine part of political bargaining" (Jenkins et al., 2008). The use of sub-politics, which occur at local and non-institutional levels, rather than engagements with representative democracy and traditional avenues of party politics has been on the rise (Beck, 1992; Castells, 2004). This has meant that mainstream political actors regularly reach out to movements, NGOs, and advocacy groups in their consultations, deliberations, and development of policies (Bucek and Smith, 2000). As movements gain footholds within institutions, new mobilizing structures are established, which can be used to organize campaigns both inside and outside institutions.

Movements also spread and maintain themselves within other social movements. Activists commonly participate in multiple movements with compatible ideologies, and movements influence one another in various ways. For example, Barbara Epstein (1991) describes how feminists became active in peace and anti-nuclear power movements in the 1970s and 1980s. Recently, feminists in North America became heavily involved in the global justice movement during lulls in feminist campaigns (Rebick,

2005: 256). Indigenous struggles are, moreover, increasingly becoming a meta-level injustice that shapes the mobilization of other movements, such as environmental (Woons, 2013), women's, and leftist (Khasnabish, 2008) movements.

Cultural activities and the activities of everyday life provide additional venues for the spread of movement ideology and the maintenance of movement networks. In Alberto Melucci's (1989, 1996) view of new social movements, collective identity develops within the structures of everyday life and is transformed from time to time into political action. Randolph Haluza-DeLay argues that the environmental justice movement has faced many barriers because of its inability to shape the broader culture of North American society and its petroculture (Haluza-DeLay, 2015). He argues that the movement will succeed only by creating an environmental habitus that shapes the way people see the environment and practise environmentalism in their everyday lives. Other researchers have similarly focused on social movement communities, which include cultural groups, alternative institutions, and other groups and events that spread movement ideas and provide spaces for activists to interact (Buechler, 1990; Staggenborg, 1998, 2001; Taylor and Rupp, 1993; Taylor and Whittier, 1992; Rodgers and Knight, 2011).

One of the important issues raised by this conception of social movements is how submerged networks become activated for political campaigns. Depending on the context in which the activities take place and the intentions of participants, cultural activities might either support or detract from political activities. In some cases, cultural strategies are employed to promote political change, and political campaigns reinvigorate cultural rituals. In other instances, culture may be an end in itself. The relationship between cultural and political activities is thus an important topic for social movement research.

Movement Outcomes

Questions about the outcomes or consequences of collective action are the most important of all for social movement researchers; ultimately, we want to know what impact a social movement has on a society. Outcomes are also among the most difficult aspects to evaluate, for several reasons. First, movements produce numerous types of outcomes—intentional and unintentional, long-term and short-term. Movements affect public policy, political access, culture, institutions, and opportunities for subsequent collective action. They may also provoke countermovements or other forms of opposition that in turn have a variety of impacts. Second, because movements endure for some length of time, they don't produce single outcomes but rather multiple outcomes over time, such as court rulings and legislation. It is important to take into account how the outcomes of one "round" of collective action influence future rounds by affecting subsequent resources, tactics, and outcomes (Snyder and Kelly, 1979). For example, the defeat of Canada's abortion laws in 1988 was a victory for pro-choice activists, but the government never passed new legislation protecting women's right to abortion, creating opportunities for countermovements and making access to abortion more difficult in many regions such as the Maritimes (Bissett, 2014; Strapagiel, 2014). Third, causality is difficult to determine; although social movements no doubt have impacts, other factors, such as large-scale socio-economic changes, also play a role. Certainly, the women's movement helped to open up jobs for women and bring women into the labour force, but so did large-scale changes such as the shift from industrial to service-based economies in many countries. Much of the research on outcomes of social movements looks at political and policy outcomes, which are per-haps the most straightforward changes, whereas fewer studies examine the cultural and institutional effects of social movements, which are harder to assess (Giugni, 1998: 373).

To get a handle on the numerous outcomes of social movements, research-ers have attempted to specify various types of impacts and to examine how movement strategies and organizational structures influence outcomes. In an influential formulation, Gamson (1990) offered two criteria for evaluating movement success: (1) *acceptance* of a challenging group as a legitimate rep-resentative of a constituency, and (2) *new advantages* or success in achieving particular goals, such as passage of legislation. Some theorists have expanded on this formulation by specifying other steps in the political process, such as getting issues on the political agenda, getting new policies implemented, actually having the intended effect, and transforming political structures (Burstein et al., 1995). Others have sought to identify broader cultural out-comes of social movements such as the creation of new pools of activists, new vocabularies and ideas (often disseminated by mass media), new cultural products and practices, and changes in public consciousness (Earl, 2004; Gusfield, 1981; Mueller, 1987; Staggenborg, 1995; Haluza-DeLay, 2007). For example, Johnson and Taylor (2008: 942) show that feminist critiques of body image have been appropriated by corporations creating a feminist consumerism. They analyzed Dove's 2004 "Real Beauty" campaign and found that although the company had adopted much of the language and symbolism of the feminist movement, it was still primarily concerned with selling its products and encouraging women to purchase beauty products. While the feminist movement changed the manifest discourse, it still struggles to challenge the latent structures of beauty ideals. Gamson (1998) amended his earlier categories to include measures of movement impacts on cultural change through public discourse. Arguing that the mass media are "the most important forum for understanding cultural impact" (ibid., 59), Gamson suggests that impact in this arena can be measured in terms of (1) *media standing* or acceptance as a legitimate source, resulting in opportunities to provide interpretations that are quoted in the media, and (2) *media discourse* as a reflection of new cultural advantages gained by a movement (see also Ferree et al., 2002).

Looking at movement impacts over time, scholars have examined how different types of cultural, organizational, and political outcomes influence subsequent collective action and outcomes. In a study of the influence of the women's movement on the election of women to public office in the United States, Mueller (1987) finds that the early women's movement did not initially have a direct impact on the election of women through means such as contributions of money and volunteers to campaigns. However, the movement helped to change the "collective consciousness" about the appropriateness of women running for public office as well as the collective identities of politically active women. As a result of changes in their consciousness and identity, women who previously would have played supportive roles in the campaigns of men decided to run for office themselves. Once elected, feminists helped to bring about changes in policies that benefited women and, as the movement developed, women's movement organizations began supporting feminist candidates more directly. Thus, challenges to existing ideas and cultural practices may be early outcomes of movements that later help to produce more substantive goals (ibid., 93).

Movement outcomes are influenced by factors both internal and external to movements, including the resources, organizational strength, and strategies of movements and the impacts of political opportunities and ongoing interactions with opponents and elites. In a study of outcomes of the American civil rights movement in the state of Mississippi, Andrews (2004) looked at a range of outcomes in different areas of the state, including electoral participation by blacks, social welfare policies, school desegregation, and election of blacks to public office. He finds that these outcomes are affected by the extent to which the movement has created a lasting infrastructure, by the strategies the local movement employs, and by countermovement mobilization and federal intervention. In places where the movement left behind a "local infrastructure" consisting of networks of grassroots leaders, community centres, and other organizations, as well as a resource base of activists and money, it was able to have a greater impact. The creation of such infrastructures is one of the long-term legacies of a social movement, which affects its ability to respond to opponents and win support from authorities and other elites.

Movements can increase their likelihood of success by taking advantage of opportunities and selecting vulnerable targets of collective action strategies. Opportunities are not only political but also cultural and economic. Moreover, outcomes are influenced not only by movement strategies but also by the strategies of their opponents, including both state and non-state actors.

In a study of animal rights campaigns, Jasper and Poulsen (1993) stress the pre-existing vulnerabilities of targets and their strategic responses to movement tactics. A movement campaign that targeted research on cat sexuality at the American Museum of Natural History in New York succeeded in part because the research employed a culturally popular species, cats, for what could be framed as frivolous research, but also because divisions within the museum created "an institutional vulnerability that prevented a united position to protect the research" (ibid., 648).

Movements and Media

Movements need to spread their messages "beyond the choir" of their own supporters to broaden their influence. Traditionally, they have attempted to do so through conventional print and broadcast media; more recently, movements have access to new information and communications technologies (ICTs), including social media tools such as Facebook and Twitter. While the Internet is extremely important to contemporary social movements, most still attempt to influence the conventional mass media in order to have access to a large public audience. Both conventional media and ICTs present challenges to social movements as they try to influence potential supporters and targets of protest.

It is quite difficult for social movements to get their messages across through the conventional mass media because movements are typically less powerful than media organizations in controlling images. Both social movements and media organizations frame issues, but the collective action frames offered by a movement are rarely presented in the same way by the mass media. Instead, media organizations have their own interests and routines that influence their coverage and framing of social movements. Movements generally need media coverage more than mass media need to cover movements, creating a "fundamental asymmetry" in the relations of movements with media (Gamson and Wolfsfeld, 1993: 116). Often, movement activities are not reported at all, and when they are covered, movement messages are frequently distorted by media frames. Internet technologies give movements more opportunity to deploy their own frames, which Castells (2007) calls mass-self communication, and alternative media such as blogs increasingly compete with conventional media for audiences. Nevertheless, movements continue to seek mainstream media coverage, even when they have little to show for their efforts (Sobieraj, 2011), perhaps because it is assumed that conventional media coverage is needed to influence public opinion.

Organizational and resource considerations, and journalistic conventions and values, are among the factors that influence media frames (Gans, 1979; Schudson, 2003; Sigal, 1973; Tuchman, 1978). News organizations in Western countries are bureaucracies, located within either public agencies such as the

Canadian Broadcasting Corporation (CBC) or private, profit-making firms, such as the American broadcasting networks and cable news channels, and they compete with other news organizations to attract audiences and sell air time, newspapers, and magazines. More material is collected by journalists than can be included in the news, and journalists working within news organizations have to sell their stories to their superiors. In developing stories, journalists work under organizational constraints and conform to occupational norms that do not necessarily work to the advantage of social movements seeking favourable media coverage (Gamson and Wolfsfeld, 1993; Kielbowicz and Scherer, 1986).

Deadlines and resource considerations are among the organizational constraints that influence news coverage. One important consequence of limited time and resources is the centralization of news gathering. Because news agencies cannot afford to have reporters everywhere in the world and must produce news in a timely fashion, they rely on centralized sources, including news bureaus located in central places, such as large cities; agencies, such as the Associated Press or Canadian Press, that collect and disseminate news; and news beats in established institutions, such as police headquarters and government legislatures, where reporters are routinely briefed and given press releases. Centralized organizations with accessible spokespersons get the most coverage because they make it easier for reporters to gather information and meet deadlines. Government agencies and officials are by far the most widely used sources, both because they have the resources to continuously provide news to the press and because they are generally seen as credible sources for news stories. The credibility of government officials as news sources, however, does vary historically.

The reliance of journalists on official sources creates an obvious problem for social movements in that they are not among the centralized, routine sources used by the media and therefore often do not get covered. In some cases, this results in a missed or incomplete story by news organizations. For example, during the conflict over the Canadian Meech Lake Accord in 1987, CBC news coverage focused heavily on in-fighting within the Liberal Party as a potential problem for the accord. In fact, Indigenous peoples, women's groups, and ethnic groups turned out to be the main opponents of the deal, but their reactions received virtually no coverage because these groups were located outside the prime news locations (Taras, 1990: 105).

Movement organizations such as Greenpeace (see Chapter 8) that are more centralized and professionalized, and that learn how to conform to media norms and provide information or "stories" in a format acceptable to media organizations, sometimes succeed in getting coverage. In an analysis of the media work of a local social movement against construction of the Jumbo Pass ski resort in British Columbia, Stoddart and MacDonald (2011) show that even local organizations use media strategically. In an analysis of

environmentalists' websites they find that organizations link environmentalism to animals, local democracy, scientific experts, and celebrities. But
when they analyzed dominant news media adoption of environmentalist
claims-making, the focus was on a much narrower set of issues and frames.
Those who have studied media tactics of movement organizations recognize
that this is an obstacle for movements and that to be successful in their
media work it is important for activists to consider the political economy
of media (Ryan et al., 2001).

Different types of movement organizations have employed a range of
strategies for securing favourable media coverage, with varying degrees of
success. In a study of movement organizations in Vancouver, Carroll and
Ratner (1999) describe the dilemmas associated with the media strategies of
different types of organizations. Greenpeace Vancouver put a great deal of
effort into planning events that would attract media coverage and bring support to the organization through the free publicity garnered; although the
strategy enjoyed some success, it detracted from grassroots organizing and
resulted in the use of predictable "media stunts" (ibid., 14). In contrast, a
gay and lesbian community service organization used the media less to generate support than to combat homophobia by educating the public; in doing
so, the group took a relatively conservative stance that alienated more radical
elements in the gay and lesbian community. A third organization, devoted to
"redistributive justice for the poor," had difficulty in getting across its leftist
critique of government policies through the mass media despite its use of
standard practices such as issuing press releases and making contact with
sympathetic reporters (ibid., 24).

Often, movements resort to dramatic tactics that will secure media
coverage, but the difficulty is that the standards for coverage may escalate.
In a study of media coverage of the New Left anti–Vietnam War movement
in the United States, Todd Gitlin (1980: 182) argues that, as the movement used increasingly flamboyant gestures, there was a rising threshold
of rhetoric and violence needed for coverage; whereas "a picket line might
have been news in 1965, it took tear gas and bloodied heads to make headlines in 1968." As Gitlin shows in the case of Students for a Democratic
Society (SDS), movement organizations are often ill-prepared for dealing
with the media, and media coverage can have extremely negative impacts on
movements. Because the mass media have an "event" orientation to deciding what is news (i.e., the "news" is what is happening today), it is difficult
for movements to secure coverage of long-term trends and conditions, such
as poverty or environmental degradation. They have to stage events, such
as an anti-poverty march or an Earth Day demonstration, to receive media
attention, but even then there is no guarantee of coverage. Because the mass
media are always looking for novelty, movements have to continually come

up with new tactics to stay in the news, and this may not be helpful for the pursuit of many movement goals.

The North American women's movement has long suffered from negative coverage of feminism, which often trivialized the movement (Freeman, 1975). In the 1960s, the movement was rarely taken seriously, often treated as "soft" news that was relegated to what were then labelled the "women's" sections of newspapers, consisting of features such as recipes and fashion (Adamson et al., 1988; Tuchman, 1978). Following a feminist demonstration at the Miss America pageant in 1968, at which women threw bras, curlers, and other symbols of restrictions on women into a trash can, the media began to characterize feminists as "bra burners," thereby sexualizing and trivializing women's liberation (Rosen, 2000: 160). Even as late as the 1990s, media coverage frequently neglected the content of feminist concerns and focused instead on the personal characteristics of leaders. For example, in a study of media coverage of women's groups in Canada, Goddu (1999) finds that journalists tended to cover female leaders either by providing profiles that focused on their looks, personalities, or personal lives, or by focusing on conflict, such as when "angry feminists" confronted public officials. In order to get coverage, some movement leaders felt they had to provide the media with conflict. For example, Judy Rebick, a leader of the National Action Committee on the Status of Women (NAC), found herself playing the role of the radical and outspoken feminist leader in conflict with powerful officials. Although this approach gained media coverage, it again focused attention on the leader's personality rather than on issues (ibid., 114). Thus, cultural stereotypes of women and media preferences for conflict made it difficult for the women's movement to discuss serious issues through the mass media.

Some feminists have employed strategies that help to at least partially overcome these problems. The experience of the Royal Commission on the Status of Women, which held hearings across Canada in 1968 before releasing its report in 1970 recommending many changes to improve women's rights, is instructive. While the commission suffered from some of the same trivialization and stereotyping that plagued women's groups, it was able to secure some serious coverage of women's issues (Freeman, 2001). The commissioners were mostly women and the chair of the commission, Florence Bird, was the first woman ever to chair a royal commission. Not surprisingly, media reports focused on Bird's personal characteristics, attacking her at times as "a career woman with no children of her own" and in other instances praising her "ladylike diplomacy" (ibid., 32–4). Yet Bird and other commissioners were committed to women's equality, and they employed a deliberate media strategy that took advantage of media norms and routines. The commissioners framed issues in terms of "democracy" and "equality of opportunity," which they knew would appeal to the media, rather than using the less familiar "women's rights" frame, and they cultivated relations with particular reporters. They also "tried to control which briefs would get journalists' attention" by scheduling more radical briefs during the lunch hour when they would receive less attention and using news conferences to provide the media with material that they controlled (ibid., 35–6). These strategies helped to achieve some serious coverage of women's issues, particularly in forums such as the women's pages of Canadian newspapers, but the coverage nevertheless continued to focus on conflict and the personal characteristics of leaders. In later years, feminist organizations improved coverage of women's issues by putting material resources into media communications and becoming reliable sources of information for journalists seeking to cover the movement (Barker-Plummer, 2002).

In addition to developing regular relations with the press and providing reliable information, some movements are able to get their messages across through the mass media by creating their own events and employing images that are irresistible to the press. As we will see in Chapter 8, Greenpeace became adept at using dramatic tactics to attract media coverage, creating such vivid images as whales being harpooned or baby seals being clubbed to death. These tactics have allowed Greenpeace to overcome any media framing of events insofar as the pictures leave a lasting impression on the public regardless of the text attached to them. Despite its success with the media, however, even Greenpeace has found itself limited by its media-oriented strategies.

Thus, a critical issue in social movement studies is how movements can use the mass media effectively. With the availability of the Internet as a direct form of mass media for social movements, online media tools provide an alternative way for contemporary movements to communicate their ideas to supporters and members of the public. Movements have always used internal communications such as newsletters to convey their messages, but the Internet provides a quick, low-cost means of reaching a large number of potential supporters and of organizing events through email, websites, and social media (Ayres, 1999; Myers, 1994; Schulz, 1998). Earl and Kimport (2011: 3–10) distinguish among several uses of online tools by social movements. "E-mobilizations" employ online tools to organize face-to-face protests by providing informational materials, motivating participants, and even organizing coalitions. Global movements for social justice, for example, have made extensive use of the Internet to organize international campaigns (see Chapter 9). "E-movements" are organized strictly online, sometimes with little formal organization (Earl and Schussman, 2003; Peckham, 1998). "E-tactics" such as online petitioning can be used by both e-mobilizations and e-movements (Earl and Kimport, 2011: 9).

The strengths and limitations of various forms of online organizing, which bypass the mainstream mass media, are an increasingly important topic for social movement research. Bennett and Segerberg (2013) argue that there is a "logic of connective action" that differs from the logic of traditional collective action. Online activism is more individualized than face-to-face activism in that participants frame their demands on social media in "personalized" ways, resulting in multiple demands and themes rather than a more unified frame. For example, during the Maple Spring protests that saw Quebec students mobilize against tuition increases, social media was a key tool to disseminate their messages (Bégin-Caouette and Jones, 2014). Similarly, the Idle No More movement originated with a Facebook thread (Caven, 2013; Van Gelder, 2013; Inman et al., 2013), and generated seemingly spontaneous flash mobs through its Twitter handle. While most traditional collective action and some forms of online action are directed by movement organizations, "crowd-enabled" connective action is organized without the involvement of formal organizations and its messages are personalized expressions of network participants rather than organizationally managed communications (Bennett and Segerberg, 2013: 46–8). Digital media are clearly playing an important role in contemporary movements, supporting networks that allow movements such as Occupy to spread rapidly, and they may also be changing the nature of protest frames.

Methods of Social Movement Research

The field of social movements has advanced greatly because researchers have conducted extensive empirical research on the key issues discussed above. A wide range of methods are used to study movements, including surveys, interviews, participant observation, content analysis, protest event analysis, and network analysis (Klandermans and Staggenborg, 2002). Different methodological approaches allow researchers to examine different causal factors and processes affecting social movements and their outcomes. Although many individual studies employ single methods, some benefit from the use of multiple methods, and most build on other studies using different methods. Each method has its strengths and weaknesses, and social movement theory has been developed through a combination of methods, either within or across studies. The following are a few examples of the key methodological approaches of social movement studies and their payoffs and limitations.

Because social movement researchers are interested in examining collective actions over time and often want to compare actions across movements or nations, many studies employ *protest event analysis* (Koopmans and Rucht, 2002). This method involves the coding of large numbers of protest "events" over time from sources of data such as newspaper accounts or police records. This data, which is often combined with other sources of data, allows researchers to employ statistical techniques to analyze the occurrence and patterns of protest. In one influential study, Kriesi et al. (1995) constructed a data set of protest events coded from major newspapers in France, Germany, the Netherlands, and Switzerland to explore differences in mobilization patterns across the four Western European countries from 1975 to 1989. Using a political process approach, the researchers were able to examine how the different political contexts of these countries, which they saw as quite similar socially and economically, affected the mobilization of "new social movements." They found, for example, that France is less receptive to new social movements than the other countries owing to the salience of traditional cleavages there, such as social class. Comparing across movements, they found that challengers raising more threatening issues were most likely to be met with repressive actions by authorities in all of the countries. Protest event data allowed the researchers to analyze these and other patterns over time in different political opportunity structures. As Kriesi et al. and other researchers recognize, however, the method is limited insofar as sources such as newspapers provide data on only a limited number and type of protests, and event data does not tell us about many aspects of movements, such as the motivations of participants.

Surveys are another quantitative method commonly used in social movement research. Individual-level surveys are administered to participants or potential participants in social movements about their motivations, attitudes and beliefs, behaviour, and characteristics, while organizational surveys are given to group spokespersons regarding matters such as organizational structure, strategies and tactics, and policies. Surveys are often conducted at protest events or delivered by phone, mail, or Internet to samples of activists, usually members of movement organizations. Some researchers have employed comparative designs to examine changes in participation or mobilization over time or differences across movements or localities (Klandermans and Smith 2002). For example, David Tindall (2004) surveyed members of three environmental social movement organizations in British Columbia at two different periods of time to understand the impact of social networks, communication, and identification on activism. Such surveys help researchers to understand changing individual motivations, using statistical techniques to control for individual characteristics such as gender and social class as well as variables such as social context. However, surveys make it easy for people to provide false information on sensitive matters, and they typically force respondents to select among pre-set choices without permitting them to explain themselves.

To obtain more detailed accounts from informants, researchers often use *in-depth interviews.* Unlike surveys, which require participants to provide a closed-ended answer using options provided by the researcher or a very short write-in response, in-depth interviews employ open-ended questions that encourage respondents to elaborate on their experiences in their own words. In this type of research, interviewers use a list of questions or topics to guide informants, but they typically add questions to probe answers and encourage elaboration, and they are flexible in allowing the informant to introduce new topics (Blee and Taylor, 2002). In-depth interviews are often used along with documentary sources to trace the history of movement organizations and campaigns, to understand strategic choices, and to explain movement mobilization and outcomes. For example, Lesley Wood used interviews with activists as well as content analysis of newspapers to understand the diffusion of protests tactics in Toronto and New York in the wake of the WTO protests in Seattle. She found that organizational context and deliberation among activists were central in determining whether or not tactics were adopted by movement organizations in the two cities. In-depth interviews help researchers to understand such processes, but the method is limited in a number of ways. Unlike surveys, interviews are usually conducted with relatively small numbers of people and findings typically cannot be generalized to a larger population, although they do help to build movement theories. Moreover, interviews are limited by the ability of informants to provide information about movement dynamics; even when highly motivated to be as honest as possible, interviewees do not always understand all aspects of an organization or movement and they cannot always convey in words what they have experienced. For this reason, researchers try to interview people with a range of perspectives (e.g., leaders and rank-and-file members of an organization, volunteers and paid activists), and they also try to use multiple sources of data.

Sometimes it is possible for researchers to observe movement dynamics first-hand by engaging in *participant observation*. This involves participating, to some extent, in a movement or organization, while also observing interactions among participants and between movement activists and their targets. Following periods of observation, participant observers record their observations in detailed field notes, and they both use social movement theory to analyze their observations and use their observations to extend theory (Lichterman, 2002). Often, participant observation is done in conjunction with in-depth interviews, with each providing different types of information. For example, Paul Lichterman (1996) studied environmental groups in California using both participant observation and in-depth interviews. While the interviews with participants provided information about how they saw their own activism, participant observation allowed Lichterman to see for himself "how they present themselves in everyday movement settings" (1996: 237) and to develop a theory of different styles of movement participation that he could not have arrived at by interviews alone. At the same time, interviews provide insights into individual motivations and behaviours that cannot necessarily be "seen" by participant observers. Moreover, many topics, such as the history of movement development, cannot be studied through participant observation.

Thus, various methods of social movement research have different strengths and weaknesses, and the use of multiple methods within and across empirical studies has been critical to the development of social movement theory.

Conclusion

Movements face numerous obstacles and opportunities as they seek to mobilize and maintain themselves and to have a social and political impact. Large-scale political opportunities and cultural changes, meso-level organization and resources, and micro-level interactions and choices of individuals all affect the emergence, maintenance, and outcomes of social movements. The characteristics of social movement organizations and other mobilizing structures affect the ability of the movement to attract participants and to wage campaigns. Movement campaigns and strategies result in victories and defeats in achieving goals, and they also affect subsequent mobilization. Movements survive through and influence institutions, other social movements, and culture in addition to creating political changes by targeting the state. Social movement scholars study the numerous issues involved in mobilizing effective collective action using a variety of methods, as we will see as we examine substantive movements in the following chapters.

Discussion Questions

1. How do large-scale changes, organizational structures, and collective action frames influence the mobilization of social movements?

2. Why do individuals sometimes participate in social movements rather than remain "free riders"?

3. What conditions would be necessary for a new movement organization, such as a local environmental group, to get off the ground and engage in collective action? What conditions might lead to failure to mobilize and act?

Suggested Readings

Earl, Jennifer and Katrina Kimport. 2011. *Digitally Enabled Social Change: Activism in the Internet Age*. Cambridge, MA: MIT Press. This book offers the first systematic and large-scale examination of Internet and online mobilization.

Klandermans, Bert, and Suzanne Staggenborg, eds. 2002. *Methods of Social Movement Research*. Minneapolis: University of Minnesota Press. This book includes chapters on the major methods of social movement research, written by experts in the field.

McAdam, Doug, John D. McCarthy, and Mayer N. Zald. 1988. "Social Movements," in *Handbook of Sociology*, edited by N.J. Smelser, Newbury Park, Calif.: Sage, 695–737. This excellent review essay lays out important concepts and debates in the study of social movements.

Snow, David A., Sarah A. Soule, and Hanspeter Kriesi, eds. 2004. *The Blackwell Companion to Social Movements*. Malden, MA: Blackwell. This collection contains essays on major theoretical issues and movements by well-known scholars.

4 The Protest Cycle of the 1960s

The year 1968 became known as "the year of the barricades" when turbulent demonstrations rocked many countries around the world, including France, Germany, Britain, Spain, Italy, Poland, Czechoslovakia, Mexico, and Japan, as well as the United States (see Caute, 1988; Fraser, 1988; Marwick, 1998). In France, students occupied an administration building at the Nanterre campus of the University of Paris on 22 March 1968, in response to the arrests of six members of the National Vietnam Committee; by May of that year, some 10 million students and workers were on strike. In Spain, students opposed the authoritarian government of General Francisco Franco, which closed down several universities; despite repression from the state, students joined with workers in a massive protest movement against the government. In the United States, students at Columbia University protested military recruitment on campus and occupied buildings, shutting down the university, and massive protests were held in Chicago at the site of the Democratic National Convention in August 1968. In Canada, students also mobilized that year, with a motion to rename Simon Fraser University in honour of Louis Riel (Lexier, 2007), a sit-in at the president's office at McGill, and a tent city erected on the University of Toronto Campus (Cleveland, 2009: 206).

The world was experiencing a major wave of protest and the political awakening of the baby boom generation that would have aftershocks for decades to come. The Vietnam War was an important stimulus for the insurgency, but the cycle of protest of the 1960s was more than a protest against the war and American imperialism. The American civil rights movement, which began in the 1950s, helped to provoke the protest cycle by providing a model of effective collective action and a vision of freedom and equality that was emulated by other movements worldwide.

This chapter begins by examining some arguments about the origins, decline, and consequences of the protest cycle of the 1960s. We then look at the American civil rights movement and the New Left student and anti-war movements that arose around the world and their influence on other movements of the time and the politics of the decades that follow. The social movements that survived the decline of the protest cycle, including Indigenous movements, the women's movement, the LGBT movement, and the environmental movement, are linked in important ways to the legacy of the 1960s, as are some of the right-wing countermovements that also emerged in the 1960s.

The Rise, Decline, and Significance of the 1960s Protest Cycle

Why did so many people around the world take to the streets in the 1960s? What happened to that protest? And what are the lasting consequences of the protest cycle? These are important questions that have occupied numerous social theorists. Many have pointed to large-scale changes such as the economic booms taking place in many Western countries, shifts in capitalism based on technological advances, and the dramatic expansion of higher education that helped to nourish a youth culture (Fraser, 1988: 2–3). However, no single structural explanation can account for the variations in protest found in different countries. Sidney Tarrow (1989: 4) argues that, although the 1960s protest cycle "originated in the general structural problems of advanced capitalism, its forms were conditioned by the particular political institutions and opportunities of each country and social sector." The actors who mobilized and the courses and outcomes of their protests differed greatly across nations. Numerous studies detail protests in France, Italy, Germany, the United States, Canada, and elsewhere (e.g., della Porta, 1995; Gitlin, 1987; Kriesi et al., 1995; Levitt, 1984; Tarrow, 1989; Touraine, 1971).

While recognizing that the course of protest varies from country to country, social movement scholars have nevertheless developed some theoretical ideas about the common features of protest cycles and the factors that lead to their rise and decline. Tarrow (2011: 199) characterizes a protest cycle or cycle of contention as follows:

> a phase of heightened conflict across the social system, with rapid diffusion of collective action from more mobilized to less mobilized sectors, a rapid pace of innovation in the forms of contention employed, the creation of new or transformed collective action frames, a combination of organized and unorganized participation, and sequences of intensified information flow and interaction between challengers and authorities.

During a cycle of contention, collective action and movement identity spread to many different groups beyond those initiating the cycle. Because so many new actors are mobilized and so many activists interact with one another, they commonly devise innovative tactics and new collective action frames. Innovations in repertoires of collective action and new collective action frames are widely diffused, allowing new groups to mobilize, including opponents of some of the initial movements. During the 1960s, it was not only progressive social movements that mobilized, but also right-wing opponents and groups that felt threatened by their demands and actions.

Explanations of the rise of protest cycles have focused on political opportunities for protest. A protest cycle occurs "when the costs of collective action are so low and the incentives are so great that even individuals or groups that would normally not engage in protest feel encouraged to do so" (Tarrow, 1989: 8). Political opportunities and threats include factors such as increased access to political participation, realignments of power, splits among elites, the availability of allies, and decreases in state repression. However, opportunities and threats are not simply "objective" structures that influence protest; as Tarrow (2011: 163–4) argues, "they must be perceived and attributed to become the source of mobilization." Protest becomes more attractive when activists recognize that resources, allies, and tactical opportunities are available to increase their chances of success.

For example, John Cleveland (2009), who was both a student activist in the 1960s and scholar of the New Left in Canada, argues that Simon Fraser University (SFU) was a hotbed of activism because it was an "instant university." During the mid-1960s Canada dramatically expanded its university system to accommodate the large baby boom generation, and a consequence was the creation of many new universities and institutions (Lexier, 2012: 84). Cleveland argues that this meant that universities, such as SFU, had loose organizational structures and were largely staffed by young academics who were supportive of participatory forms of democracy. This led to a division between administrations and professors and an elevated role and status for students in the institution, creating the opportunity for a strong sense of solidarity and contributing to the strongest English-Canadian student movement of the 1960s (Cleveland, 2009: 193). In another very different example, Paul Almeida (2003, 2008) shows how liberalization of the military regime in El Salvador in the 1960s increased institutional access and permitted electoral reforms, allowing for the development of civic organizations; when the reforms were later reversed, activists were able to use the organizational structures created during the period of political opportunity to mobilize in the face of threats.

Movements that arise early in a protest cycle, when successful, provide evidence to other potential challengers that elites are vulnerable and that protest is worthwhile. These "early risers" (Tarrow, 1989, 2011) are also important in creating master frames that inspire protest and can be adapted by other movements (Snow and Benford, 1992), and highly visible models of protest tactics, which are often diffused by mass media. For example, the civil rights movement was an early riser in the protest cycle of the 1960s; it created a master "rights" frame, developed new tactics, and demonstrated to a variety of groups that non-violent protest tactics could be used effectively. In some instances, the demands of early movements threaten the interests of other contenders, leading to the mobilization of countermovements. Thus, the protest cycle spreads through a variety of processes, as new contenders imitate early movements and extend or react to their demands (Tarrow, 2011).

In explaining how protest cycles diffuse, McAdam (1995: 219) distinguishes between **initiator movements** "that signal or otherwise set in motion an identifiable protest cycle," and **spinoff movements** "that, in varying degrees, draw their impetus and inspiration from the original initiator movement." He argues that political opportunities are critical to the emergence of the early riser or initiator movements, but that expanding political opportunities do not explain the rise of later spinoff movements. In fact, later movements may be at a political disadvantage in that governments are already preoccupied with the demands of earlier movements and less receptive to new movements. Moreover, some movements appear during periods of declining political opportunity. Instead of being the result of political opportunities, spinoff movements may arise from the organizational, ideological, and cultural bases created by earlier movements. For example, the Occupy movement was inspired by the actions of the Arab Spring and, in turn, the Maple Spring movement of Quebec students protesting against proposed tuition increases was largely inspired by the discourse and tactics used by student movements in other countries as well as the Occupy movement (Giroux, 2013: 529; Begin and Caouetter, 2014: 416). Networks created by one movement are often used as mobilizing structures by other movements. Collective action frames developed by early movements help to create new consciousness for other movements. And long-lived movements such as the women's movement create communities that spawn subsequent collective action and help to maintain movements after a protest cycle declines (Staggenborg, 1998). During slow periods in between visible movement campaigns, collective identities are maintained within the submerged networks of cultural groups, institutional spaces, and other elements of movement communities. As McAdam (1995: 230) notes, "enduring movements such as feminism never really die, but rather are characterized by periods of relative activity and inactivity."

While individual movements maintain themselves in various forms, periods of intense protest activity by multiple movements do not last forever. Cycles of protest decline because they eventually "produce countermovements, violence, and political backlash, new repressive strategies, and thence demobilization" (Tarrow, 1989: 9). Tarrow (2011) identifies several processes involved in the decline of protest cycles. One possibility is that activists simply become exhausted, but not all activists drop out at an equal rate. Those who are more extreme in their beliefs, and less likely to com-promise with authorities, are most likely to remain active despite exhaustion. Moderates are more likely to scale back their participation, and as they do so the movement may become more polarized between those who are willing to compromise and those who are not (2011: 206). Splits between moderates and radicals may result in "radicalization and institutionalization" occur-ring at the same time during a cycle of protest; radicals may become more violent in their behaviour while, on the other hand, moderates turn to more institutionalized actions (2011: 207). Selective repression and facilitation of movement actions by authorities are also important. Whereas authoritar-ian governments often respond with widespread repression, governmental authorities in democratic societies frequently encourage the actions of mod-erates and repress those of radicals, pushing the latter to further extremism while shrinking the movement as moderates turn to institutionalized action (2011: 209).

Despite the decline of intense periods of collective action, protest cycles continue to influence subsequent collective action in various ways. Many leaders and other participants who become active during a protest cycle remain involved in new social movements both inside and outside of institutions after the protest wave subsides. Tactics created during the pro-test cycle continue to be used by movements that persist or form after the cycle declines. For example, many activists, including gays and lesbians and environmentalists, continued to employ variants of the sit-in tactic devised by the civil rights movement. Master frames and new cultural understand-ings endure, influencing new generations of activists. Organizational bases created during a protest cycle often remain as submerged networks that can be mobilized for subsequent collective action. And opponents aroused during a cycle of contention may also endure as countermovements or sub-merged networks. Many opponents have adopted movement tactics, as in the case of anti-abortionists who have staged sit-ins at clinics. In some cases, countermovements keep particular movements alive beyond the decline of a protest cycle as the two opposing movements continue to do battle (Meyer and Staggenborg, 1996).

The American Civil Rights Movement

The American civil rights movement provides an example of an initiator movement during the 1960s cycle of protest that has had a lasting influ-ence on social movements worldwide. The civil rights movement played an important role in the rise of the New Left and the diffusion of protest. The movement has been studied extensively by historians and social scien-tists (e.g., Andrews, 2004; Branch, 1988; Carson, 1981; Fairclough, 1987; Garrow, 1986; Luders, 2010; McAdam, 1988, 1999; Meier and Rudwick,

1973; Morris, 1984), and here we provide only a very brief account that highlights key factors in the origins and impact of the movement and the protest cycle.

Large-scale socio-economic and political changes, including both international and domestic pressures, were critical to the emergence of the civil rights movement in the United States (Jenkins et al., 2003; McAdam, 1999; Skrentny, 1998). Internationally, the Cold War exerted a strong influence on American policy in the post–World War II era, and civil rights violations at home left the American government vulnerable to international criticism that its record on human rights was no better than that of the Soviet Union. With the establishment in 1946 of the United Nations Commission on Human Rights and the subsequent creation of its Subcommission on the Prevention of Discrimination and Protection of Minorities, the US record was open to challenge (Skrentny, 1998: 256). This concern prompted some American officials to support various civil rights measures, and this led to domestic tensions between the federal government and the political elite in the American South, which was committed to racial segregation. Socio-economic changes in the United States, including the decline of cotton as a cash crop and the large-scale migration of southern blacks to urban centres, also facilitated the emergence of the civil rights movement (McAdam, 1999; Morris, 1984). Many African Americans moved to northern industrial states, where they had a national electoral impact, causing both major political parties to become concerned about the black vote and creating political opportunities for blacks. African Americans also migrated to southern cities, where their concentrated numbers allowed them to support their own institutions and organizations and where the black vote also became a potential political force.

These political opportunities fuelled perceptions that change was possible, and organizational shifts related to these opportunities helped to mobilize the black community. Significantly, urban black churches, unlike rural ones, were able to support their own ministers. Although not all black ministers committed their churches to the movement, a sizable number of the new urban ministers were educated middle-class devotees to a radical theology stressing social activism, and these ministers became key leaders of the civil rights movement (Fairclough, 1987; Morris, 1984). The black church provided critical support to the emerging civil rights movement, including leadership, meeting places, and numerous cultural resources. Culturally, civil rights leaders were able to build on the participatory tradition of the black church, together with its theological emphasis on freedom, justice, and liberation (Morris, 1984, 2000). Ministers who became leaders of the civil rights movement adapted the traditions of the black church to draw members into the movement, and they also used their social networks to share information about strategies and tactics. Thus, pre-existing organizational and cultural bases, together with large-scale changes, were key factors in the origins of the movement.

Based on perceptions of political opportunities, organizational resources, and cultural understandings, the civil rights movement developed a repertoire of strategies and tactics that was critical to its growth and success, and to its influence on other social movements. In framing movement concerns and devising tactics, movement leaders and their allies deliberately took advantage of global concerns about human rights (Skrentny, 1998) in addition to drawing on themes of freedom and justice in the tradition of the black church (Morris, 2000). Movement tactics, including bus boycotts, freedom rides, sit-ins, and community-wide protests, mobilized participants, produced victories, and helped to spread the ideas of the movement by creating dramatic confrontations (McAdam, 1983, 1996). Worldwide media coverage showed images of heroic non-violent protesters facing police brutality and racist resistance, in some instances forcing federal intervention and resulting in movement victories. Tactics such as the sit-in have since become part of the contemporary repertoire of collective action (see Morris, 1981).

Movement tactics were critical to the ability of the civil rights movement to win many important victories, though there were also tactical problems that led to defeats and limitations of the movement. Some scholars have compared local civil rights campaigns to explain movement outcomes. Luders (2010) demonstrates that civil rights campaigns were most successful when they targeted vulnerable economic entities such as downtown businesses and other consumer-related industries. He distinguishes between two types of costs that targets evaluate in determining their behaviour toward social movements (2010: 3): *Disruption costs* are caused by movement actions, such as lost business revenue owing to a demonstration. *Concession costs* are the expected costs that result from a movement victory. For example, an elected official who gives into movement demands might be voted out of office or a business might lose money as a result of a movement victory. Depending on the mix of disruption and concession costs, targets are more or less vulnerable to protest and this vulnerability, Luders finds, influences both the target's response and the outcome of the protest for the movement. For example, the students who took part in the 1960 sit-ins in Greensboro, North Carolina deliberately targeted their protest at large downtown stores, which were highly vulnerable to disruption costs; although merchants initially feared concession costs, they ended up handing the movement a victory in the face of unbearable disruption costs (2010: 79–81). In a 1961–62 campaign in Albany Georgia, where the civil rights movement suffered a well-known defeat, the situation appeared similar, but the movement campaign was extremely broad, targeting elected officials rather than focusing on select businesses and failing to create disruption costs—in part because police chief Laurie Pritchett famously located jail space in the surrounding areas to avoid a crisis of capacity (2010: 92–6). Thus, the strategies of both movement actors and their opponents affect outcomes; movements need to choose their targets carefully to exploit political, economic, and cultural opportunities.

The election of African Americans to public office was one of the important outcomes of the civil rights movement. In his study comparing outcomes of the civil rights movement over time in different counties in Mississippi, Andrews (2004) demonstrates the importance of developing *movement infrastructure*, consisting of leadership, indigenous resources, and local organizations, as well as the extent of state repression and counter-movement activity in affecting movement outcomes. Andrews shows that the creation of a movement infrastructure had long-term consequences for communities, increasing the participation of civil rights activists in electoral politics by allowing them to register voters and elect blacks to office and enhancing their ability to influence public policy. The efforts of movements to create organizational infrastructures, together with the strategies and tactics of the movement and the actions of movement targets and opponents, have lasting influences.

The "Black Power" movement that emerged as a radical outgrowth of the civil rights movement in the period from 1965 to 1975 also had lasting impacts in terms of organizational structures and ideology. Black Power organizations such as the Black Panther Party emphasized black pride, strength, and identity rather than racial integration (Bush, 1999; Van Deburg, 1992). The movement spread beyond political organizations to arenas such as sports, the military, labour unions, prisons, professions, and universities (Bell, 2014; Rojas, 2007; Van Deburg, 1992). The movement also influenced Canadian activists as seen in the Congress of Black Writers in Montreal in 1968 (Austin, 2007) and the invitation of Black Panther Stokely Carmichael to Halifax by African Nova Scotian activist and later human rights lawyer Rocky Jones (Tattrie, 2010; Walker, 2012), and the Afro-American Progressive Association event in Toronto in 1970 (Harris, 2009). The movement had long-lasting effects on the Black Left and future generations of activists. The Black Power movement also influenced the American Indigenous movement, as seen with the adoption of the term "Red Power" and the radicalization of the American Indian Movement (Nagel, 1997).

The civil rights movement left a legacy of organizational structures, institutional influences, tactical models, and collective action frames. Human rights movements had begun spreading across Canada and other countries earlier in the twentieth century (Clément, 2008), but the civil rights movement helped to spread the "rights" frame to other social movements in the 1960s and 1970s (Snow and Benford, 1992; Tarrow, 1998). Themes of human rights, freedom, and social justice employed by the civil rights movement became part of a master frame adopted by Indigenous, women's,

LGBT, and ethnic and nationalist movements around the world. There is, however, some disagreement about what elements are most central to this frame. Morris (2000) disputes the characterization of the central frame of the movement as one of rights growing out of legal court challenges and instead emphasizes the "freedom and justice" frame rooted in the traditions of the black church. But both types of themes seem to have been important in influencing other social movements, and the rights theme draws on global concerns about human rights as well as legal efforts to secure civil rights.

The civil rights movement had an exceptional influence on other social movements because its activists promoted a global vision of human rights. As Gay Seidman (2000) notes, a number of civil rights movement leaders were involved in framing issues in global terms, creating linkages with activists in other countries, and speaking to international audiences about global issues of justice and freedom. Many participants in the civil rights movement "viewed their struggle in terms of an international campaign to end racial inequality globally" and connected their movement to larger issues such as pan-Africanism and decolonization (ibid., 345–6). Indeed, the philosophy and tactics of the civil rights movement were influenced by Mahatma Gandhi, who began his career fighting non-violently for the rights of workers and "coloured" people in South Africa and then India and who was a central figure in the Indian independence movement. Key leaders of the civil rights movement studied Gandhi's tactics and became convinced that the method of non-violence could be applied in the United States. After the American civil rights movement "perfected and modernized nonviolent direct action," the tactics of non-violent direct action "spread to other movements internationally" (Morris, 1999: 529).

In addition to the influence of its ideological frames and tactical models, the civil rights movement was important in mobilizing students, who were critical to the international movements of the 1960s. In 1960, large numbers of African-American students participated in waves of sit-ins that galvanized the civil rights movement and stimulated increased participation by white and black students in the northern United States. African-American students founded the Student Nonviolent Coordinating Committee (SNCC) and organized numerous campaigns, including Freedom Summer, which brought hundreds of northern white students to Mississippi in 1964 to register black voters and fight for civil rights in the state. The project had a huge impact on both the civil rights movement and the American student movement. It also had a long-lasting influence on Canadian student activists (Lexier, 2007; Cleveland, 2009). For many African-American activists in the SNCC, however, Freedom Summer ended in disillusionment owing to racial tensions on the project and to a lack of immediate success in influencing American politics (McAdam, 1988). Some turned away from non-violent protest and became committed to the Black Power movement. But for many white volunteers, Freedom Summer was a life-changing experience, and many of them returned in groups to their university campuses to become leaders in the emerging student movement (McAdam, 1986, 1988).

The Rise of New Left Student and Anti-War Movements

In the 1960s, students were at the centre of protests around the world (Caute, 1988; Fraser, 1988; Owram, 1996). The large student cohorts of the 1960s developed "an entirely new student consciousness," which led them to focus on their condition as students and on the transformation of the larger society (Ricard, 1994: 114). Their concerns varied in different national contexts but included reforms of the university, calls for free speech, demands on governments, support for civil rights, and protests against the Vietnam War. Student movements emerged in several Western countries in the 1950s in response to issues such as the Cold War, nuclear threats, colonialism, and racism as part of a New Left. The New Left consisted of the radical movements of the 1960s, which dissociated themselves from existing Communist and democratic socialist parties and the failures of the Old Left (Caute, 1988: 33–8; Owram, 1996: 226–33) and attempted to create a new kind of politics that would criticize capitalism and advocate meaningful forms of democracy. In Britain, the New Left was closely associated with the Campaign for Nuclear Disarmament, which mobilized many students through its youth wing. In Canada, students first mobilized around the anti-nuclear issue in 1959, developing a belief in "the common welfare over partial interests, of humanity over politics" and the Student Union for Peace Action (SUPA) emerged five years later as a leading organization of the Canadian New Left (Dickenson and Campbell 2008: 4). It was influential on the university movement of the 1960s (Levitt, 1984: 40–1) and also brought activism off the campus (Churchill 2010: 33). Students in Quebec were influenced by the nationalist movement there and aimed for "a sweeping change in the conduct and organization of their society" (Ricard, 1994: 119). In France, massive mobilizations of students began during the Algerian War, which lasted from 1954 to 1962, to support the Algerian National Liberation Front. In the United States, students began organizing on campuses in the late 1950s to support the civil rights movement and to protest US Cold War policies. In many countries, a postwar boom in student enrolments put university students in a position of strength and also created grievances regarding the dehumanizing nature of the "multiversity" and its role in producing workers for the capitalist elite.

At the University of California at Berkeley, what became known as the Free Speech Movement erupted in September 1964 when the university administration attempted to ban on-campus organizing and fundraising for off-campus political causes (see Heirich, 1968). Students who had been organizing on campus in support of the civil rights movement, some of whom had recently returned to campus after participating in the Freedom Summer project in Mississippi, led a protest against the policy. Highlights of the protest included the spontaneous surrounding of a police car to prevent an arrested student from being carried off, a student strike, and the use of the sit-in, a tactic learned from the civil rights movement, to occupy the administration building. By January 1965, after the arrests of over 800 students, the university relented and agreed to allow organizing and fundraising for outside causes on campus once again. The Free Speech Movement gave a huge boost to the student movement, both in the United States and internationally.

The Canadian New Left, especially in Toronto, was inspired by the civil rights movement and adopted many of its tactics and issues (Churchill, 2010). It was also influenced by the American student movement and later by draft resisters escaping the Vietnam War. In western Canada many students were more concerned about the treatment of First Nations as seen in efforts to re-name SFU Louis Riel University (Lexier, 2007: 7). SFU was an important site for the Canadian Student Movement, which gained the name "Berkley North" because of the large number of students involved in protest there (Cleveland, 2009). However, the Regina Campus of the University of Saskatchewan was also one of the more radical campuses in Canada (Lexier, 2008, 2012), and sit-ins and occupations were seen across the country. The Canadian Union of Students (CUS) offered leadership, training, and infrastructure to the students and helped mobilize them. Also important to Canadian New Left activism was the Company of Young Canadians (CYC), founded in 1965. Like other movements in the country, the relationship between the state and the student movement was blurred. The CYC was proposed by Prime Minister Lester B. Pearson as a youth program that would channel students and young Canadians into "constructive social action" (Dickenson and Campbell, 2008: 3). The connection to the state was met with suspicion linked to generational differences between older leftists with links to SUPA and younger activists joining the CYC. Tensions were also found between radical and more institutional orientations of young people more generally. Ultimately the "government funded hell-raisers," as the CYC came to be known, lost their independence from the government in 1969 because of many of these tensions (Brushett, 2009) and due to fears that it was becoming too radical. The federal government ultimately took over its administration and later disbanded it in 1977.

Student concerns about the nature of the university were linked to their concerns about the nature of society. In complaining about student alienation, overcrowded and irrelevant courses, distant professors, and university bureaucracy, students were also critiquing the large corporations and meaningless work of capitalist society (Levitt, 1984: 33). While protesting against university restrictions on their freedoms and demanding greater student involvement in university governance, students connected their struggles to larger issues of civil rights, racism, and democracy. In the United States, Students for a Democratic Society (SDS) used the slogan "A free university in a free society" to connect the Berkeley movement to these larger concerns (Sale, 1973: 168). In Canada, SUPA worked with disadvantaged communities and championed Indigenous rights in addition to organizing on campuses (Owram, 1996: 221), as did CUS and the CYC. All encouraged students and young people to act both within and outside the university. In Britain, students protested government policy in the colony of Rhodesia (later Zimbabwe), and in 1967, 100,000 students demonstrated to protest the government's plan to raise foreign student fees, a move that particularly affected Third World students and was considered racist by the student movement (Fraser, 1988: 109). In Italy, students in overcrowded universities protested lack of access to higher education for the working class as well as antiquated curricula, examination methods, and university hierarchies (Caute, 1988: 77). While students organized around their own grievances, they also questioned the policies of governments and the nature of the larger societies in which they lived.

The Vietnam War became an important focus of student protest in many countries. In the United States, student concern about the war increased greatly after the war escalated and the draft was enlarged in 1965. In April of that year SDS held a national protest against the war in Washington and in May, at Berkeley, the Vietnam Day Committee emerged out of the Free Speech Movement and sponsored a massive teach-in about the war. Throughout the country, SDS and the New Left expanded as concerns about the war mounted. In Britain, teach-ins about the war were held at the London School of Economics and at Oxford during the summer of 1965 in support of the American anti-war movement (Caute, 1988: 23). In Canada, a teach-in on Vietnam was held at the University of Toronto in October, and, following the event, student anti-war activists began raising the issue of Canada's complicity in the war through armament sales and other actions (Kostash, 1980: 46–8). SUPA became heavily involved in anti-war activities, in part as a way of radicalizing students who might not otherwise be drawn to the New Left (Owram, 1996: 221). In West Germany, the first major anti–Vietnam War demonstrations were held in Berlin in 1966, and opposition to the war was linked to anti-authoritarianism and concerns about German society (Fraser, 1988: 101–7). As demonstrations against the war spread to many countries, including France, Italy, and Japan, student movements linked criticisms of American imperialism to critiques of their own societies and the need for greater democracy.

Movement activity in the United States clearly influenced activists in other countries, even as movements in each country had their own particular concerns. Both mass media and personal contacts among individuals and organizations in different countries are important to the international **diffusion** of protest (McAdam and Rucht, 1993). In West Germany, for example, a student New Left organization called the Sozialistischer Deutscher Studentenbund (SDS) arose in the early 1960s at the same time as the American SDS was organizing. In the mid-1960s, writings of American New Leftists and descriptions of American tactics were published in the journal of the German SDS. Several activists from West Germany visited the United States, some as exchange students, and returned home to organize demonstrations in support of the Black Panthers and against the Vietnam War. The German New Left adopted tactics such as sit-ins and teach-ins, styles of dress, and their own versions of slogans from the American New Left and Black Power movements. For example, activists in Berlin turned the Black Power cry "Burn, baby, burn" into "Burn, warehouse, burn" to inspire firebombings of warehouses and other symbols of capitalism in Germany (McAdam and Rucht, 1993: 69).

In Canada, the influence of the American civil rights and anti-war movements was extensive. Some Canadians who became involved in the New Left had gone to the United States and participated in civil rights campaigns, and many Americans who were activists in the civil rights and anti-war movements fled to Canada to avoid the draft and continued their activism in the Canadian anti-war movement (see Levitt, 1984). John Hagan (2001: 35) estimates that more than 50,000 draft-age Americans moved to Canada; it was the largest exodus of Americans to the country since the American Revolution (Hagan, 2000: 609). Much of the migration was promoted by the Canadian federal government, which virtually granted amnesty to resisters. Rodgers (2014: 6) notes that about 40 per cent of those arriving settled in British Columbia. Many settled in the West Kootenays and resisters or "draft dodgers" were central to creating activist hubs such as Kitsilano in Vancouver or Yorkville in Toronto. Writings of the American New Left circulated widely in Canada, including a famous essay by Jerry Farber, "The Student as Nigger," which influenced high school students in Winnipeg to lobby for a student bill of rights (Vipond, 2004). Canadian groups such as the Labour Committee for Human Rights had ties to American organizations such as the National Association for the Advancement of Colored People (NAACP), and activists in Canada were inspired by Martin Luther King, who led the American civil rights movement.

In a collection of his writings published in 1968, Pierre Trudeau used the language of the US Supreme Court ruling in *Brown v. Board of Education*, which found the "separate but equal" principle of racial segregation in education unconstitutional, to discuss the need for linguistic equality and the integration of Quebec within Canada (Vipond, 2004: 96–7). By the late 1960s and early 1970s, American-influenced "rights talk" had become widespread in Canada. However, the frame was modified in line with a more collective Canadian "notion of rights that focused on the state's obligation to ensure equality" (ibid., 95).

PHOTO 4.1: Martin Luther King addressing a peace demonstration, United National Plaza, April 1967.

Legacies of the Protest Cycle of the 1960s

The civil rights, New Left, and anti-war movements mobilized large numbers of participants for a period of intense collective action. By the late 1960s these movements had begun to disintegrate for a variety of reasons, including internal weaknesses in movement organizations, an escalation of violence by radical factions, backlash from right-wing groups, and repression by governments (see Caute, 1988; Gitlin, 1980; Oberschall, 1978). Nevertheless, the protest cycle of the sixties had enduring influences on members of the baby boom generation, who retained their political beliefs and participation for the decades that followed (Whittier 1997; Braungart and Braungart, 1991; Jennings, 1987; 2002; Caren et al., 2011). Corrigall-Brown (2012: 123) found that 65 per cent of the 1965 American high school cohort belonged to an SMO or had participated in at least one protest, and that their level of political participation was affected by symbolic resources and biographical factors over the course of their lives.

The cycle of protest also affected subsequent movements and protests, including use of the "rights" frame, tactical models, lessons from movement campaigns, and profound challenges to the dominant culture. As Fraser (1988: 317) argues, "one of the major effects of the student rebellion has been a generalized disrespect for arbitrary and exploitive authority among the 1968 and succeeding generations in the West, a lack of deference toward institutions and values that demean people and a concomitant awareness of people's rights." Indigenous peoples, women, LGBT people, animal rights activists, disabled people, environmentalists, and many others were inspired to question authority and organize during and after the 1960s. Protest and social movement politics in the years to follow became so frequent and dominant that some, such as Meyer and Tarrow (1998), argued that North America and Europe had become "social movement societies." The cycle also influenced the rise of the neoliberal conservative movement in the 1970s, which dominated institutional politics for many years (Berger, 2010), and the more recent American Tea Partiers.

Among the movements that continued to advocate for new rights after the 1960s were numerous decolonial and nationalist movements. Although such movements often originated prior to the 1960s, many grew in strength and changed in character along with the protest cycle. In some instances, government affirmative action policies provided incentives for new groups to organize around their ethnic identities. In the United States, a variety of ethnic groups such as Indigenous peoples, Latinos, and Asian Americans were inspired by the successes of African Americans and encouraged by new government policies; as African Americans developed a new collective identity and a new rhetoric of black pride, other ethnic groups followed suit (Nagel, 1994: 166). At the same time as various ethnic groups organized to gain civil rights, however, white ethnic mobilization also occurred in response to affirmative action and desegregation efforts in the 1960s and 1970s, resulting in backlash movements such as anti-busing movements (Nagel, 1994: 158).

In Canada, the contemporary Quebec independence movement picked up steam in the late 1950s and 1960s as a result of a number of social and economic changes occurring in the province (Coleman, 1984; McRoberts, 1993). In the early 1960s, Quebec society underwent what is known as the "Quiet Revolution," a period of modernization and secularization of its educational system and culture, as well as its state and economic structures. Significantly, French-Canadian nationalists embraced economic and social development and became confident of their own capabilities (McRoberts, 1993: 129). Despite these changes, francophones in Quebec faced limited economic and cultural opportunities, and disaffected members of both the working class and the middle class were attracted to the sovereignty option. Inspired in part by decolonial and anti-imperialist movements in Algeria and the developing world, various organizations promoting independence formed and activists developed "a vision of a new Quebec that would be independent, secular, and social democratic" (Coleman, 1984: 218). Quebec labour unions, which grew in strength during the 1960s with the organization of public-sector workers, moved to the left politically and strongly supported the separatist movement. In 1968, sovereignty movement activists came together to form the Parti Québécois, which first won power in Quebec in 1976.

The Quebec independence movement provides an example of the tendency of some movements to split into militant and institutionalized factions; while part of the sovereignty movement became institutionalized, a radical element of the movement also emerged. Activists linked the Quebec struggle to the international protest movement of the 1960s (Krieber, 1989: 218), and one supporter of the Front de Libération du Québec (FLQ), Pierre Vallières, employed the American race analogy in his book *White Niggers of America*, which was widely read by radical Quebec nationalists (Vipond, 2004: 95–6). Owing to its use of political violence, the FLQ remained marginalized, "directly involving perhaps no more than 100 people in its various waves of bombings and vandalism during the 1960s" (McRoberts, 1993: 200), and was strongly discredited by its 1970 kidnapping and murder of a Quebec cabinet minister, Pierre Laporte, and its kidnapping of James Cross, a British trade commissioner. However, the struggles for liberation of the 1960s remained one source of inspiration for the larger, non-violent Quebec separatist movement, which became centred in the Parti Québécois.

Indigenous protests also intensified in Canada and other countries in the 1960s. In Canada, as we describe in Chapter 5, mobilization by Indigenous peoples accelerated in the late 1960s in response to the federal government's 1969 White Paper that proposed eliminating previously held Indigenous rights, and to changes in opportunities and resources (Ramos, 2006, 2008). Around the same time, the American Indian Movement (AIM) experienced a resurgence of activity as a result of the precedent set by the civil rights movement and the opportunities created by new government policies and programs (Nagel, 1996: 121). As ethnic identification became a source of status rather than stigma in the 1960s and 1970s, Native American peoples organized around the goal of "Red Power" in an effort to regain their cultural heritage as well as to settle various land claims (ibid., 124–5). Similar Indigenous mobilization can also be found across Latin America and other countries during the same period.

Since the 1960s other cycles of protest have come and gone, largely driven by new generations of activists. In the late 1980s Eastern Europe and other communist bloc countries witnessed the spread of contentious action sparked by reforms implemented by Mikhail Gorbachev in the Soviet Union (Mueller 1999). Ultimately this led to the fall of the Berlin Wall, which divided East and West Germany, and contributed to the fall of communism. Student protests also emerged in China, sparking the occupation of Tiananmen Square by student activists seeking democracy and eventually triggering military repression by the state (Zhao, 1998; 2000). An increase in protest was also seen in Canada with anti-NAFTA protests, Indigenous mobilization, and the sparking of the second Quebec referendum. More recently, new generations of activists have become increasingly politically active with the spread of protest from the Arab Spring, to anti-austerity protests in Greece, to the Indignados in Spain, Occupy protests around the world, and Idle No More in Canada.

Conclusion

The protest cycle of the 1960s mobilized large numbers of activists in many countries for numerous causes. It politicized a generation. Early movements, such as the civil rights movement, created collective action frames and tactical models that inspired massive New Left, student, and anti-war movements around the world. These movements generated change and conflict, and helped create new and lasting social movements, including Indigenous peoples' movements, the women's movement, the LGBT movement, and the environmental movement. Although the cycle of protest of the sixties declined, a number of movements survived, perpetuating the values, organizational forms, and tactics of the 1960s protests. Many activists from the movements of the sixties continued their activism in other social movements for decades to come. In some instances, the movements of the sixties also created countermovements, as we will see in examining the ongoing efforts of feminists and other activists. The following chapters examine the origins, organization, strategies, and outcomes of several ongoing social movements.

Discussion Questions

1.   Why do numerous social movements emerge during a cycle of contention?

2.   Why did the protest cycle of the 1960s decline? How did some movements survive beyond its decline?

3.   Have there been cycles of protest since the 1960s? What characterized them?

Suggested Readings

McAdam, Doug. 1995. "'Initiator' and 'Spin-off' Movements: Diffusion Processes in Protest Cycles", in M. Traugott, ed., *Repertoires and Cycles of Collective Action*. Durham, NC: Duke University Press. This article uses a political process model to analyze the influences of movements that come early in a protest cycle on later ones.

Palaeologu, Athena (editor). 2009. *The Sixties in Canada: A Turbulent and Creative Decade*. Montreal: Black Rose. This collection of essays examines the origins and unfolding of 1960s mobilization in Canada. It analyzes a wide range of movements from the New Left, to students, to the Waffle movement.

Tarrow, Sidney. 1989. *Democracy and Disorder: Protest and Politics in Italy, 1965–1975*. Oxford: Oxford University Press. This book examines a cycle of protest in Italy that ended in both institutionalization and violence in the mid-1970s.

5 Indigenous Protest

Social movements constantly face the problem of uniting diverse groups into a cohesive movement, and this is true for Indigenous peoples in Canada. Their mobilization is characterized by plurality and difference among actors rather than homogeneity. In fact, this is especially the case because the term "Aboriginal" refers to a number of different peoples, including status Indians (First Nations), non-status Indians, Métis, and Inuit. A number of additional differences among these groups—their history with colonization, legal status, language and culture, and urban versus rural experiences—at times conflict with one another, creating divergent interests.

Yet, despite diversity among Indigenous peoples, they have all faced common problems resulting from ongoing colonization and have all resisted the injustices that come with it. All have struggled against appropriation of land and material property, displacement to reserves (Miller, 1989), disenfranchisement (Indian and Northern Affairs Canada [INAC], 1996b, section 9.12), residential schooling (Haig-Brown, 1988), the banning of cultural practices (INAC, 1996c, section 9.5), being transferred from state to state without consultation (Grand Council of the Crees, 1998), discrimination in employment and daily life (Fleras and Elliott, 2003: 175; Ponting, 2000), and social exclusions from dominant institutions (Wotherspoon and Hansen, 2013: 16). Thus, despite differences among Indigenous peoples, government policy, practice, and social attitudes have created common injustices.

This chapter will examine tensions between divergent interests and the roles that resources, political opportunities, and collective identity play in engaging critical events. We first examine the concepts of community, bystanders, and critical events and then consider their dynamics by looking at Canadian Indigenous mobilization in the post–World War II era. The chapter examines how four events—the announcement of the White Paper in 1969, the patriation of the Constitution in 1982, the "Indian Summer" of 1990, and Idle No More in the winter of 2012–13—affected patterns of contention and relations with non-Indigenous Canadians. These events are discussed within the broader international context in comparison to

Indigenous protest in the United States and Latin America as well as in relation to other social movements. As will become apparent, despite many differences, critical events increase the potential for mass mobilization and the generation of common frames of resistance.

Communities, Bystanders, and Critical Events

As noted in Chapter 3 and by many social movement scholars, social networks play a significant role in mobilizing people. Nevertheless, just knowing someone does not translate into social action, and thus a focus on networks alone can be misleading (Snow et al., 1986: 468). Instead, people and communities define issues and mobilize, and if they are unable to generate bonds with other communities that share similar concerns, the outcome of their efforts will be minimal. This is because movements tend to be defined by supporters rather than by members alone (Staggenborg, 1998: 181). This is particularly the case for Indigenous peoples because their communities are often small, with limited resources. To achieve social change, small communities need to act with wider institutions, address injustices that have broad salience, and gain the support of bystander publics in other Indigenous communities and in the broader dominant society.

It is thus important to examine how communities, and the social movement organizations that represent them, interact with outside bystanders. Turner and Killian (1987: 216) define a **bystander public** as "a public that defines issues strictly from a bystander's perspective." Bystanders are people who have no direct stake in the outcome of a conflict, issue, or protest but may be affected by the dynamics that play out between political interests or mobilized groups. Turner and Killian go on to note that mobilization does not occur in a void and that actions by political elites, or those who challenge them, affect others who are not directly involved in the political process. Because of this, it is worth examining how bystanders respond to mobilization by supporting it, fighting against it, or remaining apathetic.

At a local level, community, identity, and support are constructed through basic group interactions. These allow people to share time and space, cultivate common interests, and in turn create bonds that can be drawn upon to generate resources, form organizations, engage political opportunities, defend identities, or even redress injustices. Nationally and internationally, however, such interactions are difficult to foster because regional and temporal differences act as obstacles to creating shared experience and common frames of reference. Because of this, commonality is constructed through processes of creating new collective identities. This involves producing common symbols for who belongs and this in turn binds communities together (Anderson, 1991). Large masses of people rarely share time and space, and thus national and international communities, as well as support for them,

are built through the engagement of common frames of reference that transcend differences.

Thus, the question of importance for small local communities, such as
those found among Indigenous peoples, is how to generate support from
bystanders in other communities and gain national and international attention. Dayan and Katz (1992) offer partial insight in their study of the role
of "media events," including coverage of celebrity and sporting events as
well as national tragedies. For social movements and resistance movements,
instances of political crisis should also be considered. Specifically, we need
to consider what role critical events play in bridging differences and building common platforms of social justice. As Staggenborg (1993: 320) argues,
"social movements are event-driven insofar as critical events alter expectations and perceptions of threats, focusing or distracting the attention of
movement constituents and other important actors on or away from movement issues." In other words, critical events provide opportunities to create
a common political environment, frame of interest, and support for a given
issue (Pride, 1995).

Others have examined similar phenomena. Ganz (2000: 1019) highlights how "focal moments" result in sudden changes that alter organizations' strategic capacities to mobilize. McAdam and Sewell (2001) show
that critical events act as poignant transformative instances that alter the
trajectory of contention and negotiation of social order. Yet others, such
as Khasnabish (2004), illustrate how "moments of coincidence" align the
mobilization of Indigenous struggles with other movements. He illustrates
this with the Zapatistas' struggle for autonomy and support from the labour
movement in Mexico. Such moments create common experience and in turn
generate support from other movements and bystanders.

Critical events, by any name, are "signalling opportunities" that contribute to frame alignment by affecting all actors in a given context simultaneously. Unlike political, legal, or economic opportunities, which re-emerge
in later cycles and involve institutions that continue to exist after the opportunity is gained or lost, critical events are defined by their immediacy and
historic significance. This is why they gain the greatest salience, offer the
ability to garner widespread response, transcend differences across a movement spectrum, and in turn demand engagement from bystander communities. Because of the shared experiences created by reactions to critical
events, such events lead bystanders to focus on issues embedded within
them. In some cases, this facilitates the renegotiation of dominant ideologies and social change. Before this occurs, a mobilized group must be able to
influence the way an event is interpreted and how bystanders interact with it
(Gamson, 2004; Staggenborg, 1993). The ability to do that is largely dictated
by the availability of resources, political opportunities, and the strength of
movement identities. As a result, if a given community or social movement

organization is able to tap into a critical event, it can be used to build coalitions with other communities, bystanders, and movements.

In the following sections we examine these dynamics through an analysis of Canadian Indigenous mobilization from the end of the Second World War to the present. As noted above, one of the biggest obstacles facing Indigenous mobilization is the lack of solidarity across groups. Consequently, much Indigenous social action lacks widespread engagement and is difficult to sustain (Ramos, 2006; Wilkes, 2004a, 2004b). There have, however, been notable exceptions, such as the protest against the White Paper, the engagement of the patriation process, the Indian Summer, and Idle No More. Each of these acted as a critical event for Canadian Indigenous mobilization, intersecting local communities, protesters, national movement organizations, and bystanders across the country and around the world.

The Rise of Contemporary Canadian Indigenous Mobilization

The post–World War II era was an unprecedented period of social change in North America and Europe. It ushered in human rights and anti-colonial discourses that forced existing nation-states, such as Canada, to reconsider their treatment and recognition of ethnic and national minorities (Niezen, 2000; Tennant, 1990: 121). At the same time, large numbers of Indigenous servicemen returning from World War II were becoming increasingly politically active and questioned their treatment by the dominant Canadian society (Fleras and Elliott, 1992: 42). They began to demand better educational opportunities, sought resources to develop communities, demanded that the federal government respect and honour past treaties, and pressured it to amend the Indian Act, which still governs the lives of Aboriginal peoples (Cardinal, 1999: 85). Similar trends were found in the United States (Cornell, 1988: 130; Nagel, 1996: 118). An instance of such mobilization in Canada can be seen in the case of Andrew Paull, chief of the Squamish in British Columbia and president of the North American Indian Brotherhood (NAIB), who criticized the 1951 amendments to the Indian Act, calling them dictatorial (Canadian Press, 1951).

Formally organized contention representing a broad range of interests, however, was the exception rather than the norm during the 1950s. Paull's actions were not followed by a surge of Indigenous protest as was the response to later proposed changes to the legislation. The NAIB actions were also "hindered by a lack of nation-wide support and suppressive government actions" that eventually led to internal administrative problems and the disbanding of the organization (AFN, 2011). Instead, during that decade, much Canadian Indigenous protest came from specific First Nations and local communities, and because of this it tended to occur around local injustices. When outsiders supported such causes, they were largely from neighbouring communities or were members of the same First Nation who were jointly affected. Mobilized communities thus reacted against issues affecting only their immediate interests, a limited number of neighbouring communities, or a specific First Nation. As a result, many actions during the period had little resonance in outside communities and yielded little broad-based support.

Few formal Indigenous political organizations emerged in the 1950s. Instead, the emphasis of many communities at this time was on creating clubs and informal meeting places that promoted Indigenous culture and on getting to know people rather than getting involved in politics. A prominent example of this was the founding of the North American Indian Club at "the Y" (YMCA) in Toronto. The urban Aboriginal community felt it was poorly represented and wanted to establish a meeting place that would generate a sense of pride and reflect an Indigenous cultural presence (Obonsawin and Howard-Bobiwash, 1997: 29). Although organizations were able to foster local identities and mobilize immediate communities, they faced difficulty in extending their concerns to outside bystanders, both Indigenous and non-Indigenous. As a result, the scope of early Indigenous mobilization was limited by the small size of communities, their organizations, and the local focus of mobilization. There were many obstacles to their efforts to recruit support across Canada, not to mention internationally.

In part, these trends are explained by a general lack of resources to promote widespread mobilization. Most of the organizing that took place was informal and focused on specific community interests rather than on larger pan-Canadian issues. This limited the pool of resources that could be drawn upon and in turn muted the potential for mass mobilization. In the 1960s, state funding became available (Miller, 1989: 329–30) and organizations began changing their mandates from fostering meeting places to being service providers and eventually to engaging the state through political action. Among the first contemporary national political organizations to emerge was the National Indian Council (NIC), established in the early 1960s (AFN, 2011). The council sought to create a movement of status Indians, non-status Indians, and Métis, but it had difficulty organizing because it was predominantly urban-based, while the majority of Indigenous people lived on reserves or in rural communities. The NIC faced other obstacles as well, such as a lack of stable funding and tensions stemming from divergent interests. In particular, status Indians did not want to be grouped with the Métis for fear of losing their treaty rights. The NIC dissolved in 1968, and its failure led to the creation of the National Indian Brotherhood (NIB), which represented status Indians alone (Cardinal, 1999: 92–3; Young, 1969). At the same time, the American Indian Movement (AIM) was founded in 1968 as a pan-Indigenous movement in the United States (Wilkes, 2006: 512). The same could be observed in Mexico with the formation of a national

Indigenous movement in the early 1970s (Brysk and Wise, 1997: 94). In all three countries, Indigenous peoples were responding to changing attitudes towards human rights, colonization, and national minorities.

The emergence of the NIB in Canada signalled a shift in how Aboriginal organizations were funded. Unlike earlier organizations, which gained much of their core resources through private means, the NIB would be almost entirely financed from government grants (Young, 1969). With the shift in organizational funding structures and new access to resources emerging in the 1960s, organizations began to move away from community donations, volunteerism, and local community building towards government grants and paid lobbyists. This was a pattern seen across many Canadian social justice organizations. As Clément (2009: 365) notes, the federal secretary of state began to play a major role in funding all sorts of Canadian organizations at that time. Many Indigenous leaders feared that these shifts would alienate the very communities they wanted to represent and in turn weaken their organizations' ability to resist the colonial policies of the federal government.

The White Paper

The 1960s ended with the Canadian government's release of the 1969 White Paper on Indian Policy and intense mobilization against it. The White Paper was a federal policy brief proposing the elimination of Indian status and the assimilation of the Aboriginal population (Cairns, 2000: 163). The federal government wanted to overcome the disparities among Indigenous peoples as well as to respond to the changing international discourse, which prized human and civil rights. The release of the White Paper presented a significant political opportunity and became a critical event that many believe marked the birth of contemporary Indigenous mobilization (Long, 1992: 121). Status Indians were concerned about losing their treaty rights as First Nations; at the same time, however, the paper also affected all other Aboriginal peoples, including non-status Indians, Métis, and Inuit. Because of this, it resonated beyond the critical mass of communities that had initially opposed it. The White Paper provided a common collective action frame, aligning goals and grievances among Indigenous peoples.

The first signs of opposition came from Alberta status Indians, who responded by drafting their own legislation, which they called the Red Paper. This document was presented to the federal cabinet in Ottawa in June 1970. It was based on the findings of the 1966 Hawthorn Report[1] and demanded "citizenship plus" (Cairns, 2000: 67)—that is, it sought recognition of Aboriginal rights as well as the rights of basic Canadian citizenship. Opposition emerged because the government had refused to accept Indigenous perspectives on the Indian Act. The federal government was interested in constructing a single policy that would integrate Indigenous peoples into Canadian society rather than preserve a multiplicity of First Nations, non-status Indians, Métis, and Inuit (Morris, 1969). The introduction of the White Paper created a common grievance and frame of resistance that garnered support among different communities. It was a critical event that generated widespread protest and it signalled a new era for contemporary Canadian Indigenous contention (Ramos, 2006: 223; Wilkes, 2006: 513).

Meanwhile, in the United States, the AIM was becoming increasingly active. During the same year, a group of Indigenous students from San Francisco State University began a 19-month occupation of Alcatraz Island. They declared themselves "Indians of All Tribes" and claimed the island on the grounds of treaty rights granted the Sioux in 1868 (Cornell, 1988; Johnson, 1996; Nagel, 1996: 131; Wilkes, 2006: 513). Like the White Paper, this event sparked much support. Joane Nagel even argues that it was of central importance as "*the* symbolic icon of Indian ethnic resurgence" in the United States (Nagel, 1996: 135).

Mobilization against the White Paper led to its eventual demise and, more importantly, to a policy vacuum on Indigenous issues in Canada. The federal government responded to events with Cabinet formally approving a core funding program in 1971 to provide Aboriginal groups with the resources they needed to promote their causes at the federal level (Canadian Heritage, 2005: 4; INAC, 2009: 32; Fleras and Elliott, 1992: 44). During this period, Ottawa officially changed its policy from attempting to terminate Aboriginal rights to supporting Indigenous organizations. Temporary funding granted to status Indians through the NIB was extended indefinitely and also offered to others. In fact, the Inuit Tapirisat of Canada (since renamed Inuit Tapiriit Kanatami [ITK]) and the Native Council of Canada (NCC—today the Congress of Aboriginal Peoples) were founded during this time. Because of the shift in political opportunities and resource availability, injustices were increasingly addressed through national-level politics.

This shift in focus incurred a number of obstacles. The federal government began to impose a number of restrictions and guidelines for organizational funding. It did not fund every Aboriginal organization but instead prioritized those organizations that claimed to represent *all* Indigenous peoples and those that were urban based. Evidence of this can be seen in the secretary of state's policy of supporting only one organization per province during the 1970s (*Globe and Mail*, 18 July 1972; Canadian Press, 1972). The federal government was willing to fund organizations, but on its terms.

As resources for mobilizing nationally increased, newly emerging organizations moved away from local communities to exploit political opportunities stemming from the defeat of the White Paper. Ottawa was in search of a viable policy on Indigenous issues that would not incur social unrest. The Liberal government was open to consultation on such matters, and as a result, during the 1970s, Indigenous organizations began spending less energy on local concerns, focusing instead on government policies. In shifting their efforts, organizations were increasingly fighting their battles in the courts, through lobbying, and in the media. This led them to spend less time building ties across communities and more time interacting with judicial and bureaucratic institutions.

The change in tactics accompanied the rise of a young Indigenous elite that had been educated in the dominant school system because of forced residential schooling. This elite was familiar with judicial and governmental institutions. Many of these leaders, however, were cut off from their local communities, and concern emerged over their ability to represent their people without being influenced by the federal government. As Taiaiake Alfred notes, "The co-optation of our [Indigenous] political leadership is a subtle, insidious, undeniable fact, and it has resulted in a collective loss of ability to confront the daily injustices, both petty and profound, of Native life" (1999: 73). In addition, some scholars have expressed concern that federal funding increased Aboriginal dependency (Gagné, 1994), while others have worried that such funding has not and will not resolve outstanding issues (Flanagan, 2000).

Nevertheless, the young Indigenous leaders of that time found that past treaties were powerful tools. They could be used to force the federal government to negotiate with Indigenous peoples and possibly remedy a wide range of social problems. Evidence of this was seen in 1970 when the NIB, Canadian Métis Society, and Indian-Eskimo Association[2] released a 300-page report warning that Indigenous people could bog down the courts with trials looking into treaty rights (Platiel, 1970). This was not merely a threat, and indeed a number of grievances were filed with courts across the country, leading to significant Supreme Court decisions during the 1970s that set legal precedents to support Indigenous struggles. The 1973 *Calder* decision, for example, provided impetus for the federal government to negotiate new treaties. In fact, Canada settled its first "modern" land claim with the signing of the James Bay and Northern Quebec Agreement in 1975. Thus, the 1970s saw an opening of the institutional political sphere for Indigenous organizations as funding became increasingly available, the courts provided a target for redress of past wrongs, and the government turned to the settlement of land claims.

Yet the 1970s were also characterized by an unprecedented number of radical protests. In part, this was the result of a series of highly publicized and innovative actions by the AIM in the United States whose effects spilled into Canada. In 1972, the AIM occupied the Bureau of Indian Affairs in Washington (Cornell, 1988: 190), and in 1973 and again in 1975, it violently occupied Wounded Knee on the Pine Ridge Reservation in South Dakota (Josephy et al., 1999: 48–9; Nagel, 1996: 171). These events sparked the Red

Power movement in the United States and led to a number of protests across that country as well as in Canada. The AIM, however, was repressed in the United States after the shooting deaths of two FBI agents at the Pine Ridge Reservation, and this repression was linked with the movement's rapid demobilization. The demise of the AIM also coincided with a move away from radical protest in Canada as the federal government continued to fund and negotiate with national-level political organizations and their leaders.

Divergences among traditional and elected leaders, between local and national interests, urban and rural Indigenous peoples, radical and mainstream groups, and differing legal statuses of Aboriginal peoples defined the post–White Paper period and remains the case today. This state of affairs was exacerbated when young Indigenous elites pursued the recognition of "rights." Existing legislation guaranteed only the rights of status Indians and, in some regards, the Inuit, but the federal government did not recognize the rights of non-status Indians, Aboriginal women, and Métis. Tensions resulting from different statuses led to mobilization around different interests instead of around common ones, and grievances around rights divided communities rather than bridging them. For status Indians, legal rights and treaties were seen as tools to gain self-determination, but for non-status groups, they provided a path to formal recognition. The two objectives were at odds, and over time they proved to be obstacles to coalition- and community-building.

The Constitution Act, 1982

By the 1980s, differences among Indigenous peoples became further entrenched through the federal government's decision to patriate the Constitution, which proved to be an immense political opportunity. In the negotiations leading to patriation, Indigenous organizations saw an opening for extending and recognizing their rights. Like the White Paper in 1969, the decision to patriate the Constitution would affect *all* Indigenous peoples, despite their differences. The patriation process was an opportunity that created a shared narrative space and provided a common target against which to frame injustices. Status Indians and Inuit saw patriation as an opportunity to obtain self-government and respect for past treaties; non-status Indians saw it as a way to be legally recognized and access benefits; Indigenous women saw it as a means of achieving legal recognition and equality with men; and the Métis saw it as a means of gaining recognition as a First Nation.

In the early stages of the patriation process, the NIB organized a delegation of 347 Indigenous leaders to petition the British parliament and queen to gain the right to sit as full participants at constitutional discussions (Webster, 1979). Although this was not the first time Canadian Indigenous peoples had used international institutions to exert pressure in the negotiation of their rights, it was an unprecedented sign of unity. The delegation gained much attention and sparked a short wave of protest across the country. A highlight of these actions was the 1980 "Constitution Express," a train that ran from the West Coast to the capital in Ottawa, picking up Aboriginal supporters along the way (Canadian Press, 1980). It created a symbol of pan-Indigenous unity, organization, and action.

The patriation of the Constitution provided a rare opportunity to involve bystanders among non-Aboriginal communities and to generate ties among Aboriginal groups and organizations. Like the White Paper, it was a critical event that affected all Indigenous peoples simultaneously. Either they would *all* lose their rights or they could use patriation as an opportunity to gain benefits and possibly even achieve self-determination. But, unlike the White Paper, the Constitution also affected all Canadians. As Clément Chartier, president of the Métis National Council (MNC), former president of Métis Nation–Saskatchewan (also known as the Métis Nation of Saskatchewan), and organizer for the NCC, recalled, "[O]nly eight provinces supported patriation. In order to justify patriating the Constitution [Prime Minister] Trudeau needed the support of the public and it was very important that they had the support of the Aboriginal people" (quoted in Ramos, 2004: 107–8).

There was also increasing support for Indigenous rights among the general public. By 1990, a survey conducted by the *Globe and Mail* found that the majority of Canadians supported Aboriginal issues, with 78 per cent of English Canadians and 69 per cent of French Canadians believing that constitutional amendments should address Aboriginal concerns (*Globe and Mail*, 9 July 1990). The constitutional process was thus a critical event for Indigenous mobilization because it raised the bystander public's consciousness of grievances. In other words, the process led to an extension of Indigenous collective action frames and to the potential alignment of the dominant population with their concerns. Yet, despite signs that the Constitution would include a broader community of actors, the legal language surrounding it limited its potential to generate ties among Indigenous peoples. Unity created through actions such as the Constitution Express was thus quick to dissipate.

By the early 1980s the federal government began showing signs that it was prepared to give the NIB (representing status Indians) a seat as a full participant at the constitutional discussions. Other national organizations worried that the NIB would gain the *only* seat open to Aboriginals, fanning tensions among divergent interests. The three main national organizations—the NIB, NCC, and ITK—had different views on what should be incorporated in the Constitution. By April of 1981, differences had become apparent. The NCC, mostly representing urban non-status Indians, began lobbying independently of other organizations (Canadian Press, 1981). The coalition among groups was weak and eventually broke apart. In 1983, the Métis formed their own organization, the MNC. They worried that their demands could not be repre-sented if lumped together with those of the non-status urban Indians of the NCC. Another source of tension came from the Native Women's Association of Canada (NWAC), which feared that recognition of Aboriginal rights would exclude them. They were concerned that the reaffirmation of the Indian Act and negotiations by male-dominated organizations would fail to recognize the injustices they faced. During the same period, in 1982, the NIB changed its name to the Assembly of First Nations (AFN).

Despite these differences and tensions among national organizations, the major Aboriginal groups were incorporated into sections 25 and 35 of the Constitution Act, 1982. However, the success of gaining recognition was marred by further division among organizations. The definition of "Aboriginal" adopted was vague and did not concretely set out what rights Aboriginal peoples were entitled to. It also did not clarify whether there would be equal recognition of men and women, previously unrecognized in the Indian Act. In order to resolve these problems as well as other outstand-ing issues, the federal government hosted several additional constitutional conferences between 1983 and 1987. Aboriginal peoples were invited to a number of these, and Indigenous mobilization during the 1980s moved fur-ther into the institutional realm.

The decade closed with government cuts to Indigenous education and organizations, as well as a failure to gain more specific recognition of Aboriginal peoples in post-constitutional conferences. At the final confer-ence, in 1987, the Meech Lake Accord was negotiated, to be ratified by 1990. The accord was intended to amend the Constitution to better incorporate Quebec but also to deal with broader issues such as Senate reform, immi-gration, and Supreme Court appointments. Despite the accord's grand vision, it was opposed by the women's movement, trade unions, anti-poverty groups, and, not least, Indigenous groups. All felt that their rights were being ignored.

The Indian Summer of 1990

As Ramos (2006, 2008) and Wilkes (2004a, 2004b, 2006) note, 1990, the year the Meech Lake Accord was to be ratified, saw the greatest level of Indigenous protests in Canada since World War II. As in 1969, with the announcement of the White Paper, and the early 1980s, with the patriation process, this was a period of intense political mobilization on the part of Indigenous peoples. The Indian Summer was the result of a series of events that sparked widespread Indigenous protest and led to the generation of a number of new organizations.

The first notable event occurred when status Indians from Manitoba used the ratification process of the Meech Lake Accord as a means to threaten and eventually prevent its adoption. Elijah Harper, an Oji-Cree chief and New Democratic Party (NDP) member of the provincial legislature, under the advice of the Assembly of Manitoba Chiefs, used the process as a way to draw attention to Indigenous injustices. By withholding his vote "on the grounds that procedural rules were not being followed" (Dickason, 2002: 402), he effectively blocked the accord, as each province had to ratify it before 23 June 1990 or the agreement would collapse.

Harper's battle attracted significant media coverage and brought Indigenous issues under the spotlight of Canadian politics. Like the patriation of the Constitution, it brought bystanders into the negotiation of Indigenous grievances. Because Harper's fight was based within the country's legal structures, was grounded in the discourse of the greater Canadian society, appealed to common sense, and was against an agreement that many other Canadians also did not accept, his plight resonated within the dominant society. It aligned Indigenous interests with the dominant population's master frame. Indigenous people saw Harper's stand as a tremendous achievement, signalling their ability to resist unequal relations and fight ongoing colonization.

Less than a month after the defeat of the Meech Lake Accord, Mohawks in Kanesatake, Quebec, faced off against provincial police in a violent standoff dubbed the "Oka Crisis." The Sûreté du Québec (SQ) attempted to break a barricade outside the town of Oka that Mohawks from Kanesatake had erected to prevent the expansion of a golf course on land they claimed was a traditional burial ground. When the SQ moved in with force, Mohawk warriors defended the roadblock, exchanging gunfire that left one SQ officer dead and resulted in a 78-day armed standoff.[3] Mohawk warriors from the neighbouring community of Kahnawake, in support, blocked roads going into their reserve as well as the Mercier Bridge, a major link between the suburbs of Montreal and the city. The standoff escalated over the summer to the point where the Canadian army was brought in to quell the protest.

Like Elijah Harper's actions, those of the Mohawk gained increasing media coverage, which again raised the profile of Indigenous issues. The Oka Crisis opened the public sphere to injustices and colonization and created a shared collective action frame. Because the standoffs happened soon after Harper's victory, they gave the appearance of a powerful and well-connected pan-Indigenous movement. Further, because the events in Kanesatake and Kahnawake took place within the suburbs of Montreal and were violent in nature, they brought Indigenous issues to the forefront of national media and a wide array of bystander publics were engaged. These actions jointly formed another critical event that Canadians watched unfold on their televisions.

The period was branded the "Indian Summer" because Indigenous peoples in communities across the country protested in support of the Mohawks in Kanesatake and Kahnawake. To give just a few examples,

members of the Six Nations Reserve in southern Ontario erected blockades on highways and across Canadian National rail lines, threatening to
maintain them until the Canadian army pulled out of Oka; likewise, 50
Aboriginals on the Bruce Peninsula in southwestern Ontario blocked
a road to their community to put pressure on the federal government to
act; Natives at the Tyendinaga Reserve near Belleville in eastern Ontario
blocked a bridge to Prince Edward County in support; and Ojibwa from
the Saugeen and Cape Croker reserves set up roadblocks as well (*Globe and
Mail*, 6 September 1990). Even non-Indigenous people and the international
community showed support; for instance, the Paris-based International
Human Rights Federation sent observers to monitor the conflict (Poirier,
1990). The events of that summer inspired a new generation of Indigenous
and non-Indigenous activists and leaders and they shaped Aboriginal politics
for the decades that followed (Rice, 2010).

The Oka standoff in particular was rife with iconic imagery that would
shape both Indigenous protest and the way the media portrayed it for years to
come. Perhaps the most iconic image of the standoff was "Face to Face," shown
in Photo 5.1. As Wilkes and Kehl (2014) note, it portrayed both Indigenous
and non-Indigenous conceptions of justice and nationalism. The image of
Mohawk warriors in military fatigues, the spread of the warrior flag at protest
events across the country, and radical action came to frame Indigenous mobilization in the dominant media for decades to come, often delegitimizing it and
failing to recognize that most struggles were against ongoing colonization.

CP Images/Shaney Komulainen

Photo 5.1: Face to face

The standoff ended in the fall of 1990 and the federal government responded by announcing a Royal Commission on Aboriginal Peoples a year later. The commission was given the mandate of investigating the evolution of the relationships among Canada's Indigenous peoples, the Canadian government, and society as a whole (INAC, 1996). It was one of the largest commissions conducted in Canada and lasted several years, offering unprecedented visibility for national Indigenous organizations and their leaders. The rest of the 1990s reflected both increasing institutional action, by both Indigenous elites and the national organizations, and the increasing use of more radical tactics by non-formally organized actors in local communities. The Indian Summer created a policy vacuum in Indigenous–non-Indigenous Canadian relations and led to more opportunities for Indigenous peoples to engage in dominant Canadian politics. As a result, the rest of the 1990s saw significant gains in the recognition of Aboriginal peoples and their rights. This was seen, for instance, in the signing of the Nunavut Land Claims Agreement in 1993 and the creation of Nunavut as a Canadian territory in 1999; in the 1996 creation of Canada's National Aboriginal Day, June 21; and in the Supreme Court of Canada's 1997 *Delgamuukw* decision, which set precedents for Aboriginal title and legitimized Indigenous oral history. The close of the decade also saw the Supreme Court, through its 1999 *Marshall* decision, uphold the 1760–61 treaty between the Mi'kmaq and the Crown that ensured their fishing rights. All these examples represent important shifts in Indigenous relations.

However, despite such gains, the close of the decade also saw a number of radical and even violent actions, as witnessed by the standoffs at Gustafsen Lake, British Columbia, and Ipperwash, Ontario in 1995 and the Mi'kmaq lobster crisis, which affected much of Atlantic Canada, in the fall of 1999. Each of these high-profile conflicts reflects a common pattern in Canadian Indigenous mobilization, one that sees local or small-scale groups act in defence of land and/or rights, only to be met with large-scale repression and even violence. In the case of Gustafsen Lake, rancher Lyell James[4] called for the Royal Canadian Mounted Police (RCMP) when a group of 21 Indigenous people and their supporters held an annual sun dance on contested land (Wilkes et al., 2010: 331). This led to a 31-day standoff and one of the largest and most expensive Royal Canadian Mounted Police operations in Canadian history (Lambertus 2004: 3). At its conclusion, 18 people were arrested on charges ranging from mischief to attempted murder (ibid.).

The Ipperwash crisis had roots as far back as 1993, when members of the Stony Point First Nation first began to reclaim parts of a military base in southern Ontario on land that had once belonged to them (Morden 2013: 510). During the summer of 1995, the First Nation's grievances and occupation gained national attention when the army barracks on the base were systematically occupied. In the fall of that year, the military withdrew from the base and on Labour Day, a number of protesters with ties to Stony Point occupied nearby Ipperwash Provincial Park (ibid.). The Ontario Provincial Police (OPP) had been used to monitor the occupation of the military base and had generated a plan for managing a potential occupation of the park—titled "Project Maple" (Linden, 2007: 14–18). Two days after the occupation of the park began, a violent confrontation outside the park led to the fatal shooting of protester Dudley George by the OPP. Acting Sergeant Kenneth Deane was later convicted of criminal negligence causing death and, after years of repeated calls by Indigenous groups, a provincial inquiry into the shooting was launched in 2003. The by-product of the inquiry was a change in narrative around the Indigenous protest and occupation of stolen lands and a greater understanding of the history of colonization by non-Indigenous Canadians. The protesters also secured a land transfer agreement. As Morden (2013) notes, although such an outcome is unprecedented, it is limited to the Ipperwash conflict rather than achieving social justice for Indigenous Canadians more broadly.

Violence also occurred in the fall of 1999 when Mi'kmaq fishers began to set lobster traps out of season in Miramichi Bay, off the coast of New Brunswick, after the Supreme Court of Canada overturned lower-court rulings against Donald Marshall Jr for illegal fishing and sale of eels. The court upheld a 1760–61 treaty and set a precedent that the Mi'kmaq interpreted as opening the lucrative commercial fishery to their peoples after years of largely being shut out (Coates, 2000). However, their entry into the fishery was met by fear and violence by non-Indigenous fishers, who worried that they would lose their livelihoods if the decision led to full-scale involvement of Indigenous people in the fishery. It is important to note that the decision came at the end of a decade that had seen serious losses to the fisheries of the region and moratoriums (ibid.). Indigenous fishing was thus vigorously protested, and for roughly two months there was tit-for-tat violence and mischief between Indigenous and non-Indigenous people across the Atlantic provinces (Ramos, 2007). The dispute was especially concentrated in the communities of Burnt Church and Indian Brook in New Brunswick and Nova Scotia, and ultimately the Supreme Court offered a "clarification" on its landmark decision, making it much more limited in scope.

Clearly, the mobilization of the 1990s illustrates the divergent interests that persist among Indigenous peoples and the setbacks that came with victories.

Idle No More

Indigenous mobilization continues to reflect successes by national organizations and a greater interest in and awareness of Indigenous issues among the dominant Canadian population. But it has also seen radical action born out of frustration over persistent grievances, long-standing stalemates, and ongoing colonization. The first two decades of the twenty-first century have witnessed a mix of successes and setbacks for national organizations, the threat of radical action by a number of local communities, and rapidly changing demographics among Indigenous communities which have all contributed to the emergence of Idle No More.

The start of the 2000s was met with much excitement about potential progress on Indigenous issues. In 1999, Nunavut came to fruition as Canada's first Aboriginal-majority territory. Some claim it is the largest and most comprehensive Aboriginal settlement in Canadian history (Légaré, 2008: 336). Its creation saw division of the Northwest Territories and control of roughly 18 per cent of the new territory ceded to the Inuit of the Central and Eastern Arctic (ibid., 446). Just a year later, the Nisga'a Final Agreement came into effect, resolving a 113-year dispute (Nisga'a Lisims Government, 2010). The agreement is also the first modern-day treaty in British Columbia, a province that has historically signed very few treaties, and it is a benchmark in Indigenous relations. It sets out the right to self-government and the authority to manage resources (INAC, 2010a). Soon after, the Ontario Court of Appeal in 2001 and the Supreme Court in 2003 offered the *Powley* decisions, which upheld Métis hunting and fishing rights and also set precedents for how to interpret the definition of "Métis" in the Constitution Act, 1982. The rights of the Métis and non-status Indians, moreover, were further affirmed in a 2013 Supreme Court decision that recognized that they are "Indians" under the Constitution Act, 1982.

The 2000s have seen not only unprecedented land claim settlements and court decisions but also a commitment on the part of the federal government to address long-standing Indigenous grievances and the staggering obstacles facing a young and growing Aboriginal population. This ultimately led to the negotiation of the Kelowna Accord in the fall of 2005, an unprecedented and historic series of agreements among federal, provincial, and territorial governments and Indigenous leaders and organizations to improve education, employment, living conditions, and health care through government funding and new programs (Webster, 2006). The Accord committed $5 billion in spending over 10 years (Patterson, 2006; Webster, 2006). However, it was never implemented because the government fell, and the newly elected Conservative regime, led by Stephen Harper, decided to abandon it to instead focus on the needs of the growing urban off-reserve Aboriginal populations (Ratner and Woolford, 2008). The sense of achieving a long-awaited success with the Kelowna Accord was abruptly brought to a halt, and much of the strategy and momentum in Indigenous politics shifted as a result.

Whereas national organizations continued to engage with the political opportunities presented by courts and the federal government, local

Indigenous peoples continued to struggle, often out of frustration, to have decades-old injustices resolved. In the middle of the decade, national attention peaked when a group of Six Nations protesters in Caledonia, Ontario erected tents and began an occupation of disputed land that was set to be developed by Henco Industries, a land developer. In March 2006, the developer sought a court injunction to have the protesters removed. The OPP subsequently arrested a number of protesters in April of that year, an action that was met hours later by several hundred supporters setting up roadblocks, burning tires, and reoccupying the land. This led to an escalation in the dispute that saw supporting protests by Mohawk communities in Ontario and Quebec. In June of that year, the Ontario government bought out the land developer, but the occupation continued and the summer was tense, filled with clashes, often violent and at times racist, between Indigenous and non-Indigenous protesters (for a timeline of the events, see CBC, 2006).

A year later, frustration over inaction on Aboriginal land claims and social issues could even be found among leaders of national organizations. This led the AFN to call for a National Day of Action on 29 June 2007, "designed to raise awareness and support among the general public and the government for urgent action to address First Nations issues" (AFN, 2007). Mentioned in the call for action were concerns over living conditions, rights, the new Conservative government's failure to adopt the Kelowna Accord, the continued failure of governments to resolve land claims in a timely manner, and the reversal of Canada's position with respect to the United Nations' draft Declaration on the Rights of Indigenous Peoples. However, the call for action prompted individual bands and aggrieved groups to threaten blockades and standoffs, which sidetracked the media coverage leading up to the national protest. For instance, Chief Terry Nelson of the Roseau River First Nation gained much attention with threats to block rail lines in Manitoba, which led the AFN to appeal to the railway companies to shut down for the day (CTV, 2007). Another example is the threat issued by Mohawk activist Shawn Brant to use armed force to block sections of major highways and railways in Ontario. Activists followed through by erecting temporary blockades the night before the day of action (CBC, 2007). Yet, despite such actions, the day saw hundreds of peaceful events across the country, and radical actions were few and short-lived.

The rest of the decade and now the 2010s can be characterized by a mix of successes and failures. The AFN negotiated the creation of the Specific Claims Tribunal (SCT) with the federal government to help resolve some of the enormous backlog of specific land claims. The SCT, an independent body with adjudicative powers, replaced the Indian Specific Claims Commission, which had previously made non-binding recommendations on disputes over specific land claims. Established in the fall of 2008, the

SCT "has all the powers, rights and privileges that are vested in a superior court of record" (SCT, 2009) and can thus make a "binding decision on the validity of and compensation for specific claims" (INAC, 2010b). It is seen as a major step forward in accelerating the pace at which land claims are resolved. The same year, Stephen Harper's government issued an official apology in Parliament for the policy of residential schooling that scarred generations of First Nations children, and it launched the national Truth and Reconciliation Commission in 2008 to investigate the abuses associated with that policy and to promote healing (Wotherspoon and Hansen, 2013). The commission issued its final report in the spring of 2015 with 94 recommendations on reconciling the broken relationship between Indigenous and non-Indigenous Canadians and the ongoing effects of colonization.

However, at the same time, the Conservative government voted against the United Nations Declaration on the Rights of Indigenous Peoples in 2007, leaving Canada and the United States as the only two countries of the Americas to vote against it. The federal government refused to open an inquiry into the systemic problem of murdered and missing Indigenous women despite ongoing mobilization (Canadian Press, 2014). As examined in detail in Chapter 6, the NWAC has campaigned for an inquiry into this systemic tragedy, documenting cases of women who have disappeared without proper investigation by police and other authorities (NWAC, 2010). The organization and other groups have been holding annual vigils to focus attention on this issue since the 1990s. The RCMP more recently admitted that there have been 1,186 cases of murdered and missing Indigenous women in Canada over the last 30 years (Jackson, 2014). The federal government has also begun issuing omnibus legislation that affects Aboriginal rights without consulting Indigenous peoples and has questioned the accountability and funding of Aboriginal communities and organizations.

Two pieces of legislation, Bill C-38 and C-45 (the *Jobs, Growth and Long-term Prosperity Act* and the *Jobs and Growth Act*), had a profound impact on contemporary Canadian Indigenous mobilization. Both were issued in 2012, were 450 pages long, and were seemingly aimed at non-Indigenous issues. However, couched within each piece of legislation were infringements on Indigenous land rights, water rights, and treaties with little to no consultation, and this was considered a form of ongoing colonization and social exclusion (McMillan et al., 2013: 430; Wotherspoon and Hansen, 2013).

The first bill received royal assent in June of 2012 and the second, Bill C-45, was slated to pass through Parliament in the late fall of the same year. Four women from Saskatchewan (Jessica Gordon, Sheelah McLean, Sylvia McAdam, and Nina Wilson) began brainstorming via email and turned to Facebook under the thread "Idle No More" to challenge the legislation (Caven, 2013; Van Gelder, 2013; Inman et al., 2013). They later initiated the #idlenomore hashtag on Twitter. They felt they needed to protect the environment and Indigenous rights, and together they organized a teach-in at Station West, a community enterprise centre in Saskatoon. The event was successful but received little mainstream media attention.

From there the women continued to mobilize and the #idlenomore hashtag remained active, sparking rallies and protests throughout the Prairie Provinces (Caven, 2013). The movement that emerged expanded beyond the legislation and the four women that initiated it. With a loose organizational structure and the tactical use of social media, mirroring other movements of the 2000s and 2010s such as the Arab Spring, Occupy, and the Maple Spring, the #idlenomore hashtag and meme gained traction. It held resonance as a call to Indigenous peoples to resist colonization and return to their traditional teachings. The meme also extended to non-Indigenous bystanders who were concerned over protection of the environment and the undemocratic practices of the Harper regime in issuing omnibus bills to achieve its ends.

Idle No More called for a national day of action on 10 December, which coincided with the United Nations Human Rights day and came days before the Senate would vote on Bill C-45. A day later, Chief Theresa Spence from Attawapiskat, in Northern Ontario, embarked on a hunger strike in a teepee erected on an island in the Ottawa River behind Parliament Hill. She did this in the name of Idle No More and to gain attention for the injustices faced by Indigenous peoples. A few years earlier, Spence gained national attention by calling a state of emergency in her community because it faced a housing and infrastructure crisis and she felt this was the only way to get the federal government to act. Spence said that she would continue her hunger strike until she could speak with the Prime Minister and Governor General in a nation-to-nation meeting.

The mainstream media mistakenly declared Spence as the leader of the movement. The increased attention offered by the media amplified the hashtag and movement, leading to hundreds of protests across the country and around the world, both by Indigenous peoples and by non-Indigenous bystanders who had become supporters of the movement. Many of the actions took new forms, expanding the repertoire of Indigenous protest to include flash mobs and teach-ins as well as more established actions like marches and highway and rail blockades.

Idle No More, however, was a grassroots movement and because of that it triggered the politicization of a new generation of activists that mobilized in concert with Elders and established activists. Unlike earlier waves of Indigenous protest, many of the main actors driving the movement were women, changing the image of Indigenous activist from young men in camouflage with warrior flags to young, often university-educated, women. The movement also sparked the imagination of other movements, and solidarity was expressed by environmentalists and those in other social justice movements, which we explore in Chapters 8 and 9. The rapid and widespread rise of Indigenous protest under the Idle No More meme led many to compare it

Ossie Michelin, APTN (Aboriginal People's Television Network).

PHOTO 5.2: A new iconic image of Indigenous protest?

to the Indian Summer of 1990 (Woons, 2013: 172), thus making it a critical event in Canadian Indigenous mobilization.

The federal government was taken aback by the rapid mobilization in the name of Idle No More. Prime Minister Harper was initially reluctant to meet Theresa Spence or other chiefs concerning the injustices driving the grassroots protests. This too amplified the movement and Aboriginal organizations, such as the AFN, increasingly began invoking the meme and speaking on behalf of the movement, thereby shifting the discourse of what had until then been a largely grassroots movement. Idle No More responded to this by making a post on its blog on New Year's Eve distancing the movement from Spence and what it called the "leadership" of Indigenous communities. This was the beginning of the movement's demobilization.

Through a series of negotiations the Grand Chief of the AFN, Shawn Atleo, secured a historic meeting for a small delegation of chiefs from different provinces and territories, representatives from the organization's youth, women's, and Elders councils as well as the Prime Minister and senior cabinet ministers on 11 January 2013. Theresa Spence and a number of chiefs, however, felt that Governor General should be at the meeting because of an orthodox understanding of treaties being signed with the crown and the fact that the Governor General is the official head of state. A number of Manitoba chiefs, moreover, disagreed with the location of the meeting and the process in which it was negotiated. That day Idle No More organized a protest on Parliament hill drawing about 3,000 demonstrators.

Despite the meeting Spence continued her hunger strike until 24 January, for a total of 44 days. Idle No More organized a global day of action for 28 January to coincide with the return of Parliament. That day protests occurred across the country, however, participation and media coverage was less intense than earlier events. In part this was because of the cleavages that were seen in the movement through Spence's demand to meet with the Prime Minister. Many began questioning if the movement had coherence and whether a meme was enough to spark long-term change.

Since the winter of 2012–13, the differences among Indigenous peoples and tensions increased between grass roots activists, formal organizations, and elected chiefs, as well as between chiefs holding to orthodox interpretations of treaties versus those willing to work with the government. The differences among chiefs led to the launch of the National Treaty Alliance in July 2013, representing at least 85 chiefs from Ontario, Manitoba, Saskatchewan and Alberta. The alliance felt that the AFN did not place enough emphasis on treaties and did not engage in enough consultation with communities (Barrera, 2013). These differences ultimately came to a head over the First Nations Education Act in the spring of 2014.

The act was negotiated between the AFN and the federal government and was set to transfer $1.9 billion in federal money to First Nations education. Many chiefs and communities, however, felt that the organization did not speak for them and did not have the authority to make such an agreement. They also felt that the Grand Chief, Shawn Atleo, worked too closely with the government that had forsaken their rights and treaties. This ultimately led to tension within the organization and in the spring of 2014, Atleo stepped down as Grand Chief because of mounting pressures. This has led some to ponder whether the AFN has a future (CBC, 2014). Divergent interests among Indigenous peoples continue to present obstacles to widespread or unified mobilization and shared identity (Lawrence, 2003).

International Attention and Indigenous Political Parties

While the 1970s were characterized by the intense mobilization of the AIM in the United States, the period from the 1980s onward was relatively uneventful in terms of Indigenous protest in that country. By contrast, internationally a number of opportunities began to emerge. For example, the Working Group on Indigenous Populations was founded in 1982 at the UN; in 1989, the International Labour Organization issued Convention 169 on Indigenous and Tribal Peoples in Independent Countries, opening opportunities for Aboriginals to pursue their grievances in an international forum (Speed and Collier, 2000: 881). In 1990–91, Indigenous groups in Colombia gained unprecedented legal rights, which galvanized other Indigenous peoples to mobilize to seek similar rights and even demand constitutional recognition (Van Cott, 2007: 131). In 1992, two significant events took place. First, the Rio Earth Summit bridged environmental rights, human rights, and Indigenous movements (Morgan, 2004: 495). Second, the year was marked by large numbers of Indigenous peoples protesting against the quincentennial anniversary of the "discovery" of the Americas (Brysk and Wise, 1997: 95; Collier and Collier, 2005: 456). In fact, significant protests were observed in many countries, including Mexico, where there were large rallies. Whereas mobilization in the United States was less apparent during these years, it gained momentum in Latin America throughout the 1990s.

International opportunities increased further when the UN declared 1993 the International Year of the World's Indigenous Peoples and subsequently announced that 1995–2004 would be the International Decades of the World's Indigenous People. These actions provided an international forum for Indigenous activists to meet, share information, create networks, and pressure national governments to address their issues. It allowed Indigenous peoples an opportunity to question the "citizenship regimes" of countries and pursue status as nations *within* nations, aiming for self-determination within existing nation-states rather than outright independence (Niezen, 2000; Jenson and Papillon, 2000). Such actions did not lead to increased sovereignty but did raise the profile of Indigenous peoples in the national consciousness.

Elsewhere, Indigenous peoples were also using transnational institutions to raise awareness for their grievances. For instance, the Zapatistas announced their rebellion against the Mexican state on the day that the North American Free Trade Agreement (NAFTA) was to take effect in January 1994 (Brysk and Wise, 1997: 76–7; Morris, 2001: 241; Tarrow, 2005: 113). This event is analyzed in more detail in Chapter 9. With regard to Indigenous mobilization, these actions comprised a critical event that gained much international attention and was heralded by many as successful, inclusive, and transnational because it brought both Indigenous and non-Indigenous bystanders from around the world into the struggle (della Porta et al., 2006; Keck and Sikkink, 1998: 115–16; Khasnabish, 2004; Tarrow, 2005). Two years later, the San Andres Accord, an agreement on "Indigenous rights and culture" with the Mexican government, was successfully negotiated (Collier and Collier, 2005: 456); in 1998, the state of Oaxaca in Mexico passed an Indigenous rights bill (Morris, 2001: 242); and in 2001, the Mexican government did the same. However, these achievements are far from uncontested (Khasnabish, 2004: 274). The Zapatistas continue to struggle for their rights and increased recognition. As with the struggles of Indigenous peoples in Canada, their successes are tied to critical events and to the ability to bridge differences among communities, which together draw bystanders into supporting their struggles.

The rise of Indigenous mobilization in Latin American countries was also tied to the fall of the traditional left after the collapse of the Soviet Union. Marxist-inspired movements played a significant role in the mobilization of *campesinos* (peasants), who were largely Indigenous or Mestizo (of mixed heritage). In some countries, these populations are quite significant; for instance, Indigenous peoples make up 43 per cent of Ecuador's population, 47 per cent of Peru's, 66 per cent of Guatemala's, and 71 per cent of Bolivia's (Van Cott, 2007: 128). Traditional left-ist organizations downplayed ethnic and cultural differences, which partially explains why Indigenous movements were less prominent in earlier decades. With the fall of the left, new politics around identity and Indigenous beliefs began to emerge, so much so that they became viable alternatives to the neoliberal regimes of the region and began to gain the attention of young leftists in the global North, especially after the Zapatistas successfully linked their struggles with protests against global trade (Van Cott, 2010: 387). Khasnabish (2010), among others, examines how that struggle in particular inspired social justice activists by offering a new vision of politics and struggle. In other words, the Zapatistas helped forge transnational networks in Latin America and around the world.

The success of Indigenous mobilization was also witnessed in the adoption of Indigenous rights in almost all Latin American countries, with a few countries even acting as sites of the rise of Indigenous-backed populist candidates and regimes. This was especially the case in countries with large Indigenous populations that could mount nationally viable campaigns. Beginning as early as the mid-1990s, Bolivia and Ecuador witnessed the ascendancy of the Assembly for the Sovereignty of the Peoples (ASP), the Movement toward Socialism (MAS), and the Pachakutik Plurinational Unity Movement (Pachakutik). Ecuador also witnessed the unprecedented formation of the Confederation of Indigenous Nationalities of Ecuador, which helped mobilize support for political parties and presidents and has been involved in strikes and in the junta that overthrew the country's president in 2000. The strength of Latin American Indigenous organizations and movements can also be seen in the election of Evo Morales as president of Bolivia in December 2005. Representing MAS, he became the country's first Indigenous leader. Yet, despite their rise to power, Indigenous governments in Latin America have not been without their critics. Some have been characterized as authoritative, sexist, and inconsistent in their delivery of justice (Van Cott, 2007: 139). Indigenous movements and political parties in Latin America need to come to terms with being in positions of power and find a way to avoid a repetition of the failures and injustices of previous regimes.

Conclusion

As noted throughout this chapter, a constant challenge for Indigenous mobilization, in Canada and globally, is the need to bridge the divergent interests of different Indigenous peoples. By tracing Canadian Indigenous protest and organizing from the post–World War II period to the present, this chapter has demonstrated that critical events like the White Paper, the patriation of the Constitution, the Indian Summer, and Idle No More raise the consciousness of activists and generate support from bystander publics. Such moments engage many communities simultaneously, drawing them into the negotiation of the events, increasing mobilization, and extending Indigenous collective action frames.

However, the ability to manage critical events successfully is dictated by access to resources, the creation of shared collective identities, and political opportunities. During the 1950s and 1960s, because of aggressive colonization policies, many political opportunities emerged but Canada's Indigenous peoples lacked the resources and solidarity needed to act on them. When the White Paper was announced in 1969, creating a critical event, status Indians mobilized and garnered some support, but they lacked the resources and shared identity required to fully engage it. The event signalled a transition in Indigenous–non-Indigenous relations. During the 1970s, resources and organizations emerged, as did a young Indigenous elite who took advantage of new opportunities. Thus, when the patriation process was announced, Canada's Indigenous peoples were able to engage it successfully as a second critical event.

Yet the increasing institutionalization of mobilization moved efforts away from local communities. Moreover, the recognition of different Aboriginal statuses and various community and regional concerns inhibited the creation of a unified pan-Indigenous movement. These factors led to demobilization. As the 1980s ended, however, another opportunity emerged with the Meech Lake Accord. Mobilization against the accord by status Indians led to another critical event, which was compounded by the Oka Crisis in Quebec, together launching the Indian Summer of 1990. Since then, Canadian Indigenous mobilization has consisted of a mix of successes and setbacks for national organizations, together with threats and actions by local groups seeking more rapid change. More recently the rise of the Idle No More movement signals a new era of Indigenous protest and resistance to ongoing injustices and colonization. It also shows how Indigenous mobilization increasingly intersects with women's, environmental, and social justice movements.

The ongoing struggles of Canada's Indigenous peoples are far from resolved, and increasingly, many non-Indigenous people believe that Aboriginal status grants privileges that they are uncomfortable supporting. In 2010 only 37 per cent of Canadians felt that settling land claims was "very important" and only a quarter, 25 per cent, felt the same about Indigenous self-determination (Environics Institute, 2010: 35). Consequently, as before, the Indigenous peoples of Canada still find it necessary to bridge their concerns to bystander communities and to negotiate commonalities among divergent interests. Like all movements seeking change, they must extend their claims in an inclusive manner that yields support from bystanders committed to equity and social justice.

Discussion Questions

1. What roles do bystanders play in social movement actions?

2. Which collective action frames lend themselves to the alignment of social movement issues with dominant interests?

3. How did resources, political opportunities, and collective identities influence the successful use of critical events by Indigenous peoples?

Suggested Readings

Nagel, Joane. 1995. "American Indian Ethnic Renewal: Politics and the Resurgence of Identity," *American Sociological Review* 60, 6: 947–65. This is a key article on Red Power and its impact on Native American ethnic identity.

Van Cott, Donna Lee. 2007. "Latin America's Indigenous Peoples," *Journal of Democracy* 18, 4: 127–41. This article provides an overview of Indigenous mobilization across Latin America.

Wilkes, Rima. 2006. "The Protest Actions of Indigenous Peoples: A Canadian–U.S. Comparison of Social Movement Emergence," *American Behavioral Scientist* 50, 4: 510–25. This article presents an important analysis of Canadian and American Aboriginal mobilization.

6   The Women's Movement

The "second wave" of the women's movement emerged in many countries during the protest cycle of the 1960s, mobilizing large numbers of activists and creating many social changes. By the late 1970s, however, some observers were already declaring feminism "dead," and journalists and commentators were soon describing young women as the "post-feminist" generation (Hawkesworth, 2004). Scholars and movement sympathizers have also assessed the fate of the women's movement as feminist activism became less visible (e.g., Epstein, 2001; Reger, 2005; Staggenborg and Taylor, 2005). Despite concerns and changes, the movement made significant gains in Canada during the 1970s and 1980s and there is evidence of continued growth of the movement. This can be seen through the formation of new types of movement organizations, the rise of feminism within institutions and universities, feminist participation and influence in other social movements, the development of feminist culture and collective identity, the creation of new collective action campaigns and tactics, the expansion of the transnational women's movement, and the rise of a new generation of women acting contentiously. Perceptions of the women's movement depend in part on our conception of a social movement; if we understand social movements only as publicly visible contentious politics, we miss much of this ongoing feminist activity.

This chapter examines how the women's movement has grown and survived since the late 1960s and early 1970s, particularly in North America. We begin by looking at the origins of the contemporary movement in the "first wave" of the movement and in the protest cycle of the 1960s. We then consider some areas of feminist activity that originated with the "second wave" and that remain highly important today, notably reproductive rights and violence against women. Other forms of ongoing feminist activity, including what has been called the "third wave" of the women's movement and the global women's movement, are also examined. Finally, we consider challenges to the women's movement from conservative movements and men's organizations that have co-opted the language of the movement to counter its successes as well as tensions among generations of activists interpreting feminism in divergent ways.

Origins of the Second Wave

Women's movements emerged in many Western countries in the nineteenth century as large-scale changes associated with industrialization changed women's roles in the family (Buechler, 1990). More middle-class women began to pursue higher education and many women became involved in various social reforms, including temperance and abolition movements. Women gained valuable political experience through their work in such movements, and they also came to feel sharply the limits of their political influence as women. Consequently, many women became participants in the first wave of the women's movement, which advocated women's suffrage, education, property and custody rights, and other reforms. Although strongest in the West, incipient women's movements emerged in countries around the world, and by the 1920s, women had won the vote in many countries (Chafetz and Dworkin, 1986). After suffrage was won, women's movements typically became less visible, though various groups survived the decline of the movement's first wave.

In Canada, the women's suffrage movement began in the nineteenth century and won the vote for women in 1918, two years before American women won the vote in 1920 (though women in Quebec did not win the provincial vote until 1940). The women's movement in North America, as elsewhere, was less visible after suffrage was won, but remained alive during the "doldrums" (Rupp and Taylor, 1987). In their analysis of what happened to the US women's movement, Rupp and Taylor (1987) argue that an "elite-sustained" organization, the National Women's Party, maintained the feminist movement between the suffrage victory in 1920 and the 1960s. In Canada, women who had been active in the suffragist movement also continued their activities after enfranchisement, and traditional women's associations gradually developed feminist positions (Black, 1993). In 1960, Canadian women founded Voice of Women, a peace organization that became one of the organizational bases for the new feminist movement of the 1960s. In the United States, a women's peace organization called Women's Strike for Peace was founded in 1961, and later in the 1960s, many of its activists also became receptive to the message of the women's movement (Swerdlow, 1993).

Although women's movements never disappeared after the first wave, they did not become highly visible again until the second wave of the women's movement emerged in the 1960s. Large-scale socio-economic and political changes, organizational factors, and related changes in women's consciousness were all critical to this revitalization of the women's movement. Increases in women's labour force participation and higher education, a decline in the birth rate, and increased divorce rates in many Western countries created new interests and grievances among women. Employment discrimination, for instance, became a major issue for the new women's movement. As Jo Freeman (1975: 15–17) argues, middle-class women with professional aspirations, in particular, felt an increased sense of *relative deprivation*. Although the ideological justifications for male dominance were eroding, women felt deprived when they compared themselves to their male peers. At the same time that women felt these grievances, they also found *organizational vehicles* through which to organize a variety of different types of feminist groups. These included liberal women's organizations, some of which had their origins in the first wave; radical feminist groups connected to the New Left; support from unions; and feminist groups arising out of various nationalist and ethnic movements (see Rebick, 2005; Roth, 2004; Springer, 2005).

The US women's movement, by far the best-researched national case, provides a good example of the importance of political opportunity and pre-existing organizational structures to the development of a movement, as well as a good example of the influence of the civil rights movement and the New Left. In *Inviting Women's Rebellion*, Ann Costain (1992) argues that electoral realignments in the 1950s and 1960s made political parties and government officials receptive to women as a constituency even before the women's movement organized to lobby for change. Shakeups of electoral coalitions, caused in part by the civil rights movement and the desertion of southern Democrats from their party, resulted in efforts by the Democratic and Republican Parties to court new voters in order to forge an electoral majority. While urban African American voters became increasingly important, women also represented a large block of votes. Consequently, Presidents Eisenhower and Kennedy, a Republican and a Democrat, respectively, made reference in their speeches to sex discrimination without prompting from the women's movement, and in the early 1960s, more bills dealing with women's concerns began to be introduced into Congress. In 1961, President Kennedy established the President's Commission on the Status of Women, which spawned state-level commissions on the status of women. When the 1964 Civil Rights Act was passed, Title VII prohibited discrimination on the basis of sex as well as race, ethnicity, and religion.

Political opportunities combined with organizational structures and ideological bases to support the rise of the contemporary women's movement. Two distinct branches emerged in the United States, including an "older" or "women's rights" branch, which was founded largely by professional women concerned about employment issues; and a "younger" or "women's liberation" branch, which was made up of students and other young women concerned about a wide range of issues, such as women's health and sexuality (Carden, 1974; Freeman, 1975; Hole and Levine, 1971). The older branch, formed earlier and including somewhat older women, spawned organiza-tions such as the National Organization for Women (NOW). These groups were organized in a traditionally formal manner—with elected officers, bylaws, boards of directors, and parliamentary procedure—based on the experiences of their founders in conventional voluntary associations and political parties. The state commissions on the status of women were an important mobilizing structure for the older branch, as many of its activists met one another and discussed their grievances through the state commis-sions. In contrast, the younger branch created informal organizations based on ideas about participatory democracy espoused by the civil rights move-ment and the New Left. These earlier movements provided an organiza-tional base and communications network for younger feminists. A number of independent feminist groups formed, including small consciousness-raising groups, which allowed women to discuss their personal experiences in political terms. Experiences of sexism in other movements, as well as changes in consciousness resulting from their work in the earlier movements, attracted many young women to these groups (Evans, 1979; Freeman, 1975). Although many of the women who became active in such groups were white and middle class, working-class women and women of colour also organ-ized their own feminist movements through separate community networks, including black nationalist and Chicano movement networks (Roth, 2004).

In Canada, political opportunities and mobilizing structures were also important to the emergence of the new feminist movement and its subsequent decline (Chappell 2000; Mann 2008; Masson 2009; 2006). Women already active in organizations such as Voice of Women pushed the government to create the Royal Commission on the Status of Women. Although few women's issues were on the public agenda before women's groups pushed for them, political opportunities were present because the Liberals headed a minority government, with the left-of-centre New Democratic Party (NDP) holding the balance of power, when it agreed to the royal commission in 1967 (Bégin, 1992). The activist Liberal government was eager to integrate women's con-cerns and quite receptive to women's groups that brought together women from Quebec and the rest of Canada (Vickers et al., 1993: 16). As had been the case with the US commission, the cross-country hearings held by the royal commission provided a communications network that helped to organize the new women's movement. The royal commission played an important role in sparking the National Action Committee on the Status of Women (NAC), which emerged as an ad hoc committee responding to the commission and pressuring governments to implement its 167 recommendations (Bashevkin 1998). The NAC later became a national umbrella organization, which at its peak included a coalition of over 700 organizations (Rodgers and Knight, 2011). It was also successful in developing and promoting employment and pay equity policies and the inclusion of women's rights in Canada's Constitution.

The relationship between women's organizations and the Canadian state has been somewhat unusual. In an effort to build civil society in Canada the federal government began offering formal women's organizations core funding in the 1970s to support their efforts (Bashevkin, 1998, 2009; Rodgers and Knight, 2011). The patriation of the constitution was another important opportunity for the women's movement (Vickers, 2010), as were funds available through the court challenges program (Chapell, 2000) and opportunities to challenge inequities through the Constitution and Supreme Court. Also important to the movement were unions and other institutions, such as the growing university sector that accommodated the baby boom generation, and liberal and socialist feminists of the second wave.

Like their counterparts in the United States, young women who had first become politically active in the Canadian student movement and in leftist politics often found themselves in subordinate positions in these movements. They began to organize independent feminist organizations, starting with the Toronto Women's Liberation Movement in 1967. Black women in Toronto organized through African liberation movements and later through multiculturalism projects. The francophone feminist movement in Quebec used networks of the labour movement and the Quebec independence movement (Rebick, 2005: 3–13).

In other countries, radical branches of the new feminist movement built on the organizational structures and ideologies provided by movements that had come earlier in the protest cycle of the 1960s, while many liberal feminists had connections to pre-sixties women's organizations and peace movements. Women commonly encountered sexism in the New Left, and they initially attempted to challenge organizations such as the German SDS and the American SDS (Fraser, 1988: 304) before forming their own organizations. In France, young women involved in the May 1968 protests responded to the contradictions between the New Left rhetoric of equality and their experiences as women in the movement by forming a new women's liberation group, the Mouvement de libération des femmes (Duchen, 1994). Thanks to the women's movement which survived the 1960s, New Left ideals and organizational forms also endured, influencing other social movements from the 1970s to the present.

Although the New Left and other pre-existing social movements provided tactical models and mobilizing structures for the new women's movement, they were not the only places from which contemporary feminism took root. Enke (2007) argues that we cannot truly understand the second wave of the women's movement by looking for feminism only in obvious places, such as self-professed feminist organizations. She looks at how feminism emerged in a variety of different places, including commercial spaces, such as bars, and civic spaces, such as public parks. Her work shows that a broad-based movement such as the women's movement emerges in many different venues and affects many different elements of culture.

Mobilizing Issues of the Second Wave

To get a new movement off the ground, activists need to organize around issues that people care about deeply enough to want to join in collective action. This means tapping into genuine grievances, framing issues in ways that make potential participants excited about the possibilities for change, and providing ways for people to become involved in movement campaigns. Grievances, frames, and campaigns were key ingredients in the mobilization of the modern feminist movement, a movement that emerged out of the protest cycle of the 1960s as a new and creative force for change facing a world of gender relations very different from those of today. Women lacked access to many educational and occupational opportunities; they had difficulty obtaining birth-control information and safe and legal abortions; problems such as rape and wife-battering were not widely acknowledged; and there was a great deal of sexism in everyday life. These grievances provided the early movement with many unifying issues and stimulated the formation of numerous organizations that engaged in a wide range of activities.

The goals of the new women's movement included political and legal ones, such as anti-discriminatory legislation. They also included broader cultural objectives in that the movement was fundamentally redefining gender relations and challenging cultural attitudes and values as well as seeking to change laws and secure economic opportunities and political power for women. The idea that "the personal is political" was a central collective action frame for the second-wave movement, which raised issues related to sexuality, domestic violence, and gender roles in the family that had previously been considered outside the political sphere (Evans, 2003: 3). This insight, as we will see, would continue to influence third-wave feminists and the transnational women's movement after the heyday of the second wave.

To achieve its goals, the second-wave women's movement mounted numerous campaigns, which helped to mobilize movement participants. Although not all collective campaigns result in changed laws or other new advantages, they often affect movements by creating new networks, strengthening organizations, introducing new tactics, and changing political opportunities (Staggenborg and Lecomte, 2009; Tilly, 2008). Feminists have been active on numerous issues, such as employment and pay equity, child care, abortion, lesbian rights, the rights of disabled women, and, particularly in Canada, the rights of Indigenous women and the investigation of violence against them. The Canadian second wave also played a significant role in pursuing institutional reform by campaigning to mold equality language in the Charter of Rights and establishing funding for the country's Court Challenges program to shore up those rights (Bashevkin, 2009: 123–4). These have been some of the biggest successes of the movement and they came with the support of the union movement, which was linked to socialist feminism in Canada. Although the women's movement changed after the highly visible years of the second wave, a feminist collective identity continues to be shared and developed by new generations of feminists, and important ideas and issues developed by second-wave feminists continue to stimulate activity in a variety of arenas. Two of the most important and enduring issues for feminists involve women's health and reproductive rights and violence against women.

Women's Health and Reproductive Rights

Many women's movement campaigns and tactics have focused on women's health and reproductive rights, including abortion rights. Before the second wave of the women's movement, very little information was available to women regarding sexuality, contraception, childbirth, and abortion. Consequently, women who became active in the new feminist movement began educating themselves about their bodies and publishing research about such issues as contraception so that women could take some control of their sexual and reproductive lives. For example, McGill University students published the *Birth Control Handbook* in 1968, and a feminist press, the Montreal Health Press, published a revised edition. This publication was distributed across North America and was one of the first sources of information on birth control available in a format that encouraged women to make their own choices about sexuality and birth control. The *Handbook*, which was also translated into French, was enormously successful and in 1970–71 sold close to two million copies, allowing its publishers to help finance the initiation of a women's liberation group in Montreal (Cherniak and Feingold, 1972: 110). Another important publication was *Our Bodies, Our Selves*, written by a group of women who had begun discussing sexuality in a women's liberation group in Boston called Bread and Roses. Calling themselves the Boston Women's Health Book Collective, the women gathered information about women's health and distributed it in pamphlet form in 1969. They later expanded the information into a book that demystifies medical expertise and includes personal accounts by women who focus on sexual self-determination (Evans, 2003: 48). *Our Bodies, Our Selves* has been revised and updated over the years, translated into a number of languages, and used in many schools and health clinics, diffusing a feminist perspective on women's health and sexuality to a broad audience.

These and other efforts were part of a larger women's health movement that involved efforts to give women control over their bodies. Feminists critiqued traditional models of health care delivery, in which doctors simply told their patients what was best for them, preferring instead a new model in which women were actively involved in making decisions about their own health care. Feminists developed many women's health centres and services that sought to deliver health care in a manner that gave women more control over experiences such as childbirth and abortion. For example, the women's movement inspired a trend towards home births and alternative birthing centres and the use of midwives in childbirth. Abortion became a major issue for the women's movement of the 1960s, and numerous countries eventually reformed their abortion laws in response to pressures by feminists and other abortion law reformers (Francome, 1984).

In Canada, Dr Henry Morgentaler played an important role in making abortion available by opening clinics, doing jail time, and bringing lawsuits—culminating in the 1988 Supreme Court decision that struck down Canada's restrictive abortion law (Morton, 1992). Feminists were also heavily involved, and the first nationwide action of the new women's movement was the 1970 Abortion Caravan (see Brodie et al., 1992; Rebick, 2005: 35–46). Abortion was illegal in Canada until 1969, when Parliament passed a law allowing abortions for health reasons in accredited hospitals with approval from a therapeutic abortion committee of four doctors. Feminists wanted much broader access to abortion, with the woman making the choice, not doctors. Seventeen members of the Vancouver Women's Caucus, one of the earliest Canadian women's liberation groups, travelled to Ottawa to protest the 1969 abortion law. Their Abortion Caravan traversed the country, stopping for rallies along the way and garnering a great deal of media attention. As planned, the Caravan arrived in Ottawa in time for Mother's Day, to much excitement. About 300 supporters marched on Parliament Hill, and a coffin was delivered to the prime minister's residence to symbolize the women who had died following illegal abortions. About 30 women chained themselves to their chairs in the galleries of the House of Commons, using a tactic that had been employed by British suffragists a century before (Rebick, 2005: 36). The campaign generated a huge amount of media publicity and helped to stimulate the Canadian women's movement, as new groups formed to participate in the Caravan (Jenson, 1992: 44). Feminist groups also played an important role in raising awareness over women's reproductive freedom through the promotion of gender rights in the Charter of Rights and Freedoms, and this was a key factor in the ground-breaking Morgentaler decision (Vickers 2010).

In both Canada and the United States, feminists provided referrals to women for both legal and illegal abortions. In Montreal, students who produced the *Birth Control Handbook* became heavily involved in abortion counselling, as did the Front de libération des femmes, which counselled French-speaking women (Cherniak and Feingold, 1972). In Chicago, a group of women connected to the Chicago Women's Liberation Union formed an abortion collective known as "Jane" in 1969 (see Kaplan, 1995). They first developed a list of doctors who would do abortions and who were considered "safe" and then worked with an abortionist who turned out not to be a doctor. However, he taught the women how to perform abortions themselves, and the collective ended up providing abortions to hundreds of women, including poor women who couldn't afford to travel to states such as New York, where abortion was legalized in 1970. Jane developed a supportive and non-judgmental health service that, like other feminist health projects, was sensitive to women's needs and tried to empower its clients to make informed decisions about their sexuality and reproduction. Jane became famous in feminist circles, particularly after seven of its members were arrested in 1972 and feminists organized in support of them.

Feminists in North America and Western Europe supported many abortion-related demonstrations and service projects, in addition to lobbying for legalization of abortion along with other abortion reformers. Because of their visibility and successes, abortion rights activists also provoked a powerful countermovement opposed to changes in the abortion laws. Anti-abortion movements typically include a variety of constituents, including liberal Catholics as well as more conservative fundamentalist Christians. However, some anti-abortionists are part of a larger anti-feminist movement opposed to various changes in gender relations championed by the women's movement. This anti-feminist movement is in turn part of a larger conservative movement opposed to gay and lesbian rights as well as feminist goals, both of which are seen as threatening the "traditional family."

In the United States, opponents of feminism battled successfully against the Equal Rights Amendment (ERA) to the US Constitution, defeating it in 1982 when the deadline for ratification expired (see Mansbridge, 1986). Many opponents of the ERA also became active in the US anti-abortion movement. In Canada, some conservative women were shocked when the Charter of Rights and Freedoms was passed in 1982 with an equal rights provision; in response, they founded REAL Women (Realistic, Equal, Active, for Life) in an effort to counter feminist goals, including abortion rights (Erwin, 1993).

Although anti-feminist activity has been detrimental to the achievement of some feminist goals, including unfettered access to abortion, the opposition has also served to keep feminists mobilized. Reproductive rights issues thus remain critical for feminists and arouse a great deal of passion among both movement and countermovement activists. New generations of women continue to defend what many now consider a basic women's right. In both the United States and Canada, numerous challenges to abortion rights have generated much feminist protest along with anti-abortion activity (Meyer and Staggenborg, 1998). In Canada, where the political parties exert greater control over individual members, the issue has generally been kept out of national politics; however, the 1988 Supreme Court *Morgentaler* decision struck down existing laws on abortion but did not replace them with new legislation protecting women's reproductive rights. This contributed to local conflicts over abortion clinics, conflicts in the courts, and countermobilization by conservative groups. For example, in two high-profile Canadian cases in 1989, the former boyfriends of Barbara Dodd in Ontario and Chantal Daigle in Quebec attempted to block their abortions, but temporary injunctions and court rulings ultimately upheld abortion rights (Morton, 1992). Access to abortion continues to be limited in some provinces; no doctor is currently willing to perform an abortion in Prince Edward Island, New Brunswick will not fund abortions in private clinics, and conservative organizations regularly protest against them. During the summer of 2014, Halifax was the site of anti-abortion protesters carrying graphic images of unborn fetuses, which sparked concern by residents and also triggered countermobilization by pro-choice supporters. Abortion remains an important issue for feminists, arousing a great deal of passion among both movement and countermovement activists. In Canada, however, the conflict over abortion has been less intense than in the United States, in part because the threat of Quebec separation has outweighed concerns about abortion in the arena of federal politics (Vickers, 2010).

Violence against Women

Violence against women is another issue of continuing importance addressed by the second wave of the women's movement. In North America and in Western Europe, the women's movement played a key role in bringing issues of rape and domestic violence to public attention and in changing public views as well as the practices of police departments and courts. Before the second wave of the women's movement, rape victims were often considered somehow responsible for the crime owing to provocative dress or behaviour, and many rape trials were humiliating experiences for the victims. Consequently, rape was not seen as a common occurrence because so few women reported it. Domestic violence, similarly, was not considered a serious and widespread crime until feminists changed public perceptions of the problem in the 1970s (Tierney, 1982; Walker, 1990). Feminist writings such as Susan Brownmiller's (1975) influential book *Against Our Will* helped to spread a radical feminist analysis of rape and other violence against women, viewing these acts as means by which women were kept "in their place" (Rebick, 2005: 69).

In the early 1970s, feminists in countries such as Britain, Canada, and the United States began to set up rape crisis lines and battered women's shelters or "transition houses." They also publicized the high incidence of violence against women. In 1971, for example, a group known as the New York Radical Feminists held a "speak-out" at which women spoke publicly of their rape experiences; the purpose of the event was to turn feelings of shame among rape victims into anger and action. Feminists questioned the treatment of rape victims by police and hospitals, and objected to such legal requirements as a woman having to prove that she had resisted the rape in order for her report to be credible (Rosen, 2000: 182). In the late 1970s, feminists in cities across North America began holding annual "Take Back the Night" marches to publicize violence against women. In addition to creating new services and helping to change public discourse about rape and domestic violence, feminists helped to change rape laws that failed to recognize rape within marriage and that permitted defence attorneys to question rape victims about their sexual histories (Rebick, 2005: 70).

Issues of violence against women, like reproductive rights, continued to mobilize women after the 1970s. Pornography, which first became a feminist issue in the 1970s, was the focus of much activism in the 1980s connected to concerns about violence against women. A group called Women against Violence against Women formed in Vancouver in 1982 and soon became active in a number of North American cities as feminists became increasingly concerned about the expanding pornography industry. Canadian feminists made the film *Not a Love Story*, which was released by the National Film Board in 1981 and shown all over North America. Although the issue of pornography created division among feminists, with some organizing against the censorship that they thought resulted from campaigns against pornography, feminists created a new consciousness about pornography as a form of violence against women. Activists battling against pornography also worked on raising consciousness about sexual harassment. For example, law professor Catharine MacKinnon, a well-known feminist active on the issue of pornography in North America, publicized the problem with her 1979 book, *The Sexual Harassment of Working Women*. Once feminists had succeeded in drawing public attention to the issue, they were able to convince government agencies and workplaces in countries such as Canada and the United States to implement sexual harassment policies. In 2014, however, issues of work place harassment and abuse of women continued to gain front-page headlines in Canada with the firing of CBC radio host Jian Ghomeshi over allegations of sexual abuse (Wilms, 2015) and the Dalhousie Dentistry scandal, in which misogynistic Facebook comments by male dentistry students sparked the #dalhousiehateswomen hashtag (Hampson, 2015).

As a result, although the women's movement raised awareness about violence against women, the struggle is ongoing, especially for Indigenous women in Canada. As noted in Chapter 5, the Native Women's Association of Canada (NWAC) has been particularly active in exposing the disproportionate violence against Aboriginal women and has attracted widespread national and international attention by Amnesty International (2004) as well as the UN. In its *Sisters In Spirit* campaign NWAC systematically documented the number of murdered and missing Indigenous women in Canada (Barker, 2008), finding that between 500 and 600 Indigenous women have gone missing since 1980 (NWAC, 2010: Gilchrist, 2010: 273; Dickinson, 2014: 229). The movement's efforts triggered an internal RCMP investigation of cases, which confirmed NWAC's findings but set the figure higher at 1,186 murdered and missing Indigenous women over the last 30 years. The report also found that Indigenous women are over-represented among those murdered and considered missing (RCMP, 2014; APTN, 2014). Some, such as Gilchrist (2010), note little coverage of the problem in mainstream media. Even so, the UN Special Rapporteur on the Rights of Indigenous peoples has called on Canada to launch a national inquiry into murdered and missing Indigenous women (Anaya, 2014), and this echoes calls by NWAC (see 2014) and other women's and Indigenous movement organizations. Such calls, however, have been rejected by the Conservative government.

Thus, the women's movement has brought a number of issues to public attention and created new ways of looking at behaviours that were previously socially acceptable or not addressed publicly. Issues such as reproductive rights and violence against women, however, continue to be important both for feminists at home and for the growing transnational women's movement.

Feminist Survival among New Generations

The women's movement made great progress in a number of areas, and its successes contributed to a decline in grievances among women and a feeling among many young women today that feminist activism is no longer necessary. Indeed, the fate of the women's movement has frequently been debated (see Reger, 2014b for a review). On the one hand, the movement has been declared "dead" since the decline of the visible period beginning in the 1960s. On the other hand, many scholars have disputed the use of a "wave" metaphor because it neglects less visible activities and also the efforts of women of colour and others outside of the white middle class. When a wide variety of activity by multiple actors in many venues is considered part of the movement, we can see more continuity in feminist activity, both between the first and second "waves" and since the second wave. Because the goals of the women's movement were so far-reaching and because the movement was targeting many different "structures of authority" (Snow, 2004), the women's movement of the 1960s never really died, but instead spread into many different cultural and institutional arenas. Feminists have been active on numerous issues, such as employment and pay equity, child care, abortion, sexual violence, and lesbian rights.

In fact, although the women's movement has changed since the highly visible years of the second wave, a feminist collective identity continues to be shared and developed by new cohorts of feminists, and important ideas and issues developed by second-wave feminists continue to stimulate activity in a variety of arenas. In the mid-1980s, however, socialist and radical feminist events began to proliferate in Canada largely in reaction to those feeling excluded by liberal feminism (Bashevkin, 1989: 365–6).

In the 1980s, feminists in a number of countries faced conservative political regimes—for example, the governments of Margaret Thatcher in Britain, Ronald Reagan in the United States, and Brian Mulroney in Canada. As "new conservatives advanced a pro-achievement, pro-individualist position that ceded little room to competing traditions of collective action, social protest, and progressive political engagement," feminists and other progressive activists were put on the defensive (Bashevkin, 1998: 14). Faced with anti-feminist countermovements and governments hostile to many feminist goals, the women's movement often had to defend existing gains, such as abortion rights, and to fight cutbacks in funding for women's groups and services.

The rise of REAL, as a conservative "pro-family" organization, seriously challenged NAC and second-wave feminist movement organizations in Canada. Unlike NAC, it was supportive of the neoliberal political turn and also began to challenge the national organization by applying for federal money—and receiving it. During this period NAC was almost 90 per cent funded by the federal government (Bashevkin, 1998: 200), which meant that loss of core funding had serious implications on its ability to mobilize. REAL, which was less reliant on public funds, began to play an increasing role in the development of Conservative party policy (Rodgers and Knight, 2011: 527) and federal level policy more generally. During this period a younger generation of socialist and radical feminists began to position NAC and the women's movement against the government and its policies, such as the contentious free trade agreement of the early 1990s (Bashevkin, 1989). It also pushed the organization and movement into an increasingly oppositional political space with increased use of direct-action tactics. The collective identity of the movement also continued to shift in the 1990s, creating something of a "generation gap" between second- and third-wave feminists but also sustaining the movement.

Not all observers agree, however, that it is useful to refer to a third wave of feminism—or to identify a fourth or fifth wave—and some scholars prefer to examine "overlapping generations" of feminists (Reger, 2014b: 45). The idea of a third wave originated in the mid-1990s, when a number of anthologies began to be published by young women in the United States and Canada who declared themselves to be different types of feminists from those of the second wave (e.g., Walker, 1995; Findlen, 2001; Heywood and Drake, 1997; Baumgardner and Richards, 2000; Mitchell et al., 2001). Some of the authors claimed to be part of a third wave of activism that was already underway, while others called for a third wave (Reger, 2005: xvii). This new wave of feminist activity, which began in the late 1980s, was not so much a visible new burst of movement activity (like the second wave had been) as an assertion of feminist identity among young women. Feminism had not died out in the 1980s—it was relevant and important to many women—but young feminists were declaring their generational and ideological differences from the second wave (Henry, 2004). North American women born after the early 1960s took many victories of the women's movement for granted and felt there was less need for a collective orientation to feminism. Self-declared third-wavers did not reject feminism, but they wanted to recast it on their own terms.

For some third-wavers, those terms were more individualized and personal than collective and overtly political. Arguing for an inclusive type of feminism, a number of feminist writers in the 1990s rejected what they saw as the dogmatic approach of the second wave and argued that women could define feminism for themselves (Henry, 2005). Whereas second-wavers declared that "sisterhood is powerful," third-wavers challenged the idea that women have similar interests, focusing instead on diversity and the need to include women of colour, transgender people, poor women, and others in the feminist movement. Third-wavers also argued that their brand of feminism is distinguished from second-wave feminism by its approach to sexuality, which emphasizes "women's pleasure and power over their victimization" (Henry, 2004: 22). And in Canada, French-speaking Quebec women and movement organizations began asserting their resistance to the English-speaking liberal feminists and NAC for their failure to recognize Quebec's distinctness. Such tensions ultimately contributed to the Fédération des femmes du Québec (FFQ) withdrawing from the larger NAC umbrella (Bashevkin, 1998: 222). This was significant given that the FFQ was one of NAC's original founding organizations.

A changing political climate and generational change contributed shifting scales of political engagement by the third wave, which is still prevalent today. Dominque Masson (2006, 2009) shows that, increasingly, the local and regional political spheres have become important for women's organizations and feminists in Quebec. This is due to both the political opportunities that emerged at that level, with regional tables and provincial funding, and the identities and goals of the movement that operate on that scale. While women's organizations have scaled down, they have also scaled up, pursuing transnational opportunities and solidarity (Dufour and Giraud, 2007a, 2007b). The nation-state is no longer the only political arena in which to challenge power and this has also meant a diversification of how politics is practised.

The third wave generated new organizations and activities, including many cultural activities with political intent. For example, a group of art activists calling themselves the Guerrilla Girls organized in 1985 to protest an exhibition by New York's Museum of Modern Art that included only a small number of female artists. They donned gorilla masks and took on the names of dead women artists, making posters and using humour "to convey information, provoke discussion and to show that feminists can be funny" (www.guerrillagirls.com). Since 1985, the Guerrilla Girls have written books, engaged in street theatre, and developed various projects dealing with art, popular culture, and discrimination. Another example of third-wave activism is the Riot Grrrls, a network of young women in the alternative rock music scene that started in Olympia, Washington, in 1991 and quickly spread across North America through band tours, zines (self-published journals), word of mouth, and the Internet. In 1992, there was a Riot Grrrl Convention in Washington, DC, with workshops on a number of topics, including sexuality, rape, racism, and domestic violence (Evans, 2003: 216).

The Vagina Monologues, which started as a one-woman play by Eve Ensler, is another cultural and political activity that has engaged the energies of young feminists (Reger and Story, 2005). The play consists of a series of monologues based on interviews with hundreds of women, celebrating women's sexuality and dealing with issues such as rape, body image, menstruation, and the genocide of Natives in North America. In 1997, Ensler created V-Day, a non-profit organization with the goal of stopping violence against women by acting as "a catalyst that promotes creative events to increase awareness, raise money and revitalize the spirit of existing anti-violence organizations" (www.vday.org). In 1999, V-Day began the College Initiative to encourage colleges and universities to perform the *Monologues* as a benefit for local organizations fighting violence against women. Since then, feminist students at hundreds of colleges and universities in North America and around the world have performed the *Monologues*, as have hundreds of community groups. In addition to performing the *Monologues*, V-Day groups have held workshops, shown films, and carried out various campaigns opposing violence against women and building networks in Latin America, Africa, the Middle East, and Asia as well as in Europe and North America.

In *Everywhere and Nowhere*, a study of contemporary feminism in three US communities, Jo Reger (2012) describes how feminism today is both invisible in many places ("nowhere") and taken for granted ("everywhere"). She finds that feminism among young women is alive and well, but that it takes different forms in different local environments. In a conservative Midwestern town with a somewhat conservative university, where the movement is largely invisible, feminism existed within a relatively small network, and a campus feminist organization focused on raising awareness and attracting support through activities such as annual productions of the *Vagina Monologues* and participation in the Clothesline Project, which creates visual displays of t-shirts with messages from survivors and supporters about violence against women. In a liberal East Coast town, in contrast, college students felt that feminism was "everywhere" and that there was less need to focus on specific issues. They tended to engage in "submerged feminism" around issues of "racism, homophobia and gender fluidity" (Reger, 2012: 45). In a larger and more diverse city in the Northwestern United States, feminism was often linked to queer activism. While feminist activities and identities differed in each setting, Reger located new generations of feminists in all three places.

To express their ideas and spread feminist views, contemporary feminists published books, developed websites, and created zines that often built on the notion of the personal as political (see www.grrrlzines.net). In this regard, third-wavers are similar to second-wave feminists. Both have recognized that women's movement activities often are unreported in the mass media and that when the mass media do cover movement issues and activities, women are frequently portrayed in stereotypical ways and the coverage of movement issues lacks seriousness (Goddu, 1999). Second-wave feminists responded to this problem in various ways, such as developing in the early days of the movement an informal rule of speaking only to female reporters and using feminist newsletters to spread word of the movement (Freeman, 1975; Tuchman, 1978). Contemporary feminists have avoided reliance on mass media by organizing through social media and the Internet and developing internal movement publications such as zines or numerous "cyberfeminist" sites (Reger, 2014b).

Thus, young feminists have continued to engage in innovative collective action, and many issues of concern, including violence against women and abortion rights, provide clear connections between the second and third waves of the women's movement. In Canada, for example, the 6 December, 1989 Montreal Massacre—when 14 female engineering students at the École Polytechnique at the University of Montreal were murdered by a misogynist gunman who then took his own life—has served as a focal point for protests against violence against women through annual commemorations to remember the tragic event and to draw attention to continued violence against women.

Young feminists, however, have also expanded the repertoire of tactics and the framing of feminist issues, as seen in the "slut walks" that began in Toronto and later spread to other countries (Reger, 2014). The first "slut walk" was a protest in reaction to a police officer who was addressing the issue of campus rape at York University and said, "I've been told I'm not supposed to say this; however, women should avoid dressing like sluts in order not to be victimized" (Rush, 2011). Women in Toronto in turn mobilized against the comments and against sexual profiling, victim-blaming, survivor shaming, and rape culture (Reger, 2014, 2014b: 44). With the use of the Internet and social media, slut walks have been organized in countries all over the world. While the SlutWalk was an innovative tactic and introduced new framing of issues, it built on the discourse and tactics of the earlier waves of the women's movement, including "Take Back the Night" marches that were an established part of the movement's tactical repertoire

Richard Lautens/GetStock.com

PHOTO 6.1: SlutWalk, Toronto 2011

(Reger, 2014). The SlutWalk provoked criticism as well as support within the women's movement, but nevertheless it demonstrated that the issue of violence against women, as well as abortion rights, continues to mobilize young feminists.

Other actions of young women have also provoked debate. McRobbie (2009) worries that young women are increasingly adopting a pro-capitalist femininity that plays into male-heteronormative stereotypes and degrades the victories and efforts of older generations of feminists. Johnston and Taylor (2008) and Taylor, Johnston and Whitehead (2014) also find that younger generations of women have to grapple with the co-optation of feminist goals by corporations that use feminism as a way to sell beauty products, clothes, and other merchandise through a consumerist feminism.

Despite such concerns, many young feminists continue to fight for the rights of women and are active in other social movements, including the environmental, LGBT rights, anti-racist, and global justice movements, bringing a feminist perspective to them. Moreover, other movements, as seen in Chapter 5 with Idle No More, have been driven by women and have sparked the imagination of a new generation of activists and approaches to feminism. Young feminists have also joined with more seasoned activists in expanding the global women's movement.

The Global Women's Movement

Although the transnational women's movement dates back to the nineteenth century (Rupp, 1997), in recent decades the global women's movement has expanded significantly. Not all women's groups within the transnational women's movement are feminist, but they are becoming increasingly so. Ferree and Mueller (2004: 577) distinguish between *women's movements*, which they define as "mobilizations based on appeals to women as a *constituency* and thus an organizational strategy," and *feminism*, which has "the *goal* of challenging and changing women's subordination to men." They note that many women's movements start out concerned about issues such as peace or social justice and later become explicitly feminist, while some feminist movements later expand their goals to include issues such as racism and colonialism. Both dynamics are important to the expanding global women's movement.

The expansion of the global women's movement can be traced to the creation of an organizational infrastructure that aided the formation of transnational women's networks (Antrobus, 2004; Keck and Sikkink, 1998; Moghadam, 2005; Rupp, 1997; Ferree, 2006). Owing to the efforts of first-wave feminists involved in transnational women's organizations early in the twentieth century, such as the Women's International League for Peace and Freedom, the United Nations established offices to deal with women's issues early in its history. In response to pressure from women's groups, the UN declared 1975 International Women's Year, and worldwide conferences were held under UN sponsorship. The first official UN women's conference was held in Mexico City in 1975, using the themes of equality, development, and peace. Although this first conference focused on such issues as literacy, education, and health rather than violence against women, sexuality, and sexual orientation, these more controversial issues "were to appear in subsequent meetings as women found the confidence and power to advance them" (Antrobus, 2004: 42). Most importantly, the 1975 conference resulted in a call to the UN General Assembly to declare 1975–85 the Decade for Women, and thus a mid-decade conference was held in Copenhagen in 1980 and an end-of-decade conference in Nairobi in 1985. On the recommendation of the Nairobi conference, a fourth UN World Conference on Women was held in Beijing in 1995. With resources from the UN, activists met to follow up on the plans for action formulated at the conferences and to plan for subsequent conferences, in the process creating a strong global network of activists. Most significantly, this network included activists from the global South as well as the North, and leaders emerged from developing countries as well as from the developed world. Feminist leadership also came from UN personnel and government delegations, and the UN conferences provided an opportunity for women to interact with government officials and to develop resolutions and challenge governments (ibid., 61).

With each conference and with the expansion of transnational women's networks, more and more issues were added to the movement agenda. Feminism was increasingly recognized as relevant to women around the world, rather than only to privileged women from the West, and the feminist movement was broadening its concerns in response to the increased participation of women from developing countries. Although important divisions existed among women from the North and the South, efforts were made to overcome them. As Keck and Sikkink (1998) argue, one of the concerns that first helped to create unity was "violence against women," a category that included a wide range of issues, such as rape and domestic battery, female genital mutilation, female sexual slavery, dowry death in India, and torture and rape of political prisoners in Latin America. Bringing together these various issues "implied rethinking the boundaries between public and private" and giving consideration both to activities carried on in households and to public and state violations of women's rights (Keck and Sikkink, 1998: 173). The issue of violence against women resonated with many women around the world, and it underlined the continued relevance of the second-wave women's movement's focus on the *personal as political*. The transnational women's movement successfully used opportunities such as the UN Conference on Human Rights in 1993 to campaign for the recognition of women's rights as human rights and to place the issue of violence against women on the human rights agenda. These efforts resulted in concrete achievements, such as the adoption in 1993 of the Declaration on the Elimination of Violence against Women by the UN General Assembly as well as the strengthening of regional women's human rights networks (Antrobus, 2004: 91–4). The General Assembly has become a venue for activists to address the organization and raise awareness on the continued discrimination faced by women around the world. Malala Yousafzai, for instance, a young woman who was shot and left for dead in Pakistan because she blogged about life under rule by the Taliban and her views on promoting education for girls and women (Robison, 2013), addressed the assembly on her sixteenth birthday and, at age 17, became the youngest person ever to win the Nobel Peace Prize. Her efforts are also documented in a biography she wrote about her experience and her views (Yousafzai, 2013). Her activism has gained widespread attention with of the meme "We are all Malala" that has spread across social media, though some have argued that in fact her case is an exceptional one and that many more women are harmed without global recognition (Rahman, 2014).

Transnational women's networks have also been active on issues of sexual and reproductive rights, which are complicated and sometimes divisive. Women's groups have opposed forced family planning methods, and they have argued against blaming the fertility of poor women, rather than economic inequality, for environmental and economic problems in the global

South. At the same time, women's groups have argued in favour of safe and accessible health programs for all women. Formed in 1984, a network of feminists in developing countries known as DAWN (Development Alternatives with Women for a New Era) has argued that women's health should be addressed in the context of socio-economic, cultural, and political conditions (see Antrobus, 2004; Mayo, 2005). Feminists have clashed with the Vatican and Islamic fundamentalists over abortion and contraception, and an ongoing countermovement, fuelled by the spread of religious fundamentalism, opposes many efforts of the transnational women's health movement. Activists from the Christian right have become involved in the UN process in recent years in an effort to counter feminist domination in that arena (Butler, 2006).

Along with issues of violence against women and reproductive rights, the global women's movement has focused on economic issues in a way that emphasizes connections between the personal and the political. Feminists have critiqued policies associated with neoliberalism, the economic policy championed by countries such as the United States and Britain that became prominent in the 1980s. Neoliberal economic strategies rely on trade and free-market mechanisms, rather than investment in social services and education, to promote economic growth. Developing countries seeking loans and international aid were forced to scale back government services and focus on debt reduction in order to receive assistance from the International Monetary Fund (IMF), the World Bank, and, later, the World Trade Organization (WTO), which was formed in 1995. Women in both developed and developing countries were affected by neoliberal economic policies, and the transnational women's movement was spurred on by their concerns. Feminists in global women's networks developed analyses explaining how women's unpaid labour was required in order to compensate for cutbacks in government services and how these economic policies affected the everyday lives of poor women. DAWN, in particular, has drawn on the skills of academic feminists to conduct research, prepare policy papers, and conduct workshops at international conferences (see Mayo, 2005: 139–52). Whereas second-wave feminists had conceived of the personal as political primarily in terms of individual experiences, international feminists were expanding this insight to connect macro-level economic policies to women's everyday lives (Antrobus, 2004: 45).

While most women's movements operate within national contexts and direct their demands at local, regional or national targets, the number of countries in which women's movement are active worldwide has expanded greatly, in both democratic and authoritarian contexts (Basu, 2010; Ferree 2012; Moghadam 2012). Several global forces have aided the international spread of women's movements, including transnational advocacy networks, the growth of international funding for NGOs, global feminist discourse, and international conferences sponsored by the United Nations (Basu, 2010: 5).

Transnational feminist networks continue to address numerous issues such as women's political participation, poverty, sexual violence, and discrimination in education around the world.

Maintenance and Growth of the Women's Movement

As the above description of ongoing activities shows, feminism is far from dead; the women's movement has maintained itself into the twenty-first century and even expanded in some areas. Factors identified by theories of social movements help explain the origins and ongoing activities of the women's movement. The grievances emphasized by collective behaviour theorists have combined with the pre-existing organizational structures, resources, and political opportunities emphasized by resource mobilization and political process theorists to fuel the modern movement. Once important gains were achieved, it was natural for the movement to lose some of its urgency and visibility, but feminist issues—and, in some cases, specific events—have continued to attract new generations of women. New commitments to an evolving collective identity, emphasized by new social movement theory, along with ongoing mobilizing structures and political opportunities have kept the movement alive. As Jo Reger (2014, 2014b) shows, young women remain politically active and are changing the frames of feminism and the women's movement. Internationally, grievances created by neoliberal policies and mobilizing structures and resources provided by the UN and other international organizations have expanded the global women's movement. Enduring issues and collective action frames such as "the personal is political" have proved relevant to broad constituencies of women. Opposition to the movement from anti-feminist countermovements and governments made it difficult for the movement to achieve some of its goals. For instance, conservative women's organizations have increasingly challenged dominant organization's funding (Bashevkin, 1998; Knight and Rodgers, 2011) and men's groups, or masculinism, have emerged as a challenge to feminism and the frames of the women's movement (Blais and Dupis-Déri, 2012). Across campuses a number of masculinist groups such as the Canadian Association for Equality (CAFE) have emerged. Although CAFE does not claim to be a men's rights group, the organization claims its "focus is currently on men and boys because that issue receives much less attention than equal rights for women" (CAFE, 2014). Although such countermobilization challenges the women's movement it also mobilizes feminists to fight threats to women's rights.

While existing theories of social movements help to explain the maintenance and growth of the women's movement, the trajectory of the movement suggests a need to go beyond theories of social movements that focus primarily on the public face of movements in interaction with the state (Staggenborg and Taylor, 2005). Although contentious politics are critical to social movements, so are the submerged networks emphasized by new social movement theorists. To explain the maintenance and development of a movement such as the women's movement, we need to look for social movement activity in a variety of venues rather than only in publicly visible protests targeted at states. While feminism is not always visible, it has diffused into the culture in many different venues (Reger, 2012). And, although it is convenient to talk about the "waves" of the women's movement and "cycles of protest" generally, we need to recognize that many social movements continue to exist even when periods of heightened protest subside and their activities become less visible. In the case of the women's movement, ideologically structured action (Zald, 2000) and collective challenges to authority (Snow, 2004) have kept the movement going. Moreover, the movement is still capable of large-scale collective action campaigns even though it does not continually engage in contentious politics.

Much ideologically structured action in support of feminism occurs within institutions. Indeed, scholars have shown that movement activity within institutions occurs at various stages of movement development, aiding the emergence, maintenance, and growth of movements. Before the public emergence of the second wave of the women's movement in North America, women working within government agencies, civil liberties organizations, foundations, churches, unions, and traditional women's organizations such as the YWCA pushed for women's rights and spread feminist ideas to members of their organizations and the larger public (Adamson et al., 1988; Hartmann, 1998). Once the contemporary women's movement was underway in the late 1960s and early 1970s, feminists created footholds within established institutions. In a study of feminism within the US military and the Catholic Church, Mary Katzenstein (1998: 19) found that "feminists have created organizational habitats (formal groups and informal networks) within which feminists (mostly women) share stories, develop strategies, and find mutual support." In universities, feminists have established organizational habitats, such as women's studies departments and research centres, which continue to develop feminist discourse and disseminate movement ideas to new generations of students. Often, activists inside institutions work with outsiders to promote changes, and organizational habitats may serve as mobilizing structures for the larger movement. In the transnational women's movement, feminists employed by the United Nations or national governments have worked with feminists in networks such as DAWN (Mayo, 2005). Thus, feminist activism within institutions has helped the women's movement to maintain itself and to develop in new arenas.

Feminist activism within other social movements is another means by which the movement has survived and spread. As some second-wave organizations declined and women's movement activity became less intense in the 1970s and 1980s, many feminists put their energies into peace, anti-nuclear power, environmental, gay and lesbian, disability rights, anti-racism, and ethnic and community movements, to name a few (Epstein, 1991; Meyer and Whittier, 1994). As seen in examples cited above, they have also worked with the Indigenous movement and have had ties to the sovereignty movement in Quebec. Through their participation in other social movements, feminists helped to keep alive the participatory democratic tradition championed by movements of the 1960s, and they helped to maintain and spread a feminist collective identity. For example, R.W. Connell (1990) found that feminist pressures in the Australian environmental movement led men in the movement to re-examine their ideas about masculinity and to engage in collective projects. Feminist participants, including young women, have influenced a wide variety of movements, including the recent global justice and Occupy movements.

Feminists have also been heavily involved in cultural and service activities, which are other means by which a movement remains alive. For example, feminists continue to be active in battered women's shelters, rape crisis lines, women's centres, feminist book stores, spirituality groups, theatrical performances, women's music festivals, writers' groups, and women's presses. During times when there are few active campaigns, such activities maintain feminist networks and collective identities. Third-wave feminists have participated in a wide range of cultural and political activities around issues such as sexual harassment, sexuality, body image, eating disorders, violence, racism, and sexism in popular culture (see Reger, 2005, 2012). They have been particularly focused on connecting sexism to issues of race, class, and sexuality in cultural and political projects. However, they have done so with the frames and energy of a new generation of activists (Reger, 2014b).

In addition to its ongoing cultural and service activities, the women's movement also maintains explicitly political organizations and campaigns. The European Women's Lobby, an umbrella organization of some 4,000 women's associations in the European Union, co-ordinates the lobbying efforts and campaigns of European and international feminist organizations (www.womenlobby.org). Worldwide, feminist networks continue to expand, coalitions organize collective action, and, in some instances, provincial or national organizations become active internationally. The FFQ became an important player in the global women's movement after spearheading, at the World Conference on Women in Beijing, the formation of an international coalition to stage a protest march known as the World March of Women (WMW) in 2000.

The World March of Women provides a good example of an international campaign that has expanded feminist collective identity and helped to bring together local and international activists around issues of economic justice and women's rights. The campaign came about after the FFQ organized the Quebec Women's March against Poverty, known as the Bread and Roses March, in 1995. This highly successful province-wide campaign helped to bring together feminists and community organizers around the issue of poverty and was very inspiring to participants. Soon after this success, members of the FFQ travelled to Beijing for the UN World Women's Conference, where they gave a workshop on the Bread and Roses March that was greeted with much enthusiasm by participants (Rebick, 2005: 245). An international coalition, including representatives from more than 15 countries and led by the FFQ, was subsequently formed to organize the World March of Women. After successful demonstrations were held around the world in 2000, focusing on the issues of poverty and violence against women, the coalition continued to build a global collective identity among women, and in 2005, the coalition staged another campaign; with this one, a Women's Global Charter for Humanity was relayed around the world (Dufour and Giraud, 2007a, 2007b). In 2010, the World March of Women again organized marches around the globe to call attention to a wide range of social justice issues (www.worldmarchofwomen.org).

In the United States, the NOW, founded in 1966, continues to maintain many active chapters and a large national membership (Barakso, 2004). NOW and other US feminist organizations have successfully organized large-scale collective actions from time to time, including the March for Women's Lives in 2004, which brought over a million women to Washington, DC, in one of the largest women's marches in US history. In Canada, NAC continued to be active, but along with other feminist projects, suffered greatly from cutbacks in government funding beginning in the 1980s and continuing in the 1990s (see Bashevkin, 1998). In part this was related to the increasing prominence of socialist and radical feminists extending the organization's activism against free trade and other conservative policies. This shift made the organization vulnerable to cuts in government funding and also generated internal tensions (Bashevkin, 1988, 1989: 368–9). NAC, as a result, went through a period of internal conflict in the 1990s with a new generation of feminists wanting the organization to move beyond what was often pejoratively labeled "mainstream" or liberal feminism to pursuits of diversity and greater inclusion of women from a wider range of backgrounds (Bashevkin, 1998: 222). Many argued that the organization's reform-based approach until the mid-1980s excluded Indigenous, visible minority, disabled, and working-class women and their interests. By the 2000s, NAC had become less prominent and now no longer even hosts a website. Despite the loss of the national English-Canadian organization, much mobilization has scaled down to a more regional level and also scaled up to pursue transnational opportunities (Masson, 2006; DuFour and Giraud, 2007a; 2007b). In Montreal and Quebec, the 2000 World March of Women was an important campaign that helped to reinvigorate the local and provincial women's movements

(Staggenborg and Lecomte, 2009). After playing a major role in organizing the World March of Women in 2000 and 2005, the FFQ continued to expand and change, working in the international network of women's groups involved in this effort. These regional and international campaigns built on grassroots feminist action and helped to stimulate local involvement in the women's movement (Staggenborg and Taylor, 2005).

Conclusion

Despite the decline of the cycle of protest of the 1960s, the women's movement remains vital. This chapter points to some important reasons for the continued survival and growth of the movement. The second wave of the women's movement organized around critical issues, including reproductive rights and violence against women, which remain relevant to women around the world. Along with these grievances and collective action frames, pre-existing organizational structures and political opportunities helped to mobilize the movement, and ongoing mobilizing structures, new opportunities and frames, and an evolving feminist identity have maintained it. While issues such as abortion have generated much conflict, countermovement activity has helped to maintain feminist abortion rights activities. Issues of violence against women have united women's movements around the world. An extensive international women's movement has developed, and feminism is increasingly viewed as important to women in both developing and developed countries. Feminist frames, such as the idea that the personal is political, have been adapted to new issues, linking macro-level economic policies, for example, to women's everyday lives. The women's movement has targeted many different systems of authority and has become institutionalized in many different arenas. Internationally, feminists have worked within the United Nations, national governments, and many organizations and agencies to advance movement goals. Feminists have also worked through a variety of other social movements, spreading feminist ideas and creating coalitions. The women's movement continues to spawn many cultural activities and collective action campaigns, attracting new generations of women to the movement.

Discussion Questions

1. How and why might women's movements turn into feminist movements?

2. To what extent has the women's movement declined since the years of the "second wave"? What explains the endurance or decline of the movement?

3. What are the challenges involved in the continued expansion and development of the global women's movement?

Suggested Readings

Bashevkin, Sylvia. 2009. *Women, Power, Politics: The Hidden Story of Canada's Unfinished Democracy.* Don Mills, ON: Oxford University Press. This book offers a brief history of women and Canadian politics and also identifies gaps that persist in the ongoing feminist struggle.

Ferree Myra Marx and Aili Mari Tripp (eds). 2006. *Global Feminism: Transnational Women's Activism, Organizing, and Human Rights.* New York: New York University Press. This book contains a collection of chapters that look at the intersection of feminism and globalization and also deal with questions of global rights and transnational organizing.

Rebick, Judy. 2005. *Ten Thousand Roses: The Making of a Feminist Revolution.* Toronto: Penguin Canada. Rebick documents the history of Canadian feminism using extensive interviews with activists.

7 The LGBT Movement

Since the emergence of the "gay liberation" movement out of the social movements of the 1960s, movements to improve the lives of lesbian, gay, bisexual, and transgender (LGBT) people have made enormous strides in many countries, particularly in the Western world (Adam, 1995).[1] LGBT activists have battled against discrimination in areas such as employment and housing. They have also fought for recognition of same-sex relationships, including rights to partner benefits, custody and adoption of children, and marriage or civil unions. Activists have responded to violence against gays and lesbians and have battled against the deep-rooted stigma attached to homosexuality. Gays and lesbians also had to confront the AIDS epidemic, targeting both medical practices and governments. In all of these battles, the LGBT movement met with opposition from an anti-gay countermovement, although the nature of the opposition has varied in different political and cultural contexts.

Focusing primarily on North America but also drawing some comparisons with other countries and regions, this chapter examines some of the struggles to legitimize same-sex relationships and to achieve equal rights for gays and lesbians. It begins with a discussion of the origins of the contemporary LGBT rights movement in the context of the 1960s protest cycle and then examines important movement battles and their results. We attempt to explain how these struggles and their outcomes are influenced by political and cultural opportunities as well as by movement organization and strategy.

Origins of the LGBT Movement

The contemporary LGBT movement mobilized in the late 1960s and, like the contemporary women's movement, survived the decline of other sixties movements. World War II provided opportunities for gay men and lesbians to meet one another in the armed services, in the war industries, and in the growing gay subcultures of cities where wartime allowed a greater freedom to socialize in places such as bars (D'Emilio, 1983; Kennedy and

Davis, 1993). Networks formed during the war helped to support urban gay subcultures after the war, and gays and lesbians in Western Europe and North America formed some organizations before the 1960s, including the Mattachine Society in Los Angeles in 1951. McCarthyism and the Cold War created a repressive political climate in North America and Western Europe, which led early organizations that advanced the rights of gay people, known as "homophile" groups, to take a cautious, assimilationist approach (Adam, 1995: 69). However, public consciousness about homosexuality began to shift with publications on sexual behaviour such as the Kinsey studies, which reported in the late 1940s and early 1950s that homosexual acts were fairly common. In Britain in 1954, the government struck the Committee on Homosexual Offences and Prostitution, which recommended the decriminalization of consensual homosexual acts between men who were at least 21 years of age (Engel, 2001: 71). In the 1960s, support for the civil rights of homosexuals broadened, as organizations such as the American Civil Liberties Union "accepted the principle of a basic right to private consensual sex" (ibid., 37). The political opportunities and organizational bases for an LGBT rights movement expanded before the 1960s in a number of countries, and homophile groups, such as the Vancouver Association for Social Knowledge, organized in 1964, appeared in Canada and elsewhere (Adam, 1995). These organizations sought to educate the public and gay people about the acceptance of diverse sexualities and played an important role in decriminalizing homosexuality, but soon gave way to the more radical gay liberation movement (Knegt, 2011).

That transition and the contemporary gay rights movement are often dated from the Stonewall Rebellion of 1969, when gay patrons at the Stonewall Inn in New York City rioted in response to a police raid on the bar. McAdam (1995) views the gay rights movement as a "spinoff" movement that came late in the protest cycle of the 1960s, and he suggests that, at least in the United States, there were no obvious political opportunities that affected the emergence of the movement. After Richard Nixon was elected president in 1968, the political climate became hostile for progressive social movements. In comparing the LGBT movements in the United States and Britain, however, Engel (2001) shows how features of political institutions and opportunities in the two countries affected the emergence and outcomes of the movement in each country. In particular, the separation of powers in the US system of government provides multiple points of access but also multiple veto points for social movements, while the British parliamentary system allows a receptive ruling party to take action and an unsympathetic government to avoid action despite public opinion and interest group lobbying. In Canada, although the 1982 Charter of Rights and Freedoms created new opportunities for the LGBT rights movement, the movement had taken off in the early 1970s, growing out of the counterculture of the 1960s and using legal strategies to raise consciousness even before the political opportunity associated with the Charter came along (Smith, 1999). The movement was also spurred by police harassment, state repression, and violent raids on gay bath houses in Toronto in 1981 as well obscenity charges laid against *The Body Politic*, the leading gay and lesbian liberation magazine of the 1970s and 1980s (Smith, 2005: 335; Knegt, 2011). The Charter, however, opened up greater legal opportunities during the late 1980s and 1990s and the movement was able to make important strides, putting Canada far ahead of the United States and many other countries in establishing LGBT rights.

Regardless of political opportunities, the protest cycle of the 1960s had an important impact on the development of a gay liberation movement. Many activists in the movement had first been active in other social movements, including the civil rights movement and the New Left. They had been radicalized by these experiences and were ready to apply the new collective action frames and tactics to gay liberation (Warner, 2002). The militancy of other movements of the 1960s helped gay groups overcome their previously cautious approach and led to new rhetoric and tactics, such as the emphasis on gay pride and the use of "sip-ins" to demonstrate the right of gays to go to bars without being harassed by police (Adam, 1995: 74–8). Before the night of the Stonewall raid, other incidents of street violence had occurred following police raids on gay bars, but these earlier incidents happened before an extensive protest environment developed (Duberman, 1993). By the time of Stonewall, a movement subculture was present, ready to support the protesters and to inspire the formation of Gay Liberation Fronts (GLFs) across North America and Western Europe.

Shifts in collective identity, emphasized by new social movement theory, were critical to the birth of a new gay and lesbian movement, especially the emergence of a liberation politic and the empowerment strategies taken by activists in the 1970s and 1980s. Gay men and lesbians began to identify as part of a group or collectivity, and that shared identity encouraged interaction with and participation in the movement. Many gay liberationists adopted a flexible leftist ideology from the New Left, and they built on this ideology to create a new "gay identity" and new collective action frames around gay liberation and other themes (Valocchi, 1999, 2001). Collective action frames from the 1960s that emphasized *rights* and *liberation* were important to the spread of LGBT movements. Although these frames represented different perspectives, ones that sometimes created divisions between activists who advocated the radical idea of liberation and those who employed the more mainstream idea of rights, the ideas coexisted and liberationists often used civil rights frames strategically. As Warner (2002: 70) explains, "civil rights were simple to understand," and the movement used civil rights battles as a way of attracting gays and lesbians to the movement and fighting homophobia, even if, for liberationists, these struggles were never an end in themselves.

In Canada, provincial human rights frameworks created opportunities for LGBT rights activists to use the strategy of advocating that the human rights laws include protections on the basis of sexual orientation. Miriam Smith (1999) shows that, influenced by the American civil rights movement, the Canadian movement used the language of equality in a broad way to develop political consciousness, rather than as a narrow set of legal goals. In addition to talking about gay rights, the Canadian movement also began to use litigation as a tactic in the 1970s "despite the fact that the chances of success were dismal and that the financial and organizational resources of gay liberation groups were meager" (Smith, 1999: 42). Litigation had been used successfully by the civil rights movement in the United States, but in Canada, prior to the adoption of the Charter of Rights and Freedoms in 1982 and the coming into effect of its equality rights guarantee (section 15) in 1985, there was little opportunity for movements to use the courts. However, the use of litigation before the Charter was strategic; it was a way of generating public discussion of homosexuality by using the rights frame. At a time when many gays and lesbians were still in the closet, the tactics were important in raising their consciousness and laying the groundwork for a movement that would later experience great success in changing Canadian laws relating to LGBT rights. Some activists, however, argue that the cost of the success of the rights frame has been the "normalizing" and regulation of homosexuality, leading to an assimilationist and conservative approach to advocacy that fails to recognize the unique and diverse features of LGBT cultures (Kinsman, 1996, 2001; Smith, 2007).

LGBT Liberation

The gay liberation movement spawned by the New Left raised issues of gender and sexuality and connected the struggle for gay liberation to other social movements. From 1969 to about 1972, a number of gay liberation groups formed in North America, Western Europe, Australia, and New Zealand. Like the women's liberation movement, gay liberationists formed consciousness-raising groups that produced "immense anger, joy, pride, and a boiling over of new ideas" (Adam, 1995: 83). Gay liberationists did not conceive of themselves as a minority group seeking civil rights, but rather as people who were challenging conventional notions of sexuality. In the liberationist analysis, homosexuality was seen as "a natural and normal alternative sexuality that must be liberated from oppression imposed by the church, state, and medical institutions, rigid gender-role socialization, and the supremacy of the nuclear family" (Warner, 2002: 64). Many of the early groups called themselves Gay Liberation Fronts in solidarity with the revolutionary movements of the 1960s, such as the Vietnamese National Liberation Front, and they saw the gay liberation struggle as part of a larger movement against numerous forms of oppression. To tackle oppression on many fronts, gay liberationists felt they had to be militant and highly visible, "coming out" in many arenas.

Activists engaged in a variety of confrontational tactics aimed at challenging authorities and educating the public. In the United States, the 1969 Stonewall Rebellion inspired a great deal of movement activity. Because activists considered the event worthy of commemoration, they worked to ensure that it was commemorated every year, eventually with gay pride parades in cities across North America (Armstrong and Crage, 2006). In the year following Stonewall, gay liberation groups picketed a wide variety of institutions associated with the oppression of gay people, including the *Village Voice* for refusing to print the word "gay," airlines for their discriminatory employment practices, and Macy's department store for allowing police to entrap gay men in its washrooms (Adam, 1995: 85). Activists staged a number of demonstrations at the sites of professional meetings to protest against the medical definition of homosexuality as a social pathology, and in 1973, as a result of gay protests, the American Psychiatric Association voted to change its official diagnostic manual so that homosexuality was no longer classified as a psychiatric disorder (Kutchins and Kirk, 1997).

New York Public Library

PHOTO 7.1: Stonewall Rebellion

The Stonewall Rebellion was not as immediate an event in other countries, such as Canada and Great Britain, but it was nevertheless highly symbolic and led to much publicity and the wide dissemination of movement
literature, stimulating the growth of Gay Liberation Fronts (Warner, 2002:
66). Gay liberation activists around the world were influenced by the movements of the 1960s, but protests in particular countries took on unique characteristics, and organizations formed in response to local and national events.
In Britain, gay liberationists tended to be "far more concerned with personal liberation and cultural development" than with political goals because
consensual homosexual relations had been legal in England and Wales since
1967 (Engel, 2001: 85). For a short time, British activists promoted "radical
drag," a unique gender-bending fashion style that included the mixing of
dresses and beards (Adam, 1995: 90; Engel, 2001: 85). In Canada, the first
gay liberation groups organized in the country's largest cities. The Front de
libération des homosexuels was formed in Montreal in 1970 as a response to
police raids and the closing of gay bars in the context of the War Measures
Act, which was invoked by the Trudeau government in response to the kidnapping of a Quebec cabinet minister (who was later killed) and a British
diplomat by the Front de libération du Québec (FLQ) (Warner, 2002: 66).
The Gay Liberation Front emerged in Vancouver in 1970 (Knegt, 2011) and
Toronto Gay Action was founded about a year later along with a national
monthly gay liberation magazine, *The Body Politic*, which began publishing
in Toronto in 1971 (Warner, 2002: 67). Gay liberation groups also formed in
universities across Canada.

Gay liberationists engaged in a range of militant and visible actions
aimed at challenging mainstream culture and constructing a positive collective identity for gays and lesbians. Movement frames and strategies were
affected by ideological positions and network connections to the New Left,
and gay liberation organizations helped activists to connect issues of sexuality to larger political goals. Participants were attracted to gay liberation
organizations both because they provided one of the few spaces at the time
where gay men and lesbians could come out of the closet and openly express
their sexuality and because they offered a vision of social change relevant
to the times (Lent, 2003: 44). As an activist in the Gay Liberation Front in
London, England explained,

> (t)he GLF made us aware of our sexuality as a political issue. So I could
> then see the links to other struggles. I wouldn't put it in the same terms
> today but then the idea was that gay lib would operate as part of social and
> structural revolution which was the wave of the future. In 1970 we really
> believed that the whole world was going to crash down and that revolution
> was on the cards. We wanted sexual revolution to be part of that. (Quoted
> in ibid., 38–9)

Early gay liberation organizations tended to be very short-lived, however, as they often lacked sustaining organizational structures. They were also torn apart by ideological debates and internal conflicts over issues such as sexism. Because gay liberation groups tended to be preoccupied with issues affecting gay men, lesbians in the early 1970s began to withdraw from gay liberation groups to form autonomous organizations (Adam, 1995: 99). Whereas gay men enjoyed many of the privileges of other men, lesbians suffered from the discrimination that affected all women, and they were drawn in large numbers to the women's movement. Lesbian feminists created many alternative institutions, such as women's bookstores, presses, music festivals, and theatres, which became part of "cultural feminism" after the early years of the women's liberation movement (Echols, 1989). These enterprises provided ways for lesbian feminists and other women to continue their involvement in the movement (Taylor and Rupp, 1993). Moreover, Vancouver's Little Sister's Book and Art Emporium played a prominent role in challenging the application of Canadian customs laws and promoting freedom of expression during the 1980s and 1990s. The Supreme Court recognized that the store was the target of harassment by the Canadian Border Services Agency, which repeatedly seized what it deemed indecent material bound for the bookstore. Despite such recognition, the court did not strike down the law that was being abused and the matter was left largely unresolved (Knegt, 2011).

The gay liberation movement did not end with the decline of its early organizations, but it did change its strategies. Gay liberationists had wanted to overcome set categories of gender and sexuality, but the goal of liberating sexuality conflicted with the need to create a gay and lesbian identity for political purposes (Smith, 1999: 45). Ironically, liberationists ended up helping to create gay communities and a gay identity, which entrenched many of the categories they fought to overcome (Epstein, 1999: 42). In major cities gay culture was organized around services, restaurants, bars, bathhouses, and other community organizations and businesses. Armstrong (2002) argues that gay activism in San Francisco underwent an important transformation with the decline of the New Left; the movement became focused on gay pride and identity, but in a way that promoted the acceptance of sexual and political diversity, including the pursuit of equal rights as one way of expressing gay identity and protecting individual differences. In San Francisco and other cities, the number of LGBT cultural and political organizations expanded dramatically in the 1970s, creating a strong basis for the ongoing movement. Gay liberationists remained involved in spreading gay culture in the major cities of North America and Western Europe and continued their involvement in new political organizations founded after the early 1970s. Successor organizations to the GLF groups abandoned the attempt to link gay rights to a larger revolutionary movement, however, and focused on activism surrounding specific gay issues, particularly civil rights, as a strategy for building a movement and providing opportunities for visible collective actions, such as demonstrations (Warner, 2002: 68–70).

Struggles for Equal Rights

LGBT activists have made great gains in liberal democracies by presenting themselves as a quasi-ethnic group and framing their demands in terms of civil rights. Gay rights activists built national organizations, such as the National Gay and Lesbian Task Force (NGLTF) in the United States and Equality for Gays and Lesbians Everywhere (Egale) in Canada, as well as local and regional groups, to engage in legislative, judicial, and electoral campaigns. They also pressured businesses, churches, professional associations, and other organizations to adopt non-discriminatory policies. And, as LGBT movement culture and political campaigns became increasingly visible, an anti-gay countermovement mobilized in response.

Beginning in the 1970s, LGBT activists waged campaigns to outlaw discrimination in areas such as housing, employment, and government services through local and state or provincial legislation, ballot initiatives, referendums, and attempts to add sexual orientation to municipal, state or provincial, and national human rights charters. Frequently, the movement battled discriminatory initiatives of the countermovement. LGBT rights groups also filed lawsuits to support individuals against discrimination and to attempt to overturn legislation—such as sodomy laws in the United States—that permitted police harassment and arrests of sexual minorities. In Canada, Quebec became the first province to add sexual orientation to its human rights code in 1977, after the election of the Parti Québécois (PQ) in 1976 and in the wake of public outrage against a massive police raid of a gay bar in Montreal (Warner, 2002: 148–9). However, other provinces and territories did not follow suit until the 1980s and 1990s, in part because of a backlash against LGBT rights campaigns.

In the late 1970s, an important source of opposition came from the United States, where the anti-gay countermovement employed the conservative master frame of protection of the "traditional family." In 1977, an anti-gay rights organization called Save Our Children spearheaded a successful campaign in Dade County, Florida, to repeal a new civil rights ordinance that prohibited discrimination on the basis of sexual orientation. The anti-gay rights campaign was headed by former beauty queen and evangelist singer Anita Bryant, who went on a speaking tour in the United States and Canada following the countermovement victory in Dade County and helped to defeat gay rights ordinances in several other US cities, including St Paul, Minnesota; Wichita, Kansas; and Eugene, Oregon (Adam, 1995). Bryant was invited to Canada by Ken Campbell, a Christian minister from Milton, Ontario, who campaigned with her against human rights legislation for gays and lesbians on the grounds that homosexuals recruited children and undermined families (Warner, 2002: 136). Around the same time, criminal charges were laid against the *Body Politic* for its publication of an article about intergenerational sex between men and boys, and the murder of a shoeshine boy in Toronto in 1977 was depicted in the press as the act of "depraved" homosexuals. Police raids against gay bars intensified in Canada during this period, as they did in other countries, creating a climate of anti-gay repression (Adam, 1995: 124–7).

The rise of a countermovement often helps to increase movement mobilization, and the LGBT rights movement rallied in response to the threats. In Canada, the Anita Bryant crusade "provided unprecedented opportunity" for gays and lesbians to gain a huge amount of media exposure by organizing a campaign in response—the Coalition to Stop Anita Bryant. The coalition galvanized LGBT communities in cities across the country where Bryant spoke (Warner, 2002: 136–7). Anita Bryant was at the time the national spokesperson for Florida orange growers, and LGBT activists in North America launched a boycott of Florida oranges to protest her role as a crusader against gay rights. As a result of the controversy, Bryant was dismissed from her job with the orange growers, while LGBT groups flourished as they battled the countermovement. As Fetner (2001) concludes, countermobilization offered opportunities for the LGBT movement and strengthened its activism. She also argues that by keeping LGBT rights in the news media and policy spotlight, the religious right and conservatives have contributed to a liberalizing of views toward homosexuality in North America (Fetner, 2008).

Since the 1970s, LGBT rights groups have made great strides in achieving anti-discrimination measures, while continuing to provoke opposition. In the United States, a study of gay and anti-gay rights efforts between 1974 and 1994 found that gay rights advocates were more successful overall than their opponents and increasingly so over time (Werum and Winders, 2001). Most battles were fought at the state and local levels, rather than the federal level, and gay rights supporters were particularly successful in passing local ordinances prohibiting discrimination and in using the state legislatures and courts to secure rights. Anti-gay activists were most successful with ballot initiatives and referendums, which allowed them to arouse public fears about gay rights. However, the ability of the LGBT movement to win at the ballot box also changed over time as the movement learned how to respond to its opponents. Stone (2012) details how the LGBT movement won a majority of ballot box battles between 1997 and 2003 by using increasingly sophisticated campaign tactics such as voter identification and large-scale mobilization of volunteers, made possible by a growing movement infrastructure. Between 2004 and 2012, the American LGBT movement suffered numerous defeats on ballot measures to prevent same-sex marriage, but later began to make progress in this area as well (Stone, 2012, 2013).

In Canada, sodomy as an indictable offence was dropped from the Criminal Code in 1969 as part of a package of family law reforms, influenced by British precedent (Pierceson, 2005: 172). After introducing the amendments to the Criminal Code in December 1967, then justice minister Pierre Trudeau famously remarked to the media that "there's no place for the state in the bedrooms of the nation." Although this comment attracted much attention, there was little public conflict over the change, as support for decriminalizing homosexual acts among consenting adults already existed in Canada (Warner, 2002: 44–5). In the 1970s, the LGBT movement continued to generate further support for LGBT rights. Even though there was little opportunity in Canada to make progress on LGBT rights through the courts prior to adoption of the Charter of Rights and Freedoms, Canadian activists used litigation in the 1970s to raise public awareness and create a political identity among Canadian gays and lesbians (Smith, 1999). At the same time, the movement took advantage of other opportunities for change. One such example was the creation of provincial and federal human rights commissions, which activists lobbied to include sexual orientation as a prohibited ground of discrimination in human rights codes. After the equality rights provisions of the Charter came into effect in 1985, the role of the courts in Canada expanded greatly and movements had new opportunities to use litigation to bring about legal change. The courts, moreover, have been supportive of LGBT rights claims, "increasing the incentive for LGBT groups and litigants to use the courts in pursuit of a broad range of political goals ranging from issues of censorship to same-sex marriage" (Grundy and Smith, 2005: 393). For example, between 1986 and 1999, despite opposition from anti-gay rights forces, the movement succeeded in getting the federal government, all provinces, and one territory to amend their human rights laws to prohibit discrimination on the grounds of sexual orientation (Warner, 2002: 197).

Outside of North America, LGBT activists also struggled for and won changes in human rights laws and other civil liberties measures. In 1984, the European Parliament adopted a comprehensive position on the civil rights of gays and lesbians, and a number of European countries, including France, Denmark, Sweden, Norway, and the Netherlands, passed anti-discrimination and anti–hate-crime legislation in the 1980s and early 1990s. In New Zealand, a national human rights law was passed in 1993, despite the intensive anti–gay campaign mounted by religious conservatives when male homosexual relations were decriminalized in the mid-1980s (Adam, 1995: 132–3). In other countries and regions such as Latin America, Asia, and Africa, LGBT groups have organized but they often face a great deal of state repression and societal condemnation (ibid., 165–76). In recent years a number of countries have introduced new and more punitive laws against gays and lesbians.

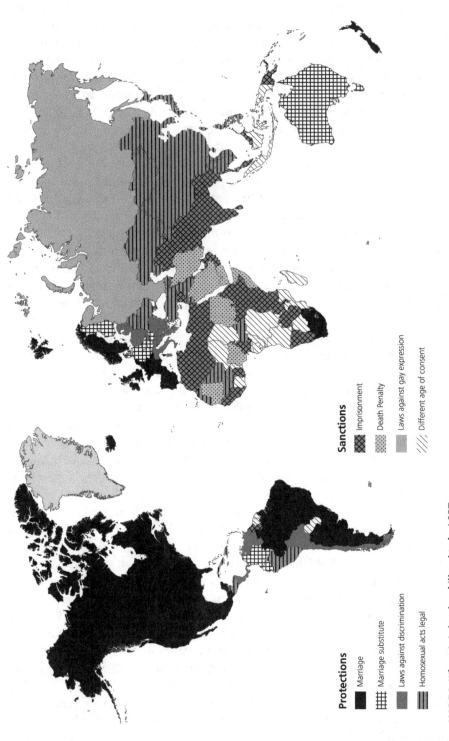

Protections

⬛ Marriage

▦ Marriage substitute

▨ Laws against discrimination

▥ Homosexual acts legal

Sanctions

⬛ Imprisonment

▨ Death Penalty

▨ Laws against gay expression

⫽ Different age of consent

MAP 7.1: Where it is legal and illegal to be LGBT

For example, Uganda passed legislation in 2014 to imprison people for life for homosexuality after originally proposing the death penalty; India reintroduced a 153-year-old colonial-era law criminalizing gay sex; and Russia banned the promotion of "non-traditional" sexuality to those under 18 just one year before the 2014 Sochi Olympics. Many feared that the Russian law was so broadly worded that it would ban any public display of LGBT symbols or sexuality and could discriminate against many of the athletes participating in the games, not to mention LGBT peoples in Russia more generally. Homosexuality is still subject to the death penalty in five countries, two others have regions that use the same punishment, and over 70 countries imprison citizens because of sexual orientation (BBC, 2014). International organizations such as the International Lesbian, Gay, Bisexual, Trans and Intersex Association have formed to assist in the promotion of human rights worldwide, but the global struggle to legitimize diverse sexualities and create equality is far from over.

AIDS Activism and Queer Politics

The AIDS crisis that began in the early 1980s profoundly affected the LGBT movement in both negative and positive ways. Most obviously, AIDS led to the deaths of many gay activists and leaders. The spread of the disease also prompted increased opposition from the conservative right in countries such as the United States, Canada, and Britain. On both sides of the Atlantic, gays were attacked for engaging in what was deemed "unnatural" and "dangerous" behaviour that resulted in a "gay plague." In the United States, conservative politicians and religious leaders spoke about AIDS as "the cost of violating traditional values" and as "an awful retribution" (Engel, 2001: 50). In 1987, Congress passed the Helms Amendment to the AIDS appropriation bill, which prohibited the use of federal money for any educational materials that "promote or encourage, directly or indirectly, homosexual activities" (Rimmerman, 2002: 94). In Britain, the Conservative government introduced clause 28 to the 1988 Local Government Bill, which did not restrict spending as the Helms Amendment did but sought to prevent local authorities from intentionally "promoting homosexuality" or teaching in schools "the acceptability of homosexuality as a pretended family relationship." The threat of clause 28 in Britain had an effect similar to the Stonewall Rebellion, resulting in an unprecedented new wave of protest that included several marches in London and Manchester of 10,000 to 30,000 protesters (Engel, 2001: 92–3).

In North America and Europe, the AIDS epidemic and opposition from the political right sparked renewed mobilization and new strategies in the LGBT movement. Owing to the crisis, increased numbers of gay people came out of the closet and gay visibility in the mass media increased dramatically. The AIDS movement spawned a large number of service organizations to assist people with AIDS, creating new forms of gay community. Many lesbians who had been disillusioned by the earlier gay movement were appalled by right-wing opposition and homophobia as well as by government inaction, and they returned to work with gay men (Engel, 2001: 48–9). AIDS movements developed both national lobbies to influence government policies and new grassroots organizations that engaged in a new round of direct-action tactics. The AIDS Coalition to Unleash Power (ACT UP) was organized in New York in 1987 and soon spread to cities across the United States, Canada, Europe, and Australia.

A number of service organizations in Canada began engaging in AIDS activism in the early 1980s and, in 1983, Vancouver held a forum on AIDS that sparked the creation of AIDS Vancouver. The AIDS Committee of Toronto (ACT) emerged around the same time; similar organizations formed in other provinces within a few years (Knegt, 2011). The first Canadian AIDS protest occurred in 1986 in front of the British Columbia legislature, and a year later Montreal's Comité des personnes atteintes du VIH du Québec emerged, as did Toronto-based AIDS Action Now!, which was the most "influential and well-known" activist group in the country (ibid., Chapter 6).

Canadian activists were inspired by ACT UP and pursued similar tactics and framing of issues. They often used street theatre, a strategy employed by countercultural movements of the sixties and the gay liberation groups of the early seventies. ACT UP and similar groups engaged in tactics intended to raise public consciousness about AIDS and to challenge the stigma attached to homosexuality (Gamson, 1989). They staged "die-ins" in which activists drew police-style chalk outlines around one another's bodies, likening AIDS deaths to murders and shifting responsibility away from the victims of AIDS. The pink triangle, which was the emblem used by the Nazis to mark homosexuals, was reclaimed by AIDS activists and used along with the slogan "silence = death" as an indictment of homophobia and indifference to gay deaths.

ACT UP converted feelings of grief into anger, which led to a period of militancy that helped to create a new "queer" identity (Gould, 2002, 2009). By the mid-1990s, the AIDS movement had made progress, and some of the anger that fuelled ACT UP subsided. ACT UP chapters were often short-lived, and in some cities, including Vancouver, ACT UP was never particularly strong compared to local groups such as AIDS Vancouver (Brown, 1997). Nevertheless, grassroots AIDS activism by ACT UP and other radical groups helped to renew liberationist challenges and sparked an important turning point in LGBT activism (Sears 2005: 99). Queer Nation was founded in New York in 1990 by ACT UP activists and others who wanted to go beyond the AIDS issue and address concerns such as homophobia and gay bashing. Bisexual and transgender politics, which had often been left out of LGBT movements, became part of the queer agenda, as activists challenged the idea of a fixed sexual identity and the assimilationist approach of trying to "fit in" to mainstream society (Epstein, 1999: 61).

Queer Nation groups formed in a number of cities in North America, and they engaged in tactics intended to raise consciousness about homophobia and heterosexism. For example, same-sex couples held "kiss-ins" in places such as shopping malls and straight bars, adopted the slogan "bash back," and called for a proactive response against violence directed against LGBT people (Sears 2005). Like ACT UP, Queer Nation groups tended to be short-lived, but they left a legacy of activism and consciousness in gay communities. Queer Nation Toronto, for example, was founded in 1990 and lasted for about two years, attracting some 200 activists. The group put up posters in downtown Toronto with messages such as "Queers are here, get used to it" and held demonstrations against the religious right, anti-abortionists, the war in Iraq, and gay bashing. Queer Nation tried to be inclusive of all sexual orientations and to work in coalition with anti-racists, feminists, peace activists, and others. However, groups such as Queer Nation Toronto found themselves lacking the processes and strategies needed to resolve differences and effect change, and they often succumbed to internal conflict over such problems as how to deal with racism and sexism when they attempted to create inclusive organizations (Warner, 2002: 259–60). Nevertheless, the movement reclaimed and popularized the use of the term "queer" and helped to launch the academic field of "queer theory" (ibid., 262).

Queer activism also helped to expand the boundaries of LGBT organizing, pushing for greater inclusion of bisexual and transgender people and raising awareness of racial and cultural diversity in gay communities. This distinguished their activism from that of earlier generations that had more constrained understandings of queer identity (Sears, 2005: 100; Gamson, 1996). Although bisexual and transgender activists had always been present in the LGBT movement, they tended to be marginalized. In the 1990s, queer theory and a dramatic increase in transgender activism influenced the movement (Munro, 2005; Stryker, 2008). This occurred in part because transgender people were recognized as a population vulnerable to AIDS, owing to risk factors such as poverty and lack of health care, and some AIDS funding was directed at transgender communities. The AIDS epidemic "significantly reshaped sexual identity politics" and helped to create new alliances among "queer" activists (Stryker, 2008: 132–4). A Transgender Nation group formed in 1992 within Queer Nation in San Francisco, and lesbian and gay groups began debating the inclusion of transgender issues (Stryker, 2008: 135–7). Although there were conflicts along the way, and both transgender and bisexual activists continued to struggle for legitimacy within the movement, the LGBT nomenclature eventually became common.

Relationship Recognition and Same-Sex Marriage

Although the AIDS epidemic sparked more overt and radical queer activism, the struggle to gain recognition and equality also persisted. As part of campaigns to secure rights, gay men and lesbians began pressuring governments, unions, and employers to provide benefits to same-sex partners and to recognize same-sex relationships. Issues of relationship recognition became increasingly important in the 1980s and 1990s, and same-sex marriage became legal in a handful of countries after the turn of the century. European countries led the way in same-sex partnership recognition, with Denmark becoming the first country to allow the registration of partnerships in 1989. The Netherlands became the first country to allow same-sex marriage in 2001 and Canada did so in 2005. Following a US Supreme Court ruling in June, 2015, the United States became the 20th country to legalize same-sex marriage.

In Canada, the public hearings preceding the enactment of section 15 of the Charter provided a major political opportunity for lesbian and gay rights advocates, who participated extensively in the hearings on equality rights (Smith, 2007, 2005, 2004: 107). Although only a few of the numerous briefs submitted by LGBT groups to the parliamentary subcommittee on equality rights concerned relationship recognition issues (e.g., regulations for pensions, income tax, insurance, and wills), these issues became a focus of much of the Charter litigation of the late 1980s and 1990s (Smith, 1999: 80–2). LGBT activists also organized within unions, particularly the Canadian Union of Public Employees (CUPE), to get same-sex benefits included in collective bargaining. At the instigation of gay LGBT activists, unions such as CUPE also launched lawsuits to secure same-sex benefits for their members, using the political opportunities created by the Charter (ibid., 121). Private sector unions were slower to act, but the Canadian Auto Workers Union, the country's largest union at the time, actively pursued equality for LGBT members in its negotiations (Hurt and Rayside 2001). Thus, Canadian unions have played a prominent role in promoting more equitable policies.

The Vancouver Gay and Lesbian Community Centre argued in its brief on section 15 that equality rights entailed a right to same-sex marriage, but this was a bold claim in the mid-1980s (Smith, 1999: 82). Other activists involved in such litigation, however, were initially careful to avoid the "M-word." A court case challenging Ontario's Family Support Act turned into a landmark Supreme Court ruling in 1999, but the lawyer who argued the case, Martha McCarthy, maintained at the time that the case had nothing to do with marriage (Graff, 1999: 23). The Canadian federal government stalled for years, but after the Supreme Court declared the Ontario law unconstitutional because its definition of a spouse excluded men and women in same-sex relationships, the Liberal government finally introduced legislation to extend to gays and lesbians the legal rights and obligations that applied to common-law heterosexual unions. At the same time, the Liberals argued that the legislation would not affect the legal definition of "marriage" as being between a man and a woman, and in 1999, the House of Commons voted overwhelmingly in favour of a motion to uphold the definition of marriage as a union between a man and a woman. However, other court rulings followed, and several provinces, beginning with Ontario in 2003, legalized same-sex marriage. In 2004, the Supreme Court of Canada cleared the way for federal legislation on same-sex marriage, and in 2005, the federal government followed the lead of the courts and passed a bill allowing same-sex marriage throughout the country.

Although there was controversy over this momentous change in Canada, same-sex marriage was the culmination of years of equity-seeking by LGBT activists, years of effort that had seen the creation of laws against discrimination and protections for same-sex relations and parenting rights (M. Smith, 2008). In the United States, in contrast, laws still permit discrimination against gays and lesbians in many states. Ten years after its legalization in Canada, same-sex marriage was finally legalized by the US Supreme Court in 2015. This occurred after a long struggle, which saw the first signs of success when several US states legalized same-sex civil unions, beginning with Vermont in 2000 following a court ruling. In 2004, Massachusetts became the first state to permit same-sex marriages and by early 2015, 37 states and the District of Columbia had legalized same-sex marriage. Progress was not continuous, however, reflecting a battle of movement and countermovement over the issue. In addition to changing legal and political opportunities, the success of the movement was affected by its frames and tactics, which were frequently altered in response to the strategies of opponents.

The LGBT movement waged a deliberate campaign to counter opposition frames through organizations such as the national Freedom to Marry organization. For example, Maine legalized same-sex marriage in 2009 and then repealed its new law in a November, 2009 referendum before it took effect. Gay and lesbian rights groups then engaged in a concerted grassroots education campaign featuring gay and lesbian couples between 2009 and 2012, when the movement won voter approval in Maine of same-sex marriage (Stone, 2013:160). In California, same-sex marriage was banned through a ballot initiative (Proposition 22) in 2000 and then banned again through a voter initiative to amend the state constitution (Proposition 8), which passed in November 2008, after the state Supreme Court had permitted same-sex marriage earlier that year. The LGBT movement worked hard to change this outcome, using a canvassing model that allowed activists to engage in conversations with voters (Stone, 2013: 159–60). Proposition 8 was challenged in the courts and ruled unconstitutional in 2010; when the Supreme Court ruled that proponents of Proposition 8 lacked standing to appeal this verdict, same-sex marriage was legalized in California in 2013.

Movement/countermovement dynamics strongly influenced the strategies of both sides in the conflict over same-sex marriage in the United States. In the early 1990s, few LGBT groups focused on marriage rights, in part because there was disagreement within the movement over the desirability of marriage, which many saw as a conservative institution, and in part because activists knew that the issue would provoke strong opposition (Fetner, 2008: 111). However, some same-sex couples were filing lawsuits over marriage-licensing discrimination, and in 1993, the issue gained a great deal of media attention when it looked as if the Hawaii Supreme Court would legalize same-sex marriage, until the state legislature stepped in to limit marriage to opposite-sex couples. Seeing same-sex marriage as a highly symbolic issue that would mobilize a great deal of support, the religious right then launched a massive campaign to prohibit same-sex marriage across the United States. This campaign in turn produced a strong response from the LGBT movement, which put aside internal differences on the issue in the face of opposition and began to organize extensively around the battle for marriage rights (Fetner, 2008: 112; Pinello, 2006). Dorf and Tarrow (2014) argue that gay rights opponents engaged in "anticipatory countermobilization" around the issue of same-sex marriage and that this in turn mobilized LGBT activists around the issue. In other words, the fears of opponents that same-sex marriage would come into being, and their opposition to this change, pushed LGBT supporters to make marriage equality a priority. Among other strategies, public same-sex weddings were used to protest marriage discrimination (Taylor et al., 2009). In 2004, when Mayor Gavin Newsom permitted same-sex marriages in San Francisco, thousands of gay and lesbian couples lined up to be married, in part as a co-ordinated strategy to make same-sex partnerships visible in the mass media.

Both sides in the battle over same-sex marriage organized in response to the strategies and victories of their opponents. In an analysis of which states were most likely to ban gay marriage, Soule (2004) found that both citizen ideology and interest group activity had an influence and, surprisingly, that states were more likely to ban gay marriage if they had previously passed some type of gay-friendly legislation. These findings point to the role of interactions between movement and countermovement; movement groups play a key role in making gains, but their victories provoke countermovement retaliation. Thus, Soule found that "same-sex marriage bans represent a backlash against policy gains made by gays and lesbians" (2004: 472). Although Soule's analysis was published before the events in California around Proposition 8, it is clearly applicable. Prior to the 2000 ban, California had enacted domestic partnership legislation. Prior to the 2008 ban, the decision by the mayor of San Francisco to issue marriage licences to same-sex couples led to the court case that temporarily legalized same-sex marriage in the state, provoking a strong countermovement reaction (*Los Angeles Times*, 8 November 2008). Proposition 8 in turn outraged and disappointed gay rights activists, leading to large protests, as well as litigation, against the measure (*New York Times*, 16 November 2008).

Despite opposition to same-sex marriage and other LGBT rights measures, marriage and equal recognition became important goals for the movement owing to new developments in LGBT communities in both the United States and Canada (Chauncey, 2004; Smith, 2008: 111). As a result of the AIDS epidemic, many gay couples were suddenly faced with issues such as control over medical decisions, health insurance, and funeral arrangements, and were thus further motivated to seek relationship recognition (Chauncey, 2004: 96). Around the same time, a lesbian "baby boom" was taking place in many major cities as lesbians began to live together openly and to have children, creating another impetus for legal protections for LGBT families (ibid., 105). In addition to these practical concerns, "the freedom to marry, including the right to choose one's partner in marriage, has come to be regarded as a fundamental civil right and a powerful symbol of full equality and citizenship" (ibid., 165; see also Hull, 2006). But "despite sociological similarities prior to the rise of the same-sex marriage debate, there were important differences in law and policy" between the United States and Canada that help to explain why same-sex marriage was legalized fairly quickly and easily in Canada in 2005, while the struggle for same-sex marriage was longer in the United States (M. Smith, 2008: 111).

In a comparison of the two countries, Miriam Smith (2008) argues that differences in political institutions best explain different outcomes in the United States and Canada regarding same-sex marriage and other gay rights measures. Although both countries have federal systems of government, their political and legal institutions differ significantly. In Canadian federalism, criminal law is controlled by the federal government, and sodomy was legalized as part of law reforms in 1969. In the United States, battles against criminal laws prohibiting sodomy had to be fought in various states until the 2003 Supreme Court ruling struck down remaining sodomy laws. While conflict over the legality of homosexuality in the United States reinforced religious and moral opposition to gay rights, in Canada the debate over same-sex marriage was framed in terms of human rights. The United States is typically considered a more religious country with a more conservative culture than Canada's, but Smith argues that the political institutions of the two countries provided different opportunities to opponents. The Christian right and other conservatives in the United States were able to fight at the federal level for the Defense of Marriage Act, passed in 1994, while at the same time fighting same-sex marriage at the state level through the state courts and legislatures, using mechanisms such as state constitutional amendments (M. Smith, 2008: 121–5).

While Canada also had an evangelical Christian movement opposed to same-sex marriage, its political system provided fewer opportunities for these Christian groups to fight against gay rights. Same-sex marriage was supported by court rulings in Canada, where "the lack of judicial federalism and the relatively unified court system" made it difficult for the opposition to challenge these rulings (M. Smith, 2008: 167). The Liberal Party, which controlled the federal government at the time, also came to support same-sex marriage. Owing to the dominance of the executive and the lack of an independent role for the legislatures in Canada, along with the operation of party discipline, opponents of gay rights had few options; tools used by US opponents, such as state constitutional amendments and ballot initiatives, were unavailable in the Canadian system (ibid., 130–1). But despite these differences in institutional opportunities and outcomes between the US and Canada, Smith (2007) argues that the frames and discourse used by LGBT activists are largely dominated by a rights-based discourse. But the success of the rights-based frame and discourse was criticized (e.g., Kinsman, 1996, 2001) for moving the movement away from more diverse and less mainstream conceptualizations of queer identity seen in earlier periods of activism.

Influences on Movement Strategies and Outcomes

LGBT movements have clearly made important gains, but they also continue to face strong obstacles. Movement strategies have played an important role in changing political and cultural climates and creating new opportunities for LGBT rights. The strategies employed by activists are in turn influenced by political and cultural opportunities, as well as by the organization and resources of the movement, and they have varied across time and place. Frequently, LGBT activists have focused on achieving equality through such means as anti-discrimination legislation and litigation to achieve equal rights, emphasizing similarities between themselves and other citizens. However, even when pursuing such seemingly "assimilationist" strategies, activists were often at the same time trying to build a movement and a collective identity (Smith, 1998). Movements can "deploy" identity for different strategic purposes (Bernstein, 1997). In some instances, activists seek to empower constituents with a sense of collective identity and to create a shared community before they engage in more instrumental action. In other instances, the goal is to transform the values, categories, and practices of mainstream culture rather than to win specific policy changes, and activists may focus on developing community and collective identity among gays and lesbians by emphasizing their uniqueness and differences from the mainstream culture.

Extreme repression of a movement, such as occurred during the McCarthy era, can lead to cautious tactics and difficulty in mobilizing support, but with the development of supportive cultural and political organizations and a positive collective identity, movements can defend themselves against opponents (Adam, 1995: 115). By the end of the 1970s, when an anti-gay countermovement emerged, the LGBT movement had created this type of infrastructure and identity in North American cities (Armstrong, 2002). Although the countermovement has created obstacles for the LGBT movement, such as opposition to same-sex marriage in the United States, it has also stimulated movement organization and strategies. Threats, as well as opportunities, have helped to mobilize the movement and to shape its frames and tactics. Opposition to same-sex marriage, as we have seen, helped to spur movement activity around the issue with the result that "marriage equality" now enjoys substantial public support.

Cross-national comparisons point to the importance of political and cultural opportunities in accounting for variations in movement strategies and outcomes. Despite many similarities between the United States and Canada, differences in the political institutions of the two countries help to account for the much greater success of the LGBT movement in achieving human rights and relationship recognition in Canada (Pierceson, 2005; Smith, 2008). Before the adoption of the Charter, there was little opportunity for Canadian activists to engage in the type of rights-seeking litigation used by movements in the United States, notably the civil rights movement. Nevertheless, Canadian activists used court cases in the pre-Charter era to raise public consciousness and to create collective identity, and then took advantage of the new political opportunity presented by the Charter to use litigation more instrumentally (Smith, 1999). Supportive rulings by the courts then helped to spread an "equal rights" frame, which further influenced public opinion in Canada in favour of gay rights (Matthews, 2005). With the passage of the Charter, the Liberal Party of Canada became identified with its "human rights regime" and LGBT rights activists gained a major political opportunity; in contrast to the "special interests" discourse that hindered activists in the United States, they were able to employ the discourse of "human rights" and "Charter values" that would become so important to Canadian political discourse (Smith, 2008: 23).

The parliamentary system and party discipline in Canada made it possible for sympathetic elites to pass gay-friendly legislation, despite lingering opposition to policies such as same-sex marriage. In the United States, some court rulings have been favourable to the movement, but the separation of powers in the American federalist system has provided more opportunities for opponents to block non-discriminatory reforms than has been the case in Canada. In the language of political process theory, opponents of gay rights and same-sex marriage had greater *political opportunities* in the United States than in Canada. As Miriam Smith (2008: 187) points out, however, the concept of a "political opportunity structure" needs to be further specified in order to show how "specific institutional features of the political system such as the separation of powers, federalism, and constitutional rules play an important role in particular policy sectors." In Canada, the constitutional entrenchment of the Charter provided the LGBT rights movement with an unprecedented opportunity to gain legal equality (ibid., 188).

In a comparison of the British and American LGBT movements, Engel found that variations in strategies and outcomes are related to both political institutions and cultural differences in the two countries. In Britain, interest groups tend to focus on the executive because there is no judicial review and the prime minister, in a majority government, can exert party discipline and control legislation in Britain's parliamentary system. Consequently, under sympathetic governments, British LGBT activists have achieved much greater national-level success in reforming laws related to sexual orientation than have American activists. In the United States, however, activists have enjoyed greater success in mobilizing, in part because the American federalist system, with its separation of powers, provides more targets for movements and interest groups. At the same time that American federalism creates more points of access for the movement, however, it also has more veto points and more possibilities of conflict with the anti-gay countermovement in different venues and at different levels of government. These differences in political institutions have structured the tactics of the movements in the two countries (Engel, 2001: 120). The cohesion and centralization of the British parliamentary system have encouraged focused campaigns and a targeting of resources at the executive when the ruling party is sympathetic. However, when the party in power is not sympathetic, the European Court of Human Rights now offers a new political opportunity to the movement. As an alternative venue to the British Parliament, this pan-European forum has established precedents sympathetic to gays and lesbians (ibid., 115). In the United States, lack of party discipline and decentralization have encouraged more grassroots activism and a wider range of strategies, including many direct-action tactics as well as institutional strategies.

Cultural factors are also critical to movement strategies, and cultural outcomes, as well as political ones, are important consequences of social movements. The political culture in the United States encouraged the LGBT movement to frame issues in terms of "rights" and to present itself as a quasi-ethnic group. In contrast, the British political culture encouraged a framing of the issue in terms of conscience and the acceptability of private behaviour, although membership in the European Union has resulted in more acceptance of a human rights frame (Engel, 2001: 135–7). In the United States, the greater religiosity of the population compared to that of

Britain has created greater institutionalized homophobia and more need for the movement to counter the frames of the Christian right (ibid., 147–50). In Canada, where religious conservatives have less influence, a culture of political liberalism made the courts receptive to the equal rights claims of the LGBT rights movement (Pierceson, 2005). Thus, movements make different strategic framing decisions and experience different outcomes, depending on the cultural contexts in which they operate.

Just as movements are influenced by larger cultural contexts, they also help to change the dominant culture. One of the accomplishments of the LGBT movement is the creation of new forms of culture and discourse regarding sexual orientation. In addition to targeting the state, LGBT activists have greatly expanded the cultural spaces available to them, such as social clubs, bars, churches, commercial services, and mass media (Engel, 2001: 126). This expanded cultural "field" of gay-friendly organizations (Armstrong, 2002) helps to maintain the movement and to spread the acceptance and inclusion of gay culture within the larger society. As the nature of LGBT organizations changes, so do the strategies of the movement. Whereas early gay liberation groups shared the values and networks of the New Left and operated in a culture in which gay sexuality was strongly repressed, by the late 1980s and 1990s, the movement had become more open to a variety of gay lifestyles, and gay men and lesbians could come out into a much more extensive cultural and commercial arena (Lent, 2003: 45–6). In recent years, the normalization of same-sex relationships, reflected in popular culture, is one of the factors influencing public acceptance of same-sex marriage (Dorf and Tarrow, 2014: 458–9).

Conclusion

The LGBT movement has created a great deal of cultural and political change in North America and Europe since the birth of gay liberation in the late 1960s. This chapter illustrates the role of key factors emphasized by social movement theorists in shaping the strategies and outcomes of a movement. The movements of the 1960s created a climate of social and political change that inspired gay liberation groups, which built on the networks and ideology of the New Left. Developing in the counterculture of the 1960s, the early movement began to create its own internal culture and collective identity. As the cycle of protest of the 1960s declined, LGBT culture continued to expand and many groups began to pursue civil rights strategies. By the late 1970s, an anti-gay countermovement had organized in response, but this development served to further mobilize the movement, as did homophobia and threats in the wake of the AIDS epidemic. Cultural and political opportunities, including political institutions and cultural values, have resulted in varying degrees of support for LGBT rights in different countries.

The organization and strategies of the LGBT movement have been critical in taking advantage of those opportunities. With major social changes such as the spread of same-sex marriage, it is clear that the movement has had a profound cultural and political impact.

Discussion Questions

1. How did public opinion on homosexuality change, and what role did changes in public opinion play in advancing LGBT rights?

2. What have "liberationist" and "equal rights" strategies each contributed to the movement and its successes?

3. How do we explain differences in movement outcomes when comparing countries such as the United States, Britain, and Canada?

Suggested Readings

Engel, Stephen M. 2001. *The Unfinished Revolution: Social Movement Theory and the Gay and Lesbian Movement*. Cambridge: Cambridge University Press. This comparative study of gay and lesbian movements in the United States and Britain employs political process theory and usefully expands the approach with its analysis of cultural factors.

Fetner, Tina. 2008. *How the Religious Right Shaped Lesbian and Gay Activism*. Minneapolis, MN: University of Minnesota Press. This book examines how the conservative countermovement helped spark reaction by LGBT activists and contributed to the ongoing struggles for recognition and equality.

Smith, Miriam. 2008. *Political Institutions and Lesbian and Gay Rights in the United States and Canada*. New York: Routledge. This is an important study of national gay and lesbian rights activism in Canada, both pre-and post–Charter of Rights and Freedoms with comparison to institutional opportunities in the United States.

8   The Environmental Movement

Environmental problems are extremely complex and long-term, and are critical to the future of our planet and its species. The environmental movement, which originated in a number of countries in the nineteenth century, is faced with the challenge of maintaining effective campaigns of action over many decades. Maintaining a vital environmental movement involves keeping activists involved, influencing public opinion and holding public attention, creating lasting organizations, and devising collective action campaigns that have a real impact on environmental problems. The stakes are extremely high: beyond long-standing problems of pollution and habitat destruction, global warming is now causing the oceans to warm and the glaciers to melt at an alarming rate, with consequences such as increased hurricanes, floods, a potentially catastrophic rise in sea levels, droughts, and accelerated loss of species. Environmentalists must tackle the causes of such devastation and, despite the urgency of the issues, the problem of motivating individuals, industries, and governments to participate in bringing about the radical changes necessary.

In this chapter, we examine some of the problems involved in sustaining an influential environmental movement, concentrating on the movement in North America. We begin with a discussion of the origins of the contemporary movement in the 1960s and then turn to mobilization of the movement over time and its ability to attract and maintain public support. Next, we examine debates over the direction of the environmental movement and consider a selection of organizations and campaigns, including Greenpeace and its media-focused efforts such as its anti-whaling campaigns, green lobbies, consumer-based boycotts, anti-logging and anti-roads direct-action campaigns, and opposition to fossil fuel industries. We also consider the movement's intersection with Indigenous issues as well as backlash against the movement by conservative governments that label radical organizations terrorist.

Origins of the Environmental Movement

Although the protest cycle of the 1960s gave impetus to new types of environmental organizations and activities, the environmental movement originated much earlier. Conservation movements emerged in a number of countries in the nineteenth century to promote national parks, wilderness preservation, resource management, and the exploration of nature (Lowe and Goyder, 1983: 15–17). In Europe, Australia, and North America, campaigns were initiated to connect environmental concerns such as sewage disposal and clean air and water with public health (Rootes, 2004: 612). In the United States, organizations such as the Sierra Club, the National Audubon Society, and the Izaak Walton League formed in the late nineteenth and early twentieth centuries. Canada's first conservation organization, the Canadian Nature Foundation, was founded in the 1930s (Paehlke, 1997: 254). Women active in Progressive Era organizations in North America supported the conservation movement by lobbying for clean air and water, pure food, and public parks.

Threats to the environment, mobilizing structures, and political opportunities all contributed to the expansion of the environmental movement in the 1960s. While environmental problems were long-standing movement organizations and writers began to call attention to these problems. In the early 1960s, activists in the women's peace movement raised environmental issues in connection with their concerns about atmospheric testing of nuclear weapons (Rome, 2003: 534–6). Voice of Women in Canada and Women's Strike for Peace in the United States created public awareness of the environmental effects of the nuclear arms race by organizing events and collecting children's baby teeth to dramatize the issue of high levels of strontium 90, a by-product of radiation, in milk (Swerdlow, 1993; Rebick, 2005). With the publication of such landmark works as Rachel Carson's *Silent Spring* (1962), which focused attention on pollution from pesticides, the concerns of the environmental movement broadened.

Although the earliest environmental groups were regionally based and narrowly focused on particular concerns, many of them expanded their missions and their memberships greatly. A number of established conservation organizations such as the Sierra Club, exhibiting extraordinary longevity, served as mobilizing structures for new groups formed in the "environmental" era of the 1960s (Bosso, 2005). Political opportunities helped to expand the movement, and landmark environmental legislation was passed in a number of Western countries. In Canada, in response to public concern, the federal government began taking responsibility for environmental protection, and in 1969, legislation such as the Clean Air Act and the Canada Water Act was passed (Howlett and Joshi-Koop, 2010: 476).

The cycle of protest of the 1960s thus led to a major wave of environmentalism with new environmental organizations forming in the late 1960s and early 1970s, including local, national, and transnational organizations. Greenpeace emerged out of Vancouver and then spread around the world, and Friends of the Earth formed in the UK and quickly branched out to other countries. As in the case of the women's movement, the earlier wave of the movement provided a foundation for the new one. Established conservation organizations were important to the organizational expansion of the environmental movement, as "most of the organizations that emerged during the environmental era got critical early help from an older organization" (Bosso, 2005: 45). Other social movements of the 1960s were also key, providing activists, tactics, rhetoric, and energy to the environmental movement. Many New Left activists, like women's peace activists, became concerned with the issue of nuclear arms in the 1950s and early 1960s, which helped make them receptive to environmental issues.

The counterculture of the 1960s created and supported "back to the land" rural communes, many of which were founded by activists seeking to create more sustainable communities in the wilderness of British Columbia and rural communities of Nova Scotia. The counterculture movement led to the creation of natural food restaurants and the growth of vegetarianism, as well as street theatre on environmental issues. Activists in New York, for example, held a "soot-in" at the Consolidated Edison building at which they sprayed black mist and passed out darkened flowers (Rome, 2003: 544). By the late 1960s, members of political groups such as Students for a Democratic Society (SDS) were increasingly connecting the degradation of the environment to capitalism and the Vietnam War (ibid., 544–7). Student anti-war activists formed eco-action groups on a number of North American campuses. Environmental activists who came out of the protest movements of the 1960s adopted many of the direct-action tactics used by the civil rights, anti-war, and women's movements. In the United States, massive demonstrations were held on the first Earth Day on 22 April 1970. The event was envisioned as a nationwide "teach-in" modelled on the teach-ins held by anti–Vietnam War activists, and campus activists made connections between military activity and chemical pollution (Sale, 1993: 24). Earth Day was incredibly successful and had a lasting impact on the environmental movement—stimulating grassroots activism, strengthening national political efforts, institutionalizing environmental media coverage, and inspiring environmental programs in schools, among other legacies (Rome, 2013). The influence of 1960s tactics continued in later decades, with huge celebrations of the twentieth anniversary of Earth Day in 1990 in many countries around the world. Canadian environmentalists also used tactics from the 1960s—sit-ins, for example—to protest logging in British Columbia in the 1990s.

Greenpeace formed in Vancouver in 1969 to block American nuclear weapons testing (Dale, 1996; Wexler, 2004; Zelko, 2013). The founders of

Greenpeace were Canadian and American peace activists and journalists from the protest movements of the 1960s. They were strongly influenced by earlier peace and anti-nuclear protests (Zelko, 2013) and adopted the Quaker tactic of bearing witness. The political context of the student New Left and anti–Vietnam War protest was critical to Greenpeace's first action in 1971, when activists sailed an old fishing boat from Vancouver to the site of a planned US nuclear test on the island of Amchitka in the Aleutian Islands. Because the test could potentially have created tidal waves on Canada's west coast, the Greenpeace organizers initially called themselves the Don't Make a Wave Committee, but later hit on the more media-friendly name Greenpeace (Zelko, 2013: 69). Although the Greenpeace campaign was framed to appeal to mainstream Canadian nationalism, it was also calculated to build on previous peace movement and student protests against US military tests (Dale, 1996: 16). Exploiting both Canadian patriotism and anti-American sentiment caused by the Vietnam War, Greenpeace took off during a period of expanded activism that had been generated by the movements of the 1960s.

In addition to inspiring direct action by Greenpeace and other environmental organizations, participants in the movements of the sixties also supported other forms of environmentalism. In West Germany, for example, activists from the student movement became involved in environmental issues and later founded the Green Party in 1979, which blurred the lines between the environmental movement and mainstream politics. It became the most successful environmental party in Western Europe. The German Green Party attempted to be a different type of political party, incorporating ideas about participatory democracy into its structure and rotating its members of parliament (McKenzie, 2002: 58). Thus, the cycle of protest of the 1960s helped to spawn an enduring environmental movement that influenced the laws and policies of many countries, despite the numerous difficulties the movement encountered in achieving its goals.

With the growth of environmentalism in Western countries, international environmentalism also expanded, although the pattern in developing countries differs from that of developed countries. In a study of the founding of environmental organizations worldwide, Longhofer and Schofer (2010) show that, in the industrialized West, domestic environmental organizations existed for some years before citizens began participating in international organizations. In developing countries, in contrast, memberships in international environmental organizations preceded the founding of domestic environmental groups. Thus, the creation of an international environmental movement helped to spread the movement to developing countries, "providing organizational models, resources, and legitimation that spurs formation of associations that may be quite global in character" (ibid., 526).

Mobilizing Support for Environmentalism

All long-term social movements are faced with the problem of maintaining support for the cause over time, and the environmental movement faces particular challenges insofar as many environmental problems are long-term ones that are extremely difficult to solve and may not be apparent to potential movement constituents in their everyday lives. For example, although scientists agree that the planet is experiencing climate change and immediate and aggressive actions must be taken to prevent it, 23 per cent of Canadians agree it is real but do not believe it is caused by humans, and over one in 10 Canadians don't even believe the scientific evidence (Environics, 2013: 2). Americans share similar views, with 36 per cent believing there is no solid evidence of climate change (PEW, 2013). Min Zhou (2013), using the World Values Survey, found that people with more education and knowledge about global environmental harms are more likely to be concerned about the environment. He also finds that those who are more liberal in their political attitudes have a greater concern. Recently, however, increasing numbers of extreme weather events may finally be intensifying concern among the broader public about global warming caused by human activities (Gore, 2014: 89). Over the years, public interest in the environment and membership in environmental organizations have ebbed and flowed, as has media attention to environmental issues.

Between 1965 and 1970, when numerous environmental groups formed in North America, there was a great sense of urgency about environmental issues (McKenzie, 2002: 89). Actions by groups like Greenpeace gained national and international headlines with media-savvy direct-action stunts (Dale, 1996). However, concern about environmental harms has varied since then (Leiserowitz, 2007: 9). Anthony Downs (1972) argues that there is an "issue attention cycle" whereby the public becomes alarmed about a problem and very concerned with its amelioration. Once the public comes to realize the cost of significant advances, however, enthusiasm for solutions to the problem dampens. Eventually, the decline in public interest is followed by a "post-problem phase" during which the problem may sporadically recapture public interest. In 1972, Downs wrote that the public was already starting to realize the enormity of the social and financial costs involved in cleaning up the environment.

Media attention is one factor that affects public concerns, and although there were periods of heightened media attention to the environment in North America since the early 1970s, the movement struggled to maintain ongoing and in-depth coverage of environmental problems. Media coverage of environmental issues tends to focus on dramatic events such as oil spills and nuclear power accidents, which offer striking visuals and simple causal explanations of environmental harms. For example, the 1989 *Exxon Valdez* oil spill in Alaska and the confrontations over logging in British Columbia in the 1990s were major stories (Hacket and Gruneau, 2000: 169). However, even environmental disasters such as oil spills do not always attract or maintain media and public attention—or even action from environmental movements. For example, the BP oil spill in the Gulf of Mexico in 2010 received the most attention from the news media, environmental groups, and government during the phase of the disaster when visual images and simple stories, such as a burning oil rig and oil-soaked wildlife, made environmental harms most obvious (Hoffbauer and Ramos, 2014). Later, the less visible but ongoing and serious environmental problems resulting from the oil spill received much less attention and the media focus moved from environmental damage to economic recovery. In their analysis of Canadian print media coverage of climate change over time, Young and Duags (2011) found that, although climate change is complex and multilayered, the media has decontextualized the harms by ignoring their causes, scientific claims, and impacts, focusing instead on politics and economic issues related to the environment.

Downs (1972) suggests that media coverage and public interest tend to go in cycles. For example, one study shows that coverage of global warming by the *New York Times* and the *Washington Post* increased dramatically in the late 1980s but declined in the 1990s (McComas and Shanahan, 1999). Systematic, ongoing coverage that does not involve major crises or movement-created drama is generally lacking in the North American media; the media have difficulty sustaining interest in complicated issues. This has important consequences for public attention to environmental issues and the ability of environmental movement organizations to mobilize support.

The extent of public concern about the environment also depends on competition from other concerns, such as economic problems. During periods of economic recession and high unemployment environmental concerns tend to be less salient than economic ones, meaning that they take on less immediate personal importance for members of the public. New social movement theorists have argued that support for environmental protection is associated with "post-materialist" values, which focus on quality of life and self-expression, rather than with "materialist" values, which emphasize economic and physical security (Inglehart, 1990, 1995). Some of the countries that score high on measures of post-materialism, such as the Scandinavian countries and the Netherlands, also have high levels of support for environmentalism. Within countries, individuals with post-materialist values are more likely to support environmentalism and to join environmental groups (Inglehart, 1995: 57).

The post-materialist values explanation suggests that citizens of affluent countries are likely to be more concerned about environmental protection than citizens of poorer nations. However, this conclusion does not appear to be supported by multinational survey data, which show high levels of concern for the environment in poor countries (Dunlap and York, 2008). One explanation for this contradictory evidence is that environmental concerns are based on "essentially materialist concerns with safety and security" as well as on post-materialist values (Rootes, 2004: 618). In other words, support for environmentalism is linked both to objective problems, such as water and air pollution, and to post-materialism. Thus, high levels of support for environmental protection exist in low-income developing countries where these problems are most severe as well as in developed countries that score high on post-materialism (Inglehart, 1995). But Dunlap and York (2008) question the utility of making a distinction between materialist and post-materialist values; they find that people in poor countries care about global as well as local environmental problems and that there is evidence that people in poorer countries may be even *more* concerned about the environment than those in richer countries. They conclude that environmentalism has become a worldwide movement that is not dependent on post-materialist values or national affluence. Their arguments are supported by Longhofer and Schofer (2010: 521), who find no effect of post-materialist values on the formation of environmental organizations.

It is clear that public support for environmentalism has risen to strikingly high levels worldwide (Leiserowitz et al., 2005). However, attitudinal support for the environmental movement does not necessarily translate into environmentally conscious behaviour or support for environmental organizations. Because environmental protections are a public good and because individual contributions to the reversal of large-scale environmental degradation are not likely to make a dent in the problem, the movement is, not surprisingly, faced with a free rider problem. Many more people believe in environmental goals than actively support the movement, and some surveys suggest that only 10–13 per cent of the worldwide public supports the movement by donating to environmental organizations, writing letters, and signing petitions (Leiserowitz et al., 2005: 28–9). Table 8.1 shows environmental group membership in selected countries across four waves from 1981 to 2014. Global surveys also show differences between richer and poorer societies with regard to behaviours such as recycling and selecting "green" products. For example, one survey found that among respondents from high-income countries 67 per cent reported buying green products and 75 per cent reported recycling, compared to only 30 per cent of respondents from low-income countries reporting buying green and 27 per cent reporting recycling. However, such results may reflect the lack of facilities and markets in lower-income countries, and it is unlikely that surveys adequately represent the very poor, "who are most likely to reuse and recycle as part of survival" in low-income countries (ibid., 28). Moreover, residents of wealthier countries engage in high levels of consumption and use large amounts of energy. And, as environmental activism becomes more common in many poor countries and as international environmental organizations work to spread environmental values around the world (Wapner, 2002), multi-national survey evidence shows that activism is viewed favourably by residents of poor countries (Dunlap and York, 2008: 542).

Table 8.1 Per Cent Members of Environmental Organizations

Country	Wave 1 1981–1984	Wave 3 1995–1999	Wave 5 2005–2009	Wave 6 2010–2014
Argentina	1.2	5.6	8.7	10.4
Australia	3.4	17.6	13.5	14.4
Azerbaijan		0.7		0.5
Belarus		1.9		1
Brazil			7.1	4.4
Bulgaria		1	1.4	
Canada			16.5	
Chile		18.4	13.5	8.3
China		5	12.7	2.4
Colombia		6.5	4.8	16.3
Cyprus			6.7	8.3
Egypt			1.2	0.3
Estonia		2.4		2.3
Ethiopia			27.8	
Finland	0.7	7.7	9.3	
France			14.7	
Georgia		0.5	0.5	
Germany		8.3	5	6.8
Ghana			26.1	14.2
Great Britain			15.8	
Hong Kong			2.2	20.2
Hungary		3.1	1	
India		11.9	59.4	46.9
Indonesia			35.8	
Iran			9.8	
Iraq				1.6
Italy			7.7	
Japan	0.6		4.5	3.3
Jordan			0.4	5.4

Table 8.1 *continued*

Country	Wave 1 1981–1984	Wave 3 1995–1999	Wave 5 2005–2009	Wave 6 2010–2014
Malaysia			10.2	9.3
Mexico	2.9	25.1	12.9	14.5
Moldova		4.5	7.2	
Morocco			1.9	1.4
Netherlands			15.3	10.8
New Zealand		16.5	17.9	18.9
Nigeria		29.6		22.7
Norway		6.7	7.3	
Peru		14.1	7	7.3
Philippines		12.8		28.7
Poland			7.5	4.6
Romania		6.3	0.7	4
Russia		1.6	4.6	1.3
Rwanda			18.6	24.1
Slovenia		4.4	6.8	6.6
South Africa	3	18.8	19.8	35.8
South Korea	2.7	24.9	7.5	8.4
Spain		8.7	4.7	2
Sweden	6.4	12.7	10.7	10.9
Switzerland		19.4	23.8	
Taiwan		7.7	5.4	28.1
Thailand			19.8	16.1
Trinidad and Tobago			16.6	15.4
Turkey		1.9	1.2	1.8
Ukraine		1.5	4	1.4
United States	6	25.6	15.8	17.5
Uruguay		12.5	6.2	2.1

Source: Compiled from World Values Survey (www.worldvaluessurvey.org/WVSOnline.jsp)

Note: Selected countries, based on active and inactive members in variables v33 (81/84); v33 (95/99); v29 (05/09); v30 (10/13). Additional country data available from the World Values Survey website.

Despite gaps between attitudes and behaviour and variations over time and place in levels of support, environmental organizations have attracted members and contributions, even at times when environmental concerns are low in saliency because people are preoccupied with other concerns, such as the economy or terrorism. During the 1980s, for example, support for environmentalism among North Americans remained high, but economic issues were far more salient. In 1980, when Ronald Reagan was elected president, "there was no evidence that environmental protection was a salient issue to more than a very small percentage of the general public" (Mitchell, 1984: 54). Nevertheless, threats to environmental progress by the Reagan administration elicited a great deal of financial support for national environmental groups, and a number of large American environmental organizations, such as the Wilderness Society, the Sierra Club, Defenders of Wildlife, and Friends of the Earth, experienced dramatic growth as a result (Mitchell et al., 1992: 15). In Canada, large environmental organizations such as the Canadian Nature Foundation, the David Suzuki Foundation, and the Sierra Club of Canada also expanded or established themselves and helped to place new issues on the political agenda in the 1980s and 1990s (Wilson, 1992, 2001). Worldwide, membership in environmental groups more than doubled during the 1980s and 1990s (Dalton, 2005), and in 1990 an estimated 200 million people attended celebrations of the twentieth anniversary of Earth Day held in 140 countries (McKenzie, 2002: 65).

Although such extensive participation in the environmental movement is not always in evidence, many people have attended movement events and joined environmental organizations over the years in part because "public bads" such as toxic dumps and air and water pollution are powerful motivators (Mitchell, 1979). As collective behaviour theorists argue, environmental degradation creates grievances, and these grievances help to motivate collective action, although grievances in themselves are not enough to sustain a social movement. Another reason for ongoing mobilization is that many large environmental organizations (e.g., the Wilderness Society and World Wildlife Fund) are professionalized organizations with paid staff. As resource mobilization theorists have suggested, such groups make the free rider problem less significant because they provide easy, low-risk ways for individuals to participate. For example, many people join environmental organizations by contributing money in response to direct-mail or online solicitations. Even traditionally direct-action groups like Greenpeace have transformed over the years and now rely on large professional staffs that spend much of their time seeking out donations and lobbying (Dale, 1996). Some criticize the most prominent environmental organization as "Big Green" or "Green Inc.,' saying they have lost their original mandates of challenging power holders and have become copies of the institutions they once challenged (Sklair, 1994). Others observe that organizations have been co-opted by corporate funding and resources that help such organizations maintain their "professionalized" activism (MacDonald, 2008; Sklair, 2002: 276).

There are, of course, ways for grassroots activists to participate in the environmental movement, and social movement theorists have looked at the types of organizational bases, social networks, and ideological commitments that affect participation beyond financial contributions and formal organizations. Active participation can take numerous forms, including relatively low-cost and low-risk behaviours such as attending rallies, writing letters, and signing petitions as well as more costly and risky activities such as joining illegal blockades, participating in "tree-sits," and setting up protest camps. In predicting who will participate in various types of activities, social movement analysts have explored the role of various types of attributes (e.g., ideological commitments) and structural variables (e.g., network connections and organizational affiliations). For example, in a study of relatively low-cost, low-risk participation in the British Columbia Wilderness Preservation Movement, David Tindall (2002) found that people are most likely to continue to participate if they have numerous network ties within the movement that provide them with information about movement events and issues and encourage identification with the movement. In contrast to research on high-risk activism (McAdam, 1986), Tindall found that weak, rather than strong, network ties and only minimal ideological support were conducive to low- to moderate-risk activism, such as attending non-violent demonstrations and meetings, signing petitions, or participating in information campaigns.

In a study of several environmental groups in California, Paul Lichterman (1996) looked at how political communities are developed and maintained. He found two types of foundations for community in the environmental groups that he studied: "communitarian" and "personalized" commitments. In an anti–toxic waste group located in an African-American community, for example, participation was based on pre-existing racial and religious community ties; members of the group were mostly black, church-going citizens who were already integrated into a larger community. By participating in the environmental group, they were acting as good citizens of their community who sought particular goals, and they willingly allowed community leaders to direct their participation in a traditionally organized group. In contrast, Lichterman found that members of a group associated with the US Green Movement, which organized in the 1980s to promote "green values" through green electoral parties as well as other means, did not have ties to a pre-existing community; they were acting as individuals with a "personalized commitment" to values they wanted to put into action. Their participation was not strictly instrumental, and the groups they joined tended to spend a great deal of time discussing ideology and creating structures that allowed for extensive participation and the development of collective identity. Although participants were developing their identities as activists and seeking self-fulfilment, Lichterman argues that this type of "personalism" was not simply therapeutic and did not detract from public-spirited action. Rather, individuals with personalized orientations were developing long-term commitments to political activism that would help to sustain certain types of participatory groups, such as the Greens.

This sort of value orientation to political activism clearly underlies many environmental activities. In addition to community-based local groups and national environmental organizations, the movement includes many grassroots organizations that mobilize individuals motivated by a desire to act on their personal values and activist identities. Such individuals often remain active in various groups for many years, even a lifetime. An example of the type of group supported by such activists is Earth First!, which was founded in the United States in 1980 by activists seeking to create an environmental movement based on strong commitments to the value of nature (Brulle, 2000: 198). Earth First! became known in North America for its radical environmental values and use of direct-action tactics by highly committed activists. An Earth First! group launched in the United Kingdom in 1991 became heavily involved in the British anti-roads movement and attracted activists looking for personal empowerment and committed to social justice (Wall, 1999). In Canada, Earth First! and other grassroots groups carried out radical environmental protests in a similar activist tradition, such as the Clayoquot Sound protests against logging in British Columbia in the 1990s. More recently, radical environmental groups have mobilized against the fossil fuel industries to protest practices such as coal mining via mountaintop removal and drilling for natural gas through hydraulic fracturing or "fracking."

To mobilize large numbers of diverse participants, movements typically need both large national or international movement organizations and local grassroots groups. They also need both mainstream and radical groups. On the all-important issue of climate change, the environmental movement failed for many years to organize an effective movement, but has recently made progress in mobilizing a movement to combat global warming. The climate change movement includes moderate and radical orientations and both established Big Green organizations in coalitions such as the US Climate Action Network and radical grassroots groups in the Rising Tide North America coalition.

Both national organizations and coalitions and local grassroots activists are employing a variety of strategies (Wines, 1 June 2014). Long-standing environmental organizations, such as the Sierra Club, have created campaigns to move beyond fossil fuels and encourage energy efficiency and the use of renewable energy sources. New organizations have also formed to combat climate change, including 350.org, which was founded in 2008. It took its name from the goal of keeping the amount of carbon dioxide in the atmosphere to 350 parts per million, the limit many scientists agreed was necessary to keep the planet livable. (Carbon dioxide levels have since been recorded at 400 ppm, and 350.org's goal is to reduce levels below 350 ppm.)

To mobilize a global movement around climate change, 350.org has helped to organize international days of action, such as the International Day of Climate Action in 2009, Global Power Shift summits in countries around the world, and campaigns and demonstrations against fossil fuel industry projects such as the Keystone XL pipeline in North America (see http://350 .org). National and international organizations such as the Sierra Club, 350 .org, and Greenpeace have worked with local groups in an increasingly vocal movement to combat climate change.

Debates on the Power and Direction of the Environmental Movement

Because contributions to environmental groups vary with changes in political opportunities and other socio-economic shifts, the environmental movement has not enjoyed continuous growth and stability. Environmental movements in different countries have experienced periods of upsurge and decline, depending on local and national as well as international factors (Rootes, 2004). Moreover, the power of the environmental movement is limited in the face of other factors that affect environmental outcomes, such as the influence of fossil fuel industries on local cultures and political decisions. In a study of opposition to liquefied natural gas (LNG) terminals in the United States, McAdam and Boudet (2012) found that mobilization against proposed LNG projects occurred in only half of the 20 communities they studied, and the mobilization that did occur was often minor, with only one community experiencing what they considered a genuine social movement. "Community context" variables, such as the history of the community with an industry (e.g., oil and gas development in the Gulf Coast region) or conditions of economic hardship that make communities receptive to even risky projects, played an important role in preventing mobilization in many communities. Where opposition to LNG projects occurred, however, it did contribute to the rejection of LNG terminals.

Thus, environmental movements have met with varying amounts of success in mobilizing support and influencing public policies, and serious environmental problems such as global warming remain urgent. Consequently, there have been many debates over the organization, strategies, and effectiveness of the environmental movement. One important theme in these debates is the impact of **institutionalization**, which generally refers to the tendency of movement organizations that have survived over many years to develop bureaucratic structures, to rely on professional staff, and to cultivate relations with government officials and other elites. Environmental movements in most developed countries are highly institutionalized on the basis of such indicators as size, income, formalization of organizational structures, number and professionalization of employees, and relations with government and other established actors (ibid., 624). The strategic choices of environmental movements are also a prime subject of debate, involving questions about the importance of direct-action tactics versus institutional ones, the use of media-oriented tactics, efforts to influence and work with corporate elites, and other issues.

In North America, concerns about the environment became less salient to the public in the 1990s, with few Canadians or Americans paying much attention to environmental problems until the mid-2000s (Harrison, 2007: 94). This decline in salience was reflected in low levels of membership in North American environmental groups in the 1990s. For example, out of Ontario's population of about 12 million, the Federation of Ontario Naturalists had about 15,000 members in 1995 and the World Wildlife Fund had about 60,000 members. In comparison, Britain's Royal Society for the Protection of Birds claimed one million members out of the country's population of 60 million (Cartwright, 2003: 130, n. 2). In the United States, between 1990 and 1994, membership in the Sierra Club fell from 630,000 to 500,000; membership in Greenpeace dropped from 2.5 million to 800,000; and the National Wildlife Federation laid off 100 staff (Dowie, 1995: 175).

In *Losing Ground,* an influential study of the decline of American environmentalism, Mark Dowie (1995) argues that the economic recession of the early 1990s was one factor in this decline, but he notes that the crisis for environmental organizations outlasted the economic recession. The election of the Clinton–Gore administration was another factor; because Vice-President Al Gore was an environmentalist, many people apparently believed that financial contributions to environmental organizations were less important during this period. Dowie also notes a problem with "list fatigue" in that mailing lists were being overused by national environmental groups; direct-mail solicitation ceases to work when the same people keep getting the same type of appeals from various groups. In addition, other issues, such as AIDS and homelessness, were competing with the environment for donors (ibid., 176). But Dowie argues that mainstream environmental groups also had themselves to blame for their decline: they became overly institutionalized and co-opted by government and corporate elites. Nevertheless, he is encouraged by new forms of environmental activism such as multiracial struggles for environmental justice and grassroots direct-action campaigns.

In a study of the organizational evolution of the American environmental movement, Christopher Bosso notes that, despite its shortcomings, "the organized vanguard of national environmental advocacy in the United States *has survived.* Moreover, as even Dowie admits, it has made a difference, although how much of a difference is a matter of debate" (Bosso, 2005: 6). Bosso reports that, despite the dips in membership in the 1990s cited by Dowie, in 2003 the Sierra Club boasted a membership of 736,000, while the

National Audubon Society had 550,000 members and the National Wildlife Federation had 650,000 members. These organizations, along with others (e.g., Greenpeace and the Nature Conservancy), have become "permanent fixtures in national politics" because they have adapted to changing political and economic conditions (ibid., 7–9). Bosso describes how established environmental organizations such as the Sierra Club changed their organizational structures to meet new demands and older organizations facilitated the emergence of new ones, the latter often occupying particular advocacy niches such as land conservancy or clean water. In maintaining themselves, Bosso argues, national environmental organizations have sustained an environmental presence in American politics, and this has helped to sustain policy gains and spread environmental values (ibid., 153).

Studies of environmentalism in Canada and other countries have also noted positive as well as negative effects of institutionalization (Rootes, 1999). In a report on the Canadian environmental movement, Jeremy Wilson (2001: 60–1) notes that many of the large national organizations, such as the Sierra Club and the David Suzuki Foundation, have managed to create opportunities for volunteer participation despite their bureaucratic structures. In addition, these large organizations continue to cover a range of issues, and numerous smaller local and regional organizations also thrive alongside them. Moreover, Wilson, like Bosso, notes that there are distinct advantages to institutionalization, including organizational stability and access to government insiders and other decision-makers. In their analysis of the German environmental movement, Rucht and Roose (1999, 2001) similarly argue that institutionalization helps the movement gain influence in established politics (e.g., through the Green Party) and that other types of groups also flourish in the decentralized German environmental movement. European environmental movements have generally been able to benefit from "the opportunities presented by institutionalization" while still engaging in protest tactics (Rootes and Brulle, 2013: 5).

Related to concerns about the effects of institutionalization, observers have also debated the effectiveness of movement strategies. In another widely debated critique of mainstream American environmentalism, Shellenberger and Nordhaus, in their essay "The Death of Environmentalism" (2004), claim that the movement has become overly narrow in its strategies and objectives, acting as a "special interest" that lobbies for limited legislative proposals but fails to supply the vision needed to address the global warming crisis and other major issues. They argue that environmentalists need to frame issues in new ways to create new alliances. For example, having an overall vision of creating jobs in new types of energy industries, rather than a focus on isolated technological fixes, could unite environmentalists, workers, and businesses. Instead of looking for the "short-term policy payoff," environmentalists need to offer "alternative vision and values" to support

long-term strategies such as "big investments into clean energy, transportation and efficiency" (Shellenberger and Nordhaus, 2004: 25–6). Their thesis
sparked much debate, including rebuttals to Shellenberger and Nordhaus's
contention that the movement is declining and public support is fading (e.g.,
Dunlap, 2006).

Although there is general agreement among environmentalists that
pressing problems such as global warming require new strategies, many
doubt that a reframing of the issues will lead to solutions to major problems. Brulle and Jenkins (2006: 84) point to the power dynamics and financial costs involved in addressing global warming; beyond changing values,
the movement has to figure out how to deal with "the inevitable economic
trade-offs" and "the strong vested interests and sunk costs in the existing
carbon-intensive economy." In northern Alberta, for instance, extraction
of oil from tar sands helps to drive the national economy while creating
what is perhaps "the world's largest environmental disaster zone," and is the
leading cause of Canada's increased greenhouse gas emissions (Biro, 2010:
308). Thus, the environmental movement faces huge obstacles in developing
effective strategies and tactics. In fact, the dramatic change required "in the
way the world produces and consumes energy far outstrips the capacity of
environmental groups" (Bryner, 2008: 330).

However, the movement has made progress in introducing new frames
and discourses that have created some cultural changes as well as new
political coalitions (Brick and Cawley, 2008). For example, the "climate
change" frame for the global warming phenomenon has helped people
understand that a variety of events (e.g., heat waves, hurricanes, and flood-
ing) are related, and environmental websites have shown people how to
calculate their "carbon footprints" and to change their everyday behaviours in order to reduce them (ibid., 213). Some new coalitions between
environmentalists and business leaders are also emerging as sharehold-
ers concerned about the financial implications of climate change force
some companies to address the issue (Bryner, 2008: 331). Although many
national governments failed to take leadership on climate change, there
was more action at local levels. For instance, hundreds of cities around
the world participated in the Cities for Climate Protection campaign,
aimed at reducing greenhouse gas emissions (www.iclei.org). In Canada,
the Federation of Canadian Municipalities encouraged participation in
this campaign; in the United States, where there was a deficit of sympathetic national change agencies, the connections of cities to international
environmental organizations encouraged participation in the program
(Vasi, 2007). Both nationally and internationally, numerous environmental
organizations provide educational materials and support to a growing climate protection movement (Moser, 2007). Increasingly, like activists in
other movements, environmentalists employ online networks and social

media to organize activists and communicate and debate issues such as climate change (Ackland and O'Neil, 2011; Uldam and Askanius, 2013). In fact, as the case of Greenpeace illustrates, the use of media has been important to raising environmental concerns.

Greenpeace and the Mass Media

Despite its beginnings as "a rag-tag collection of long-haired, bearded men" (Dale, 1996: 1), Greenpeace became a powerful multinational organization, capable of manipulating the global media, through the use of its trademark strategy of creating dramatic events that generate sympathetic coverage and large numbers of supporters (Brown and May, 1991; Weyler, 2004). The group got its start with a campaign to stop a US military nuclear test at Amchitka in the Aleutian Islands (see Hunter, 2004, for a detailed account). Led by media-savvy activists, the campaign exploited anti-US sentiment in Canada by emphasizing the threat of tidal waves on Canada's west coast from the nuclear test. The activists bravely sailed an old fishing boat to the test site, thereby creating a "David-versus-Goliath spectacle of ordinary people defying a morally bankrupt and intellectually unsound enterprise" (Dale, 1996: 18). The campaign provoked an enormous amount of opposition to the nuclear test among the Canadian public and an equally large amount of media coverage. Although the test proceeded as planned, the US military later announced that it would cease nuclear testing in the North Pacific, allowing Greenpeace to claim victory.

In choosing a strategy of non-violent direct action, Greenpeace leaders were influenced by their political ideology, and they framed the issue in terms of the need for organizations and individuals to stand up to corrupt and unjust governments and corporations (Carmin and Balser, 2002: 379). Through direct action, Greenpeace aimed to create dramatic confrontations that would generate media coverage and thus direct public attention to environmental issues. The Amchitka campaign proved highly successful in this regard, but in adopting this strategy, Greenpeace was already limiting its public presentation of the issues. To win the favour of the media and the mainstream public, the group had chosen to appeal to Canadian patriotism and to avoid more radical and controversial issues, such as Canada's participation in the Vietnam War effort through the sale of war materials to the United States (Dale, 1996: 20). Nevertheless, Greenpeace's media-oriented direct-action strategy allowed the group to avoid compromising its ideals in the political arena (Carmin and Balser, 2002: 381).

Greenpeace continued sailing ships to confront opponents, including whaling vessels. The organization's first big breakthrough came in 1975 when its ship confronted a Soviet whaling fleet in San Francisco Bay and a Greenpeace photographer captured Soviet whalers plunging a harpoon into the back of a sperm whale. The close-up of "blood and gore as the huge creature died" was irresistible to the mass media and "allowed Greenpeace to use the image to change the way millions of people thought about whales" (Cassidy, 1992: 169). In taking great risks, Greenpeace activists came across as "a noble and brave group of crusaders up against a heartless and barbaric band of murderers" (Dale, 1996: 150). Once again, however, the Greenpeace strategy required a certain type of frame, in this case blood and conflict, to attract media coverage. In two later anti-whaling campaigns, efforts at diplomacy and temporary success in stopping the whale hunts were not newsworthy (Cassidy, 1992: 170–1; Dale, 1996: 151).

As a result of all the media attention, Greenpeace became very "hot" as an organization and grew rapidly. It eventually developed into an organization with the kind of professional expertise among its staff that allowed it to engage in all of the "preparation, training and research" that goes into putting on sophisticated "media events" (Eyerman and Jamison, 1989: 107). This expansion and professionalization came at a cost, however; as Greenpeace transformed from a small group of activists into a large, respected organization, the group placed "new emphasis on organizational structure, merchandising, and cash flow" (Cassidy, 1992: 170). Greenpeace did develop an effective media strategy, which involved providing "emotionally charged images to counter the effects of negative framing by the mass media" (ibid., 171). Whereas many movement organizations are stymied by undesirable media frames, Greenpeace got around this problem by providing images that send a powerful message regardless of how the mass media frame the story. To hone this strategy, the organization invested enormous resources and acquired the technological expertise to meet the production needs of television (Dale, 1996). Greenpeace learned to create an event, film it, and deliver a video news release designed to allow news editors to select short video clips with great ease. In this way, Greenpeace was able to get air time for important environmental issues. In 1993, for example, it created international publicity about the Russian dumping of nuclear waste in the Sea of Japan by catching the polluters in the act and beaming back live pictures using sophisticated equipment on board the Greenpeace ship (ibid., 110).

Although Greenpeace has enjoyed great success, its media strategy has some clear limitations. To maintain its media expertise, Greenpeace has had to develop a professionalized organization, making it difficult to encourage initiatives from rank-and-file activists, and some Greenpeace activists have become disenchanted with "the inflated attention they give to media coverage of their events" (Rucht, 1995: 82). One problem is that many serious environmental problems lack dramatic visuals and are thus difficult to address with a media-based strategy. Complex and long-term issues cannot easily be framed into the kinds of stories with narrative structures that appeal to the mass media, and the content of Greenpeace communications had to be limited to "easily understood and accepted messages" (Eyerman and Jamison, 1989: 108). Because it is extremely difficult for movements to present issues with any nuance through the mass media, another problem is that new constituents attracted through media presentations may have a different understanding of issues than older activists and leaders. For example, Greenpeace's anti-sealing campaigns in the 1970s used images of baby seals being clubbed, and this strategy attracted animal rights sympathizers to the cause (Dale, 1996: 94). The successful anti-sealing campaigns resulted in a collapse of seal-pelt markets, which devastated the Inuit economy in Canada. When Greenpeace tried to address these economic problems by arguing for a ban on sealing that exempted Indigenous peoples, there was a great deal of conflict and many animal rights activists eventually left Greenpeace to form a new organization.

In conveying its messages to the public through the mass media, Greenpeace is limited by the tight formats of news media and the need to frame messages in ways that appeal to mass audiences (Dale, 1996: 8). Some Greenpeace leaders have recognized the need to adopt new strategies in order to address complicated environmental issues. The organization has offices in both the global North and the global South, and staff in regions such as Latin America have helped to broaden the organization's thinking about problems that cannot be addressed easily with media-oriented tactics. Consequently, Greenpeace has developed a greater understanding of the relationship between environmental degradation and globalized trade and the need to address disparities between developed and developing countries in solving environmental problems. Nevertheless, Greenpeace is structured to engage in dramatic tactics and remains reliant on media attention to generate support. Following its decline in membership in the early 1990s, Greenpeace revived itself by using its classic tactics in an anti-nuclear testing campaign against France in 1995—10 years after French agents sank Greenpeace's ship, the *Rainbow Warrior,* in New Zealand, provoking international outrage (Dale, 1996: 9). After France announced its intention to end the global moratorium on nuclear testing by resuming its test program in the South Pacific, Greenpeace deployed its ship and generated headlines to mobilize world opinion against the French. The country went ahead with the test but agreed to a moratorium on further testing, and the campaign "rocketed Greenpeace back to superstar status" (ibid., 206). Although it is rarely possible for Greenpeace to generate this level of attention, the organization has difficulty departing from the strategies that have brought it so much success.

Green Lobbies and Consumer Boycotts

Like Greenpeace, other large environmental organizations have also had problems devising effective strategies and tactics. In the United States and

Canada, large national organizations such as the Sierra Club, the World Wildlife Fund, and the Nature Conservancy lobby the federal and state or provincial governments. In both countries, the movements also include a variety of local and regional groups with diverse strategies. During periods when the national government is hostile to movement initiatives, as in the case of the United States during the Reagan-Bush years of the 1980s and early 1990s, lobbying strategies tend to be largely futile. Corporate lobbies have countered the efforts of environmentalists by opposing environmental regulations and, in the United States, by increasing their political dona-tions to congressional candidates (Beder, 2002: 34). In Canada, corpora-tions far outspend environmental lobbies, and "no Canadian environmental group has resources adequate enough to cover all of the government officials who play significant roles in the typical policy process" (Wilson, 1992: 116). Moreover, even when environmental policies are passed into law, it is often difficult to get them implemented so as to have a real impact (McCloskey, 1992). The impact is also obscured by active policies by governments that use rhetorical acceptance of environmental advocates' claims only to control how those translate into policy and practice. This can be seen in Canada through the Harper government's acceptance of climate change and expres-sion of the need to fight its detrimental affects while simultaneously expand-ing and promoting bitumen extraction and neglecting the country's Kyoto Protocol and Copenhagen Accord targets and obligations (Young and Coutinho, 2013). Consequently, North American environmental organiza-tions have found it very difficult to influence public policy, and there is a great need for them to pool their resources and work together in coalitions in order to carry out effective strategies.

Green lobbies have played an important role in putting issues on the public agenda, and they do enjoy strong public support. Michael McCloskey, a long-time activist, suggests that mainstream environmental groups could do a better job of tapping into high levels of public support if they used their own strengths at gathering information. In particu-lar, national environmental groups could use their research capabilities to gather and then disseminate information about various products, and they could engage in marketplace tactics such as boycotts, letter-writing campaigns, and protests at stockholders' meetings—tactics that could be employed in coalition with grassroots groups. McCloskey gives the example of Alar, a chemical commonly used on apples, which was the subject of a television exposé by the Natural Resources Defense Council (NRDC) in the United States in 1989. Although the US Environmental Protection Agency had debated the safety of Alar for years, no action was taken; how-ever, after the NRDC exposé, consumers revolted and refused to buy Alar-treated apples, stores refused to sell them, and growers agreed to stop using Alar (McCloskey, 1992: 86).

This kind of consumer power, in conjunction with the skills of national environmental organizations and the energies of grassroots activists, seems to hold great potential for the environmental movement. Insofar as the strategy of harnessing public concerns relies on the mass media, however, the movement risks the oversimplification of issues. This can be seen in the case of a tuna boycott organized by environmental groups in the late 1980s to protect dolphins, which are often caught and killed in tuna-fishing nets because they swim with schools of tuna. Many environmental groups used the image of the dolphin, a very sympathetic sea mammal, to get the public to boycott tuna, believing that a boycott might force the international tuna industry to adopt a new technology and use nets that would allow dolphins to escape. In 1990, the major US tuna companies announced that they would buy only "dolphin-safe" tuna, labelled accordingly. While most environmental organizations were thrilled with this outcome, "Greenpeace began to consider the social consequences of an international boycott of dolphin-caught tuna" (Dale, 1996: 161). Greenpeace had learned from its earlier boycott of seal pelts that the issues were often more complex than the survival of an attractive animal, and the organization's Latin American bureaus also offered a different perspective on the tuna boycott. They argued that the US companies were acting to protect themselves from foreign competition insofar as the industries of poorer countries did not have the technology to avoid killing dolphins and would be driven out of business by the boycott. Greenpeace wanted to try to address these economic problems and look for a long-range solution to the dolphin–tuna issue, but that position created public relations problems for Greenpeace as well as tensions with other environmental groups that wanted to declare victory (ibid., 161–3).

As this example shows, there are no easy strategies for dealing with complicated environmental and socio-economic problems. Many national environmental organizations in the United States and Canada have been working with industries to promote "sustainable development" practices to save both energy and money. Critics argue, however, that industries want to define sustainable development on their own terms, and that they assume workers will bear much of the cost of greater efficiency in the form of loss of jobs (Adkin, 1992: 138). And, indeed, many businesses lobbied against ratification of the Kyoto Protocol to the United Nations Convention on Climate Change, warning that many jobs would be lost. Nevertheless, environmentalists have worked hard to form coalitions with labour unions and others and to address socio-economic issues in both developed and developing countries. In Canada, where the Kyoto Protocol was ratified in 2002 with strong public approval, the David Suzuki Foundation collaborated with the Communications, Energy and Paperworkers Union to report on the economic benefits of Kyoto, effectively countering the "doom-and-gloom job-loss" framing by corporate lobbyists, and labour unions backed ratification together with "just transition" programs to assist displaced workers (Stewart, 2003: 42). Climate Action Network Canada is strongly committed to "a just transition for workers, First Nations and other communities affected by a change to a sustainable energy system" (www.climateactionnetwork.ca). Thus, green lobbies are pursuing a variety of strategies as they attempt to tackle global warming and other complex problems.

Grassroots Environmentalism and Direct-Action Campaigns

While many large national environmental organizations have become highly institutionalized, grassroots environmental groups have also mobilized to expand the goals and tactics of the movement. In fact sometimes groups chose to "go local" instead of global in their activism, even valorizing local food and lifestyles over more transnational objectives (Stoddart and Ramos, 2013). Some of these local groups also organize to oppose the siting of environmental hazards in their own neighbourhoods, such as "dirty diesel" trains in Toronto (Taylor, 2015). Although critics labelled them NIMBYS (Not in My Backyard), many local movements developed into environmental justice groups with a deeper understanding of the political and economic underpinnings of environmental problems (Szasz, 1994: 80). In recent years, new direct-action campaigns have emerged around climate change and opposition to fossil fuels, and even more traditional conservation organizations are engaging more frequently in direct action (Rootes and Brulle, 2013: 5).

In some instances, local environmental disasters served as critical events that helped to mobilize grassroots movements. Movement organizations were then successful in framing issues in ways that appealed to local activists, and they devised direct-action tactics that allowed for grassroots participation. In the United States, a toxic-waste movement emerged in the late 1970s, based primarily in white working-class and middle-class communities and spurred by the saga of a neighbourhood community that had been built on top of Love Canal, a chemical-waste dumpsite for a chemical plant in Niagara Falls, New York. In Canada, residents and workers campaigned against chemical pollution in highly industrialized areas such as southwestern Ontario (Adkin, 1998). Racial and ethnic communities also mobilized around toxic contamination and public health threats (Brulle and Pellow, 2006). This coincided with the rise of the environmental justice movement, which raised issues of racism and inequality, charging that the working poor and people of colour typically pay the highest price for environmental pollution in that industrial facilities and toxic-waste dumps are often placed in poor and minority neighbourhoods (Szasz, 1994: 75).

While the environmental justice movement has been linked to concerns about "environmental racism" in the United States, in Canada the movement has developed in a much different context (see Agyeman et al., 2009). Recent mobilization has occurred around the high correlation between waste disposal sites and African Nova Scotian and other racialized communities (Deacon and Baxter, 2013). Canada's different racial history, however, has meant that the environmental justice movement has tended to focus on the "considerable environmental injustice in terms of abrogation of treaties, land rights, resource management and living conditions" faced by Indigenous peoples (Haluza-Delay, 2007: 560). Although the frame of environmental justice was initially employed primarily in the United States, the movement has spread internationally, with different concerns highlighted in different national contexts. In 1991, delegates from the United States, Canada, and Central America gathered in Washington, DC, for the first People of Colour Environmental Leadership Summit (Dowie, 1995: 151). More recently, a global environmental justice movement has developed around concerns about "climate justice" and the ways in which climate change increases inequality in terms of "who suffers most its consequences, who caused the problem, who is expected to act, and who has the resources to do so" (Mohai et al., 2009: 420). Like the earlier environmental justice movement, it connects environmentalism with other inequalities. In particular the climate justice movement focuses on political-economic and underlying power dynamics that shape environmental harms (Bond and Dorsey, 2010). It challenges the relationship of capitalist and neoliberal policies shaping globalization and the long-term consequences they have in creating an unsustainable environment (Klein, 2014). Ultimately climate justice will demand that people adopt a different mindset and a more sustainable lifestyle (Haluza-Delay, 2007, 2015).

Radical environmentalists, motivated by ideology and an activist commitment rather than connections with local communities and ethnic groups, also organized grassroots groups in the 1980s and 1990s. Many of these activists were influenced by the philosophy of "deep ecology," which emphasizes "ecocentrism" (or human solidarity with nature and the rights of nature) as opposed to a human-centred view of the world (Devall, 1992: 52). Organizations inspired by the deep ecology philosophy, including Earth First! and the Rainforest Action Network, became active in North America, Europe, and Australia. Not all radical environmentalists consider themselves deep ecologists, but they advocate direct-action tactics as an alternative to institutionalized environmentalism and as a way to empower activists. These tactics have attracted many participants. Some groups, such as the US branch of Earth First!, advocated the use of such controversial tactics as tree-spiking to damage logging equipment despite criticism that this tactic endangered loggers. In recent years, new Earth First! groups have formed as part of the environmental justice movement. Rising Tide North America, formed in 2000 with roots in the deep ecology movement, is a radical coalition that brings together Earth First! and other grassroots groups (Brulle, 2015: 155).

Such radicalization, however, has come with a cost in that many environmental groups have been labelled eco-terrorists delegitimizing the claims of the movement. Joosse (2005) illustrated this through his systematic analysis of media coverage of the Earth Liberation Front (ELF). He found that ELF's strength emerged from its leaderless and local structure, which allowed it to deploy quickly and engage in large number of direct actions (Joosse, 2007). But the lack of a clear leader also meant that media messages were left to the interpretation of journalists and those outside of the movement. This often meant that the focus was on the radicalness of actions and the threat posed by the group instead of the environmental harms ELF was contesting.

Because of their visibility and apparent threat to the interests of loggers, miners, farmers, and other groups, radical environmental groups provoked countermovement activity. Recognizing the successes of grassroots environmental groups in mobilizing new supporters, opponents have mimicked their organizational forms. On behalf of corporations, public relations firms have created artificial grassroots coalitions (known as "Astroturf") to give the appearance of citizen support for anti-environmental positions (Beder, 2002: 32). The Wise Use Movement was created in 1988 when representatives of US and Canadian groups, including interest groups (e.g., the American Mining Congress) and corporations (e.g., Exxon and MacMillan Bloedel), came together to create an anti-environmental movement that was known as Wise Use in the United States and the Share Movement in Canada (ibid., 45). Industry-backed Wise Use groups have drawn attention to the radical activities of environmentalists and attempted to recruit to the countermovement rural dwellers, loggers, and other workers concerned about loss of jobs and land. By adopting the form of a social movement, anti-environmentalists are able to claim a greater legitimacy in opposing environmental policies than industrial lobbies can, and countermovement entrepreneurs can appeal to the fears of local activists by painting environmentalists as "the enemy" (see Switzer, 1997).

Opposition to social movements, particularly in the form of a countermovement, is often a sign of the movement's success (Meyer and Staggenborg, 1996). The emphasis on direct action helped to reinvigorate the grassroots environmental movement, resulting in some dramatic campaigns in the 1990s. In Canada, radical environmentalists worked in coalition with organizations such as Greenpeace to protect the forests of Clayoquot Sound, British Columbia. In the UK, Earth First! led a militant anti-roads movement, which involved many local communities in the environmental movement. In the area of climate change, a countermovement of climate change deniers, consisting of industry interest groups, conservative think tanks and foundations, front groups, conservative media, politicians, and "contrarian scientists," has managed to stall actions to prevent further climate change (Dunlap and McCright, 2013).

In the Canadian context, the Conservative federal government in 2012 amplified such countermobilization by introducing new tax laws that prevent charities from devoting more than 10 per cent of their resources for political activities. At the same time the government gave the Canadian Revenue Agency (CRA) $8 million to monitor and audit charities that fail to comply. The situation led to long-time and famed environmentalist David Suzuki leaving the board of the charity bearing his name because he feared his activism would undermine its work in the wake of the new policy (McCarthy and Moore, 2012). Other organizations, such as ForestEthics, which targeted the Canadian energy industry by encouraging large US firms to avoid the use of fuel derived from Alberta tar sands, have opted to give up their charitable status in order to ensure the ability to take a critical stance toward the federal government. During 2014 the CRA audited seven of the leading environmental organizations across the country, including the David Suzuki Foundation, Tides Canada, West Coast Environmental Law, the Pembina Foundation, Environmental Defence, Equiterre, and the Ecology Action Centre, putting them at risk of losing their charitable status and millions of dollars of resources that help them advocate on behalf of the environment (Solomon and Everson, 2014).

The Clayoquot Sound Protests

In 1993, after the British Columbia provincial government announced that it would allow clear-cut logging in much of the old-growth forests of Clayoquot Sound, on the west coast of Vancouver Island, one of the most dramatic direct-action campaigns in the history of the environmental movement was organized in British Columbia. As many as 12,000 protesters blocked access to a logging road, and some 800 people were arrested in largely non-violent protests. A local group called Friends of Clayoquot Sound, which had been fighting for preservation of the forests for over a decade, established a peace camp, and this became one base for protesters involved in the blockades. The protests drew attention from around the world, and numerous environmental organizations, including Greenpeace and the Sierra Club, became involved. A countermovement also mobilized; in the spring of 1994, as many as 20,000 forestry workers and their families lobbied the provincial legislature, and in July of that year, thousands of people held a festival designed to celebrate "timber culture," which they felt was threatened by the protests (*Globe and Mail*, 14 July 1994).

Nevertheless, public opinion was strongly opposed to clear-cutting, and the environmental campaign employed both market-based tactics and direct action, using the resources of large international organizations as well as those of local groups. After Greenpeace threatened to boycott their products, two British paper companies cancelled contracts to buy pulp from the Canadian timber company MacMillan Bloedel. The BC government eventually set stricter limits on logging in Clayoquot Sound, and the direct-action protests ended.

The struggle over clear-cutting, however, continued. In a boycott campaign led by the Sierra Club and Greenpeace against Home Depot, the huge home improvement and building supplies retailer based in the United States, environmentalists deluged the company with postcards, sent an exhibit on the Great Bear Rainforest (located on the central mainland BC coast) to a shareholder meeting, and erected a Home Depot protest billboard over a clear-cut patch near Vancouver. The campaign resulted in a major victory when Home Depot, which has over 850 stores worldwide and sells 10 per cent of the world's market supply of wood, announced in 1999 that it would phase out sales of wood from endangered forests by 2002 (*New York Times*, 22 October 1999). Boycotts also forced timber companies to agree to more sustainable practices, although conflicts over logging in British Columbia continue. Overall, the movement campaign made important gains by building on favourable public opinion, using the resources of large environmental organizations, and harnessing the energies of grassroots activists with direct-action tactics.

The Anti-roads Movement

A dramatic direct-action campaign took place in the United Kingdom in the early 1990s, spearheaded by the Earth First! network founded there in 1991. As Derek Wall describes, protests against new roads and anti-car campaigns first occurred in the late 1960s and early 1970s, when local NIMBY activists who were protesting the loss of their neighbourhoods to motorways joined with environmentalists who were framing car use in terms of global environmental destruction (Wall, 1999: 27). Activists in London and Manchester, for example, used blocked roads as a tactic to demand car-free streets and free public transportation, holding Reclaim the Streets parties on busy roads and "bike-ins" by large numbers of cyclists (ibid., 29). While some anti-car and anti-roads activity continued beyond the early 1970s, radical activists in Britain became increasingly involved in anti-nuclear protests and peace campaigns, including the well-known women's peace camp at Greenham Common (ibid., 33). In the 1980s, a "green movement" emerged in Britain, prompting some anti-roads activity. Protest accelerated dramatically in the 1990s after the Conservative government issued a call for increased road construction in its 1989 White Paper, *Roads for Prosperity*, and after the founding of Earth First! (UK) in 1991 (ibid., 37).

During the 1990s, anti-roads campaigns were mounted in a number of locations; they involved thousands of activists and resulted in major reductions in the government's plans for road construction. The first major campaign took place in Twyford Down, near the city of Winchester, in protest of the construction of the M3 motorway there. Inspired by the Greenham

Common peace camp and similar tactics used by the Australian rainforest movement, activists created an anti-roads protest camp at Twyford, attracting large numbers of activists (Wall, 1999: 67). Alliances were created between local activists and radical environmentalists from groups such as Earth First! (UK), and direct-action tactics (digging and occupying tunnels, sitting in trees, blockading roads, and so on) were employed to raise the costs of road construction. Campaigns in other locations used similar tactics, and the "green network" in the United Kingdom expanded greatly, spreading strategies and a radical environmentalist collective identity. Reclaim the Streets parties were held in many cities, and the movement built on youth counterculture as well as on environmental networks and the memberships of large groups such as Friends of the Earth and Greenpeace. The movement faced great obstacles, including countermovement activity in favour of road construction and strong opposition from the government. Despite opposition and an initial lack of political opportunities and resources, however, the movement was able to create divisions within the government (Doherty, 1999: 284). The movement spawned effective alliances between local activists and radical networks and gained a great deal of media attention with its use of innovative direct-action tactics. Activists felt empowered by the protests, and an expanded network of radicalized green activists and a repertoire of direct-action tactics are among the movement's enduring outcomes (Wall, 1999).

Fossil Fuel Resistance and Indigenous Protest

While pollution caused by the coal, oil, and gas industries has long been of major concern to environmentalists, climate change has made resistance to fossil fuel extremely urgent. Radical environmentalists are increasingly framing campaigns against fossil fuel industries in terms of "climate justice" and the need for a "just transition." That is, they are drawing attention to the enormous sacrifices that some local communities are making as a result of fossil fuel extraction and to the need to address the unequal burdens of climate change for the most vulnerable communities worldwide. Recognizing that there must be a transition to renewable energy and sustainable living, climate justice activists argue that the transition must be a just one: the main costs of climate change should not fall on low-income and racially oppressed communities, which have already suffered disproportionately from pollution and ecological crises. Internationally, global justice groups have addressed climate justice by critiquing "not just the distribution of economic goods but environmental goods and bads as well" (Schlosberg, 2007: 82).

The natural gas and oil industries are also targets of grassroots environmental groups, and strong movements have emerged to protest extraction of gas and oil through fracking and infrastructure projects such as pipelines and compressor stations. Environmentalists strongly opposed the Keystone XL pipeline project, which would carry oil from the Canadian tar sands in Alberta to Texas, on the grounds of its implications for climate change as well as risks to wildlife and communities. There have also been protests and strong opposition against the Northern Gateway pipeline, which would span from Bruderheim Alberta to Kitimat British Columbia. Both proposed projects have sparked local protests of people who would be directly affected as well as transnational campaigns. The campaign against the Keystone XL pipeline, including a large demonstration at the White House in February 2013, organized by the Sierra Club, 350.org, and others, prompted President Obama to delay permission for the project and also stimulated protests of other pipelines in the United States (Ostrander, 2014). Opposition to bitumen extraction, labelled tar sands by environmentalists, has also transcended different movements including Indigenous communities and organizations, religious groups, and the labour movement (Haluza DeLay and Carter, 2014). During May of 2014 activists across a wide range of movements held a national day of action against the proposed projects (CBC News, 2014). Earlier that year singer Neil Young announced a solidarity concert tour to raise funds for Athabasca Chipewyan First Nation's legal defence fund. While visiting the tar sands he gained national attention for comparing them to the bombed-out remnants of Hiroshima, Japan. This sparked reaction from the prime minister and a conservative backlash. Later

Andrew Burton 2014/Getty Images

PHOTO 8.1: The People's Climate March

that year actor Leonardo DiCaprio visited the area and also condemned development of the tar sands. The use of celebrities to amplify environmental concerns has also been used by other environmental movements (Stoddart et al., 2013; Stoddart, 2012).

As noted in Chapter 5, Indigenous mobilization through Idle No More is strongly linked to environmental protection. Activists originally mobilized against two budget bills, C-38 and C-45, which would affect how Canada protects land and water. The intersection of Indigenous activism and environmentalism can also be seen in the anti-fracking movement. During the 2013 Elsipogtog protests in New Brunswick, Indigenous activists from the community opposed seismic testing by SWN Resources to explore the area's potential for natural gas extraction. Ultimately the protest led to a standoff with the RCMP and violence which gained national and international attention. Given that oil and gas development in Canada will occur on land claimed by Indigenous peoples, further intersection between the Indigenous and environmental movement is likely. Throughout the United States, and in many other countries, grassroots movements have emerged to protest fracking for gas and oil, engaging in a wide range of tactics including demonstrations, divestment campaigns, and community bans. While the prospects for reversing climate change remain bleak, an increasingly large fossil fuel resistance movement is emerging (McKibben, 2013), and grassroots groups are creating a larger climate justice movement.

The strength of this movement was demonstrated on 21 September 2014, when hundreds of thousands of people—most estimates ranged from 300,000 to 400,000—descended on New York City for a People's Climate March. The march took place in advance of a UN meeting on climate change and was intended to show public concern to heads of state about the urgency of global warming. Solidarity marches took place in cities around the world as a diverse collection of environmentalists, union members, and ordinary citizens joined the demonstrations in New York (Foderaro, 2014). In Canada supporting marches were held in almost every major city and the mobilization garnered unprecedented media attention. The People's Climate March was co-ordinated by organizations such as 350.org, the Sierra Club, and the global online activist network, Avaaz. Many grassroots environmental justice groups, including members of Rising Tide North America and the Climate Justice Alliance, also participated in the People's Climate March and then organized about 3,000 people to "flood Wall Street" in a nonviolent direct action on the following day in New York's financial district. The protesters demanded support for communities impacted by climate change and a just transition away from a fossil fuel–based economy (http://risingtidenorthamerica.org).

Conclusion

The modern environmental movement has endured for decades despite shifts in its organizational strength and activity. The movement's organizational and strategic diversity is one important reason for the continued salience of environmentalism. Large national organizations have created green lobbies in numerous countries. International organizations have spread to many countries and are capable of mounting both national and transnational campaigns. Greenpeace, in particular, has become expert at generating media coverage. Local and regional groups, such as Friends of Clayoquot Sound and Earth First!, have demonstrated the potential of non-violent direct action for the environmental movement. Networks of environmental activists and collective identities endure, even when particular organizations and campaigns decline. The movement has provoked significant countermovement activities, but these responses are an indicator of environmentalism's appeal, even though they seek to harm the movement's cause.

Strong public support for environmentalism helps the movement endure by creating financial support for movement organizations and political support for movement positions. Environmental problems are subject to issue attention cycles, but the movement continues to be relevant to the public because critical environmental problems are ongoing and local populations are often affected by environmental devastation, including the increasingly apparent impacts of global warming. Public support creates the potential for a greater use of market-based strategies, but also the risk that only strategies that appeal to the mainstream public will be developed. Strategies that are difficult to convey through the mass media and that involve slow and complicated solutions may be difficult to sell to the public. Organizations that depend on donations from a great many people may fail to develop solutions that require lifestyle sacrifices on the part of the public. Moreover, even with public support to combat such enormous problems as global warming, economic interests and financial costs create major barriers. Industry's opposition to the movement and an industry-backed countermovement, including climate change denial, have stymied progress. Coalitions with labour unions and other groups are clearly necessary, as are international efforts to address the global scope of environmental problems. Many environmentalists are involved in such efforts, including the global justice movement, which is the subject of the following chapter.

Discussion Questions

1. How can the environmental movement overcome the free rider problem and get citizens to contribute to the movement and its goals, either through individual action (e.g., recycling) or through participation in collective action?

2.   What are the strengths and weaknesses of Greenpeace's media-based strategy? How might new communications technologies affect this strategy?

3.   How might the environmental movement convert public concern about the environment into cultural changes and public policies that address major issues such as global warming?

Suggested Readings

Brulle, Robert J. 2000. *Agency, Democracy, and Nature: The U.S. Environmental Movement from a Critical Theory Perspective*. Cambridge, Mass.: MIT Press. This book analyzes the major forms of environmentalism in the United States.

McKenzie, Judith I. 2002. *Environmental Politics in Canada: Managing the Commons into the Twenty-First Century*. Oxford: Oxford University Press. This book describes major trends in Canadian environmentalism.

Rootes, Christopher. 2004. "Environmental Movements," in D.A. Snow, S.A. Soule, and H. Kriesi, eds, *The Blackwell Companion to Social Movements*. Malden, Mass.: Blackwell, 608–40. This essay provides a comparative perspective, analyzing trends such as the institutionalization of environmental organizations in Western countries.

Young, Nathan and Eric Dugas. 2011. "Representations of Climate Change in Canadian National Print Media: The Banalization of Global Warming," *Canadian Review of Sociology* 48(1): 1–22. This article examines how the issue of climate change has been covered by news media and shows how it is framed and misframed.

9 Global Movements for Social Justice

A seemingly new movement burst onto the scene with massive demonstrations at the 1999 conference of the World Trade Organization (WTO) in Seattle. As many as 50,000 demonstrators, including environmentalists, labour unionists, human rights advocates, students, and feminists, descended on the city, resulting in major disruptions to the week-long conference, intense clashes with police, and a great deal of media attention. The "battle in Seattle" and subsequent protests in Washington, DC, Quebec City, Genoa, and elsewhere were manifestations of a "movement of movements" to protest the neoliberal economic policies promoted by the WTO and other global financial institutions. International financial institutions and their policies—and global capitalism more generally—became targets for multiple movements because they were seen to be worsening poverty in developing countries, burdening women and families, promoting environmental destruction, and lowering labour standards.

The Seattle protests were influential around the world, but most dramatically in North America, where "Seattle tactics" such as "black blocs, jail solidarity, blockades, and giant puppets" diffused to movements in cities such as New York and Toronto (Wood, 2012: 4–5). Initially, the emerging movement was commonly known as the "anti-globalization movement" for its opposition to global capitalism, but activists gradually defined their cause as a "global justice movement" promoting democracy, participatory governance structures, and fairer and more sustainable economic policies rather than simply opposing globalization.

From the start, the movement faced enormous obstacles in bringing together diverse participants and formulating strategies that would have an impact on global political and economic institutions. After the terrorist attacks on the United States on 11 September 2001 (known as 9/11), the movement faced even stiffer challenges in mobilizing and strategizing. By 2002, the "Seattle cycle" of protests had declined in the US and Canada (Wood, 2012: 32). Nevertheless, global justice movements remained alive in different forums around the world and protests at international summits such as G8 meetings continued to occur (Starr, Fernandez, and Scholl, 2011).

With the global financial crisis of 2008, a new cycle of protest emerged, engaging many activists who traced their participation in global justice protests at least as far back as Seattle (Bennett and Segerberg, 2013: 4). This cycle of protest was greatly aided by new information and communication technologies, such as social media, that allowed activists to share information and organize, even in repressive contexts. Protests ranged from demonstrations against banks in Iceland in 2009 to the large-scale protests in Spain inspired by Iceland's example, to the many movements that emerged as part of the "Arab Spring" of 2011, to the Occupy Wall Street movement (Castells, 2012), to the "Maple Spring" and Idle No More.

This chapter begins with a description of the origins of the global justice movement and the various protests that led up to the Seattle demonstrations, including the anti–free trade movement that began in Canada. We then look at more recent protests and consider some key factors including framing activities, mobilizing structures, social media, and international opportunities that help to explain how global social justice movements have mobilized diverse activists. Finally, the chapter examines some of the strategies and outcomes of the movements.

Origins of the Global Justice Movement

The Seattle demonstrations captured world attention in part because they occurred in the United States and consequently received a great deal of media coverage, but they were not the first collective actions targeted at international institutions and their neoliberal trade and monetary policies. Jackie Smith (2008) uses the concept of a "rival transnational network" (Maney, 2001) to show how a *democratic globalization network* emerged to contest the *neoliberal globalization network* that had formed among business, government, and other interests. The global justice movement grew out of earlier local, national, and international mobilizations involving many of the organizations and activists present in Seattle (Smith, 2001, 2008). Neoliberal economic policies, which were promoted vigorously by the Reagan administration in the United States, the Thatcher government in Britain, and the Mulroney government in Canada, provided a common target for protests around the world in the 1980s and 1990s. Moreover, some of the cultural changes associated with globalization threatened national and ethnic identities and local cultures, while new technologies such as the Internet promoted greater awareness of these issues and increased the potential for global mobilization (della Porta et al., 2006: 14–15). Thus, global economic policies and cultural threats provided numerous targets for protesters, such as intrusions on national identities and cultures; government cutbacks to social programs; and trade policies, economic projects, and corporations considered to be exploitive of workers and the environment. At the same time, activists began to see themselves as part of a global movement for social justice and a new type of "globalization from below" (ibid.).

The emerging movement was highly heterogeneous, incorporating multiple movements and identities but converging around opposition to the institutions of global capitalism and support of the right of peoples to determine their own future, quite apart from the influence of international financial institutions and transnational corporations. Among the many collective actions that targeted neoliberalism (described in Starr, 2005: 20–5), "IMF riots" or "bread riots" involving general strikes and massive protests took place in some 23 countries in the 1980s. These protests were responses to the structural adjustment programs (SAPs) promoted by the International Monetary Fund and the World Bank, which required developing countries to cut social programs and privatize services and investments in order to pay down their debts while increasing private production and trade. In 1990, the African Council of Churches called for debt relief in response to neoliberal policies, and a debt relief movement known as the Jubilee 2000 campaign mobilized in a number of countries, building largely on faith-based networks of activists (J. Smith, 2008: 101). In Europe, a variety of movements used direct action in taking control of buildings to protest policies such as welfare cuts and racism in immigration. On 16 October 1985, Greenpeace London initiated the International Day of Action against McDonald's, a day that would be observed annually in protests against McDonald's business practices, environmental damage, and treatment of animals. A movement of European farmers in support of family farming and sustainable farming practices mobilized in the 1980s, and in 1988 some 80,000 demonstrators from across Europe protested against the IMF meetings in Berlin.

Economic adjustment policies have had particularly strong impacts on poor Indigenous peoples, and in Latin America, the adjustment process following the 1982 debt crisis provoked a variety of ethnic conflicts in Bolivia, Mexico, and Peru (Brysk and Wise, 1997). In Colombia, beginning in 1992, Indigenous people protested against a drilling project by Occidental Petroleum until the project was finally withdrawn in 2002. In Brazil, the Landless Workers' Movement became very active in large-scale land occupations. In 1992, European and Latin American farmers created an international farmers' organization of small- and medium-sized producers. In other developing countries, protesters have fought against projects imposing environmental and socio-economic costs on the local population. In India, a long-term protest movement opposed a World Bank project, the Sardar Sarovar dam, which the bank pulled out of in 1993; by 1997, when the Supreme Court of India ordered a halt to the Sardar Sarovar project, the anti-dam movement had spread to other projects. Such struggles "gained intense international attention in the context of an emerging comprehensive case against corporations" and attracted environmental organizations to the cause (ibid., 24).

In North America, the 1980s movement in opposition to the Canada–US Free Trade Agreement (FTA) played an important role in creating transnational networks among activists in Canada, the United States, and Mexico. As Jeffrey Ayres (1998) describes, a coalition of "popular-sector groups" in Canada, including churches, labour unions, farmers, Indigenous peoples, and women's groups, organized to oppose the agreement. All of these groups had been affected by the economic recession of the 1980s and were alarmed by the political shift to the right when the Conservatives were elected in 1984. Aroused by these grievances and threats, popular-sector groups took advantage of the mobilizing opportunities created by public hearings on free trade and the political opportunities that resulted from divisions among the different levels of government, as well as unresolved issues between Canada and the United States that delayed the FTA and allowed opponents time to organize. Although the movement lost the battle over the FTA, Ayres argues that the form of coalition-building used by the Canadian movement spread to the United States and Mexico. The co-operative ties created among activists in the three countries through the battle over the extension of the free trade agreement to Mexico in the North American Free Trade Agreement (NAFTA) contributed to the creation of the broader global justice movement.

On 1 January 1994, the day that NAFTA took effect, a group of Indigenous people and peasants in the Chiapas region of Mexico—calling itself the Zapatista Army of National Liberation—took over a number of towns and set up autonomous zones. The Zapatistas were protesting NAFTA and the neoliberal policies of the Mexican government such as the elimination of protections for coffee prices and the dismantling of a program that provided communal plots of land to Indigenous farmers. Although the Mexican government met the insurrection with military force, the Zapatistas quickly mobilized national and international support, forcing the government to declare a ceasefire. The Zapatistas were able to generate support through their extensive network connections to peasant and other non-government organizations (NGOs) within Mexico and through connections to other activists in North America created by the anti-NAFTA coalition (Schulz, 1998: 593–4). They also generated international solidarity through use of the Internet, winning sympathy for a broad set of demands focusing on justice, democracy, and dignity. In 1996, some 3,000 activists from around the world gathered in Chiapas at a meeting hosted by the Zapatistas; this meeting led to the creation of a transnational network of activists opposed to neoliberal policies and committed to social justice, environmentalism, and women's rights, among other common values.

In the decades since World War II, the number of international NGOs has increased greatly, and they have played a key role in what Keck and Sikkink (1998: 1) call "transnational advocacy networks," which are "distinguishable largely by the centrality of principled ideas or values in motivating their formation." International NGOs have formed advocacy networks around human rights, peace, environmental, women's rights, and economic justice issues (ibid., J. Smith, 2008). Many of the participants are professionals who lend expertise and legitimacy to international campaigns that have helped to institutionalize new international norms on these issues. Advocacy networks have worked through institutional structures such as the UN, but they have also supported, and expanded along with, grassroots movements. In recent decades, transnational social movement organizations have expanded greatly and become more decentralized, in part because new communications technologies have lessened the need for centralized and hierarchical organizational structures and allowed local and national groups to connect with international networks (J. Smith, 2008: 124).

Around the world, local and national movements spread to the international level and supported emerging global justice networks, with a large number of protests occurring in the wake of the founding of the World Trade Organization in 1995 (Starr, 2005: 25–6). In Nigeria, the Ogoni people had been waging a long struggle against exploitation in their homeland but gained little notice until Ken Saro-Wiwa and other activists formed the Movement for the Survival of the Ogoni People (MOSOP) to fight for political autonomy and against ethnic, economic, and environmental exploitation by the Nigerian government and Royal Dutch/Shell, the major oil company operating in the region (Bob, 2005: 54). In 1995, large demonstrations were organized to protest the execution of Ken Saro-Wiwa and eight other MOSOP activists by the government of Nigeria following a trial on trumped-up charges and despite world condemnation. In December 1995, France saw the largest demonstrations since May 1968, in the form of massive strikes by workers, students, women's groups, and others, in protest of government plans to reform social security and in support of the welfare state; in 1998, some of the same organizations joined together to create the Association for the Taxation of Financial Transactions and Aid to Citizens, known as ATTAC (Ancelovici, 2002: 432). ATTAC became an "international movement for democratic control of financial markets and their institutions" with branches in over 30 countries (www.attac.org).

In many cities, local movement activity picked up in the 1990s, involving participants in causes that would feed into the global justice movement. In what Janet Conway (2004) calls the "activist city" of Toronto, for example, a group created in 1992, the Metro Network for Social Justice (MNSJ), brought together unions, community-based social service agencies, housing and anti-poverty activists, feminists, and others who saw connections between local problems such as cutbacks in municipal services and larger issues of free trade and neoliberal economic policies. In London, the anti-roads movement that had originally protested motorway construction and the takeover of cities by cars developed a broader anti-corporate critique. Joining with other countercultural groups, anti-roads activists promoted Reclaim the Streets parties in the 1990s as a way of reclaiming public spaces (Klein, 1999: 312–13). Reclaim the Streets also spread internationally, and in May 1998, a global street party was held simultaneously in cities around the world (rts.gn.apc.org). Police reaction to the parties varied greatly, in some cities resulting in riots, but everywhere a great deal of emotion was aroused regarding the power of the movement (Klein, 1999: 320–1). The mobilization of such local movements made the scale shift to the international protests in Seattle and elsewhere possible, and the stability of these local organizations provided a place for local activists to return to after participating in episodic transnational activism (Tarrow, 2005).

Peoples' Global Action (PGA), inspired by the Zapatista vision, was among the transnational networks of activists that were forming at this time. Created in 1998, the coalition sponsored the first "global day of action" in May 1998 to coincide with the meetings of the G8[1] in Birmingham, England, and the WTO in Geneva (Wood, 2005a, 2005b). The second global day of action was called by the PGA to protest the June 1999 meeting of the G8 in Germany, and the third global day of action was called to protest the WTO meetings in Seattle in November of that year. Thus, numerous protests organized by various networks of activists had occurred around the world before the events in Seattle in 1999. The dramatic protests in Seattle created new momentum for the movement, and a record number of organizations participated in the protests, both in Seattle and in cities around the world. After the Seattle protests, the PGA and other activist networks continued to organize protests to coincide with the meetings of international financial organizations and to target corporate symbols of global capitalism such as McDonald's and Nike.

As a result of the successful Seattle protests, many activists across North America began to experiment with direct-action tactics such as blockades in addition to more conventional demonstrations (Wood, 2012). Although the events of 9/11 slowed the momentum of the movement, particularly in the United States and Canada, a massive protest took place in over 150 cities worldwide against the WTO meetings in Qatar in November 2001 (Wood, 2005a: 80). Despite a brief pause in protests in response to the terrorist attacks of 2001, and some decline in use of "Seattle tactics" by the North American movement by 2002 (Wood, 2012), the global justice movement continued to be active worldwide after 9/11. In fact, after the US invasions of Afghanistan and Iraq, the ranks of the movement were expanded by antiwar activists around the world (Podobnik, 2005).

A number of important changes occurred in transnational activism in the "post-Seattle era" after the late 1990s. These include increased activism in the global South, decentralization of organizations, a shift to locally oriented sites of protest, and an emphasis on issue campaigns, often organized through the Internet, rather than on global institutions (J. Smith, 2008: 127). Perhaps most importantly, the expanded use of digital and social media has facilitated new transnational networks of activists involved in organizing what Bennett and Segerberg (2013) call "connective action" in addition to more traditional face-to-face collective action. Consequently, a large diversity of organizations, involving many different constituents and collective action frames, can become involved in organizing global protests. For example, the 2009 protests at the London G20 Summit involved two very different coalitions: Put People First (PPF), an alliance of over 160 NGOs, unions, and environmental, social justice, and religious groups that mobilized some 35,000 protesters for a "Jobs, Justice, and Climate" march; and G20 Meltdown, an anti-capitalist alliance of anarchists, socialists, and others that organized actions such as a protest at the Bank of England against war, climate crisis, and various financial crimes (Bennett and Segerberg, 2013: 63). While both coalitions aimed at some of the same targets, G20 Meltdown was more ideologically cohesive as an anti-capitalist umbrella group that engaged in direct actions on the street, whereas "PPF went to great lengths to encourage personalized expression through various technologies deployed on its website" (2013: 72). Extensive use of digital technologies, Bennett and Segerberg (2013: 85–6) argue, made PPF a stronger and more diverse network while still allowing the coalition to organize a large protest.

As the example of the London G20 protests illustrates, networks of global justice groups aided by Internet communication technologies continue to target international institutions. The world economic crisis of 2008 generated a great deal of anger against institutional symbols of greed and power. Along with large demonstrations at the 2009 G20 meetings in London, where the "financial district was an obvious target," protests occurred at the site of NATO meetings in Strasbourg, France, where protesters objected to spending on military campaigns rather than social welfare (Castle and Erlanger, 2009). At subsequent international meetings of the G20, in Pittsburgh in 2009 and in Toronto in 2010, activists again linked concerns about economic justice with the urgency of climate change, organizing demonstrations and staging educational events to protest the G20 and its policies.

While the earlier global justice movement remained alive, the global financial crisis of 2008 also triggered a new cycle of intense protest. Manuel Castells (2012) argues that the Internet, social media, and the occupation of physical spaces were all critical to the rapid spread of this international wave of protest that culminated in the Occupy Wall Street movement. In Iceland, the collapse of three large banks created an economic crisis, and citizens became outraged at government support for the banks. Aided by social media, the protest spread and in January 2009, thousands of people demonstrated outside Parliament by beating on drums, pots, and pans. Dubbed "the kitchenware revolution," the protesters called for an election, which resulted in a new government that was able to deal with the banks and rescue the country from economic disaster (Castells, 2012: 34–7). Later, in Tunisia, a very different type of protest occurred after a young street vendor named Mohamed Bouazizi set himself on fire on 17 December 2010, to "protest against the humiliation of repeated confiscation of his fruit and vegetable stand by the local police after he refused to pay a bribe" (2012: 22). His act sparked demonstrations by other youths and, after being posted on the Internet, the protests spread across the country, resulting in more videos of protests and police violence on social media. The movement combined free Internet communication with occupations of public space, setting up tents and holding long discussions at the public square where government ministries were located (2012: 23). The protesters demanded democracy and, after overthrowing the government, "reached the milestone of clean, open elections on October 23, 2011" (2012: 29).

The events in Tunisia inspired protests in many other Middle Eastern countries in what became known as the "Arab Spring" of 2011. In Egypt, massive demonstrations quickly emerged, with thousands occupying Tahrir Square in Cairo in early 2011 and eventually toppling the Mubarak government. In many other countries as well, governments were overthrown though democracy was not always achieved. The successes in Iceland and Tunisia also inspired protesters in Spain, known as the *indignados*, who saw "the possibility of successfully confronting the collusion between bankers and politicians through grassroots mobilization" (2012: 111). The financial crisis hit Spain hard with extremely high unemployment, and activists were indignant at the unfairness of actions taken by the banks and government. A decentralized network of protesters followed the Arab example in calling for demonstrations in the streets using social media, resulting in huge demonstrations and occupations of public squares in Madrid, Barcelona, and elsewhere.

All of these protests inspired the Occupy movement, which began with Occupy Wall Street (OWS) in New York City in September 2011. As Todd Gitlin (2012: 13–16) describes, there were actually several independent origins of OWS, including calls for "a 99 percent movement" and Operation Empire State Rebellion by a subgroup of the Anonymous network using the name A99, a march on Wall Street by a left-wing coalition called New Yorkers Against Budget Cuts, and a call by the Vancouver-based anti-consumerist magazine Adbusters to occupy Wall Street on 17 September 2011.

They all had in common outrage at rising inequality and the influence of money on government, resulting in policies that benefited the elite 1 per cent at the expense of the other 99 per cent. The pre-existing networks decided to consolidate their efforts around 17 September and, after much planning,

WHAT
IS OUR
ONE
DEMAND?

#OCCUPYWALLSTREET
SEPTEMBER 17TH.
BRING TENT.

Adbusters Media Foundation

PHOTO 9.1: Adbusters' call to occupy Wall Street

protesters set up a camp in New York's Zuccotti Park. From New York City, the Occupy movement spread to other cities in North America and around the world, as activists set up camps in public places and built a movement against inequality and in favour of real democracy (Castells, 2012). Although the Occupy camps were eventually evicted or dismantled, the movement had a lasting impact in radicalizing many young participants who had never before experienced political protest, changing the public discourse, and creating or expanding networks of activists that survived beyond the Occupy camps (Milkman, Luce and Lewis, 2013).

In Quebec, for instance, the 2012 student movement against proposed tuition increases, dubbed the "Maple Spring," was inspired by the discourse and tactics used by the Occupy movement (Bégin-Caouette and Jones, 2014). Students used social media and street theatre to paralyze downtown Montreal. Students and their supporters, like protesters in Iceland, also adopted the tactic of banging pots and pans while marching and began wearing red squares as symbols of their protest, a tactic used in earlier student protests. The Quebec government responded by issuing Bill-78, which required at least eight hours' advance notice before protests, banned masks, and restricted the freedom of assembly, protests, or picketing near universities and CEGEPs. Later that fall the provincial Liberal government that introduced the proposed tuition increases was defeated and the new government halted them.

Mobilizing Frames, Structures, and Opportunities

Theories of social movements suggest some key factors that influenced how and why these global movements for social justice emerged when they did. Global economic changes and the application of neoliberal policies created widespread *grievances* and *threats* in both developed and developing countries. Conflicts over the consequences of neoliberal policies became widespread in the 1980s and 1990s, and—significantly for the creation of a transnational movement—activists in different locations began linking various socio-economic and political problems to neoliberal policies. In other words, they were creating a *master frame* that diagnosed specific problems as consequences of neoliberalism and its practice by international financial institutions (Ayres, 2004, 2005). This "broadly interpretive, increasingly transnationally-shared diagnostic frame" helped to mobilize a global movement by linking different types of social problems worldwide to the rise of neoliberalism (Ayres, 2004: 12). Thus, problems such as rising debt loads in developing countries, austerity measures such as cuts to social programs, rising unemployment in both developed and developing countries, and instability in the international economy could all be attributed to neoliberalism. As a result, activists working on a variety of projects were able to adopt a common *collective identity* as global actors who opposed neoliberalism and sought social and environmental justice and democracy from below (della Porta et al., 2006). When the financial crisis of 2008 hit, another wave of global protest continued the fight for social and economic justice. The protests began in Europe, where citizens were "angry at austerity imposed not only by their governments but also by global markets," and became linked to protests in the Arab world and to Occupy Wall Street (Calhoun, 2013: 28). The theme of austerity became central to the master frame associated with neoliberalism for a new generation of activists.

Not only was it possible to trace many different problems to neoliberal policies, but political opportunities for transnational protest were expanded by **internationalism**, which Tarrow (2005: 25) defines as the "structure of relations among states, non-state actors, and international institutions, and the opportunities this produces for actors to engage in collective action at different levels of this system." Tarrow expands upon earlier political process theories in his analysis of how the **international opportunity structure** changed with the enlarged role of institutions such as the World Bank and the European Union (EU). Although international institutions often represent the interests of global capitalism, they "also offer an opportunity space within which opponents of global capitalism and other claimants can mobilize" (ibid., 26). Thus, the transnational global justice movement network continually interacts with international institutions (J. Smith, 2008). In the past few decades, as international governmental institutions and activities such as high-profile international summits have proliferated, so have parallel summits and global movements (Pianta, 2003). International institutions are key targets and arenas for transnational activism, and as in the case of national governments, actors within these institutions may be divided in their sympathies, creating both opportunities and obstacles for protesters.

Tarrow (2005: 32) identifies some of the important political processes involved in transnational contention. In some instances, collective action occurs in a domestic arena, but with global connections, the process of **global framing** involves the use of "international symbols to frame domestic conflicts" and **internalization** is "a response to foreign or international pressures within domestic politics." Both of these processes were involved when French farmers blockaded Euro-Disney in 1992 to protest EU agricultural reforms and the "Americanization" of Europe (ibid., 31; Bush and Simi, 2001). In **diffusion**, forms of contention spread from one site to others, as in the case of Reclaim the Streets parties. In **scale shift**, co-ordination of collective action shifts to a different level, as in the case of a local group such as ATTAC becoming international. Two other processes identified by Tarrow occur at the international level. **Externalization** involves "the vertical projection of domestic claims onto international institutions or foreign actors," as in the case of a Renault plant closure in Belgium that activists brought to the attention of the EU (Tarrow, 2005: 32). **Transnational coalition formation** involves creating a network or coalition among actors from different countries, such as Peoples' Global Action and the World Social Forum (WSF).

The WSF originated in 2001 through "upward scale shift" when activists who were engaged in local struggles created the annual global justice summit as an alternative to the World Economic Forum; since then, there has been a "downward scale shift" with the proliferation of regional, local, and national forums modelled on the WSF (Tarrow, 2005: 128–34). Smith (2008: 199) argues that the WSF process provides a space in which global justice activists from diverse movements can come together to experiment with new forms of participation, share ideas, develop skills, and cultivate a collective identity. She notes numerous difficulties in this process, including the problems of making connections between the local and the global, creating understandings between activists from the global North and South, dealing with resource disparities, and managing the large numbers of activists who have begun to attend the annual forums. However, the WSF has provided a space for activists to come together and develop a shared analysis along with particular issue campaigns. And, most critically, it has helped activists develop a global collective identity.

The global justice movement has worked to expand the WSF as both an "open space" and a "network" in which global democracy can flourish—that is, it has sought to create the type of decentralized movement form emphasized by new social movement theory (Smith et al., 2008: 27–8). In order to facilitate more localized organizing, the WSF process has expanded to local, national, and regional forums. European Social Forums have been held, initially annually and later biannually, in various European cities since 2002. The first US Social Forum (USSF) was held in Atlanta in 2007 and was followed by a second USSF in Detroit in 2010. In Canada, a forum was organized in Windsor just prior to the Detroit forum. A Quebec Social Forum (QSF) was held in Montreal in 2007, attracting about 5,000 participants from across the province. As Dufour and Conway (2010: 30) describe, the QSF was both an "event and [a] process, within the longer history of social mobilization in Quebec." It built on mobilization for the World March of Women and mobilized many feminists as well as unions, anarchists, and other groups opposed to neoliberalism. As with other social forums, the QSF experienced tensions as it attempted to create a democratic space and struggled to bring together activists who held different visions and advocated a diversity of tactics (ibid., 34). Thus, the WSF and local, regional, and national forums are ongoing experiments in creating democratic alternatives to neoliberal institutions.

As they began to create an international global justice movement, activists at different levels built on a variety of formal and informal, movement and non-movement *mobilizing structures* (J. Smith, 2008: 112). For instance, contacts in intergovernmental agencies and the meetings of international institutions served as informal and formal mobilizing structures outside the movement, while activist networks and transnational movement organizations provided structures within the movement. A large number of NGOs have been very important to the global justice movement, providing professional expertise and organizational stability to movement campaigns. Nevertheless, with the crucial help of new communications technologies, informal networks of groups and individual activists may be the most critical type of mobilizing structure for the transnational movement (J. Smith, 2008: 113).

To create a movement of movements, activists used *collective action frames* that linked the concerns of different social movements. Gerhards and Rucht (1992) analyze the mobilization processes in two protest campaigns in West Germany, one against US president Ronald Reagan's visit to Berlin in 1987 and the other against the meetings of the IMF and the World Bank in Berlin in 1988, the latter having included an alternative conference critiquing the policies of the international financial institutions. To explain how the campaigns mobilized, Gerhards and Rucht look at what they term the "micromobiliza-tion" and "mesomobilization" actors that comprised the mobilizing structure for the protest activities. **Micromobilization actors** are the various groups that mobilize individuals to participate in protests, including trade unions and environmental, religious, neighbourhood, student, peace, and women's groups. In the case of the anti-Reagan demonstration, participants were all part of a large network of local Berlin groups, whereas in the anti-IMF campaign, local groups were joined by national groups, including the Green Party. **Mesomobilization actors** work to integrate participating groups, forming co-ordinating groups to organize the micromobilization actors (Gerhards and Rucht, 1992: 558). One of the critical tasks they perform is the creation of collective action frames that allow individual groups to engage in **frame bridging** to connect their particular concerns to the larger concerns of the campaigns (ibid., 584–6). Thus, in an early example of what would become a unifying anti-neoliberalism frame, the IMF and the World Bank were portrayed as agents of a world economic order that exploits developing countries. This frame mobilized many groups, including ecological groups, which focused on how projects of the IMF and the World Bank led to the destruction of rainforests, and women's groups, which emphasized that women bear the brunt of the burden resulting from economic policies that increase poverty in developing countries.

To be successful in linking together actors from different movements and at different levels, movements need effective mesomobilization actors and frames that bridge movement concerns and link local, national, and international issues. In the global justice movement, local activists have engaged in global framing to enhance the appeal of local issues, in some instances strengthening their causes by appealing to international organizations for assistance. For example, Clifford Bob (2005: Ch. 3) shows how the Ogani, a little-known ethnic group in Nigeria facing a hostile domestic environment, sought international help in their struggle for ethnic autonomy and against degradation of their environment. The Movement for the Survival of the Ogoni People initially failed to convince major international NGOs, such as Greenpeace and Amnesty International, to take up the Ogoni cause, but MOSOP eventually learned to frame its concerns in ways that were more appealing to international environmental and human rights groups. By focusing on Shell Oil's environmental abuses of the Niger Delta, and aided by widespread concerns over deepening state repression, MOSOP convinced international NGOs to provide resources and generate publicity.

International networks of NGOs and coalition organizations such as ATTAC and the PGA have served as mesomobilization actors for the global justice movement, helping to build organizations within countries and to mobilize transnational protests (e.g., global days of action). Networks of co-operating organizations have encouraged not only participation in protests but also active participation within the network organizations, which have stressed participatory forms of internal decision-making (della Porta et al., 2006). These heterogeneous networks of organizations have been able to work together within the global justice movement because participants share a collective identity that is inclusive of diverse groups. In an extensive study of global justice networks in Europe, Donatella della Porta and colleagues show that this identity was constructed by the movement through counter-summits and documents that stress a number of values and commitments, including global citizenship, diversity, democracy from below, ecopacifism, and opposition to neoliberalism and global capitalism. This master frame resonates with activists, who share a collective identity based on these ideas (ibid., 82–4).

Although master framing helps to unite a diverse movement, resource inequalities and other North–South differences make it extremely difficult to create and maintain coalitions that include participants from both developed and developing countries. Peoples' Global Action has attempted to deal with such problems by creating "a structure and process explicitly aimed at avoiding Northern domination of the coalition" (Wood, 2005b: 99). Thus, participation at conferences by people from the developed global North is sometimes limited; the Conveners Committee, which is the PGA's only central decision-making body, is regionally balanced in its composition, and the overall structure of the coalition is decentralized to allow grassroots participation (ibid., 100–1). While there are ongoing struggles over organizational processes in the PGA, the coalition has worked to create collective identity among participants through such practices as the drafting of "living documents" that are revised at each gathering. This process allows participants "to challenge any perceived consolidation of power" and to "build trust by reworking the basis of their collaboration in new ways" (ibid., 111). Despite differences, "movements participating in the PGA increasingly see themselves as part of a connected global struggle against neoliberalism" (ibid., 113).

In addition to creating workable mobilizing structures and unifying collective action frames, global movements for social justice have organized with the aid of the mass media and particularly the Internet. Digital technology and social media have become critical strategic tools for global justice activists, allowing individuals and groups within the decentralized network structure of the movement to co-ordinate global protests and to send information around the world quickly and cheaply (J. Smith, 2008: 126). Use of the Internet helped to bring together "a variety of national and regional anti-neoliberal collective action frames" and to develop a critique of neoliberalism through the use of listservs, email, and websites, as well as face-to-face meetings (Ayres, 2004: 19). The Zapatistas won national and international support and inspired global justice activists around the world through mass media coverage and the dissemination of their messages on listservs and websites. They posted their proposal for an international communications and resistance network on a German "Initiatives against Neoliberalism" website, thereby linking their proposal to a wide variety of other struggles, such as the European March against Unemployment (Schulz, 1998: 603).

The Internet became increasingly important when it was used in North American campaigns against free trade and neoliberalism. In 1998, the Council of Canadians (COC), a public interest group with 100,000 members, was instrumental in defeating the Multilateral Agreement on Investment (MAI) in a campaign that relied heavily on the Internet to disseminate information on the MAI and to communicate with other anti-MAI activists around the world (Ayres, 1999). Whereas earlier campaigns launched by the COC and its allies against the FTA and NAFTA had relied on costly and time-consuming mailings and cross-country meetings, the anti-MAI campaign could quickly reach a national and global audience with up-to-date information at little cost (ibid., 140). In advance of the Seattle protests in 1999, websites and listservs were used extensively to mobilize participants. For example, the Ad-Hoc Student Coalition for Fair Trade was a virtual umbrella organization that sent out emails to groups across Canada, such as the Canadian Federation of Students, that in turn forwarded the emails to their own listservs. The Canadian coalition also co-ordinated with US groups, such as the Boston Center for Campus Organizing, that often sent messages to the Canadian network (*Toronto Star*, 29 November 1999). During the Seattle protests, subscribers to distribution lists (e.g., StopWTORound) received reports on the protests as they were occurring (Van Laer and Van Aelst, 2010: 1153)

Internet use became even more sophisticated in the ongoing mobilization against the Free Trade Area of the Americas (FTAA), a proposal to extend free trade throughout the Americas. The campaign, which brought tens of thousands of demonstrators to Quebec City in April 2001, used the Internet to disseminate information about the FTAA, to communicate strategies, and to pressure authorities (Ayres, 2005). Prior to the Quebec City demonstrations, listservs available in English, French, Spanish, and Portuguese, together with a protest website, posted updates on demonstration plans and "rider boards" for those looking to share rides to Quebec City, information on what to bring and expect, and "action alerts" from groups such as Public Citizen in the United States and the COC in Canada, encouraging participation in call-ins, letter-writing campaigns, and email protests directed at the US and Canadian governments (Ayres, 2005: 47). Internet communications helped to bring together activists from different cultures and geographic regions by creating a sense of solidarity and common purpose, spreading tactical innovations, and co-ordinating strategies (ibid., 48). Internet communications also aided in the creation of a coalition organization called the "Hemispheric Social Alliance" (HSA) and in the drafting of the *Alternatives for the Americas* document, which provided movement alternatives to the FTAA (ibid., 48–51).

Della Porta and her colleagues investigated a number of issues related to use of the Internet associated with the global justice demonstrations at the G8 meetings in Genoa in 2001 and at the European Social Forum in Florence in 2002. They found that the Internet played a major role in the organization of logistics and in the development of documents and ideas via websites and email. Websites available in English, French, German, Italian, Portuguese, and Spanish disseminated a steady stream of information about the events and recruited international volunteers (della Porta et al., 2006: 96–7). Although there was some evidence of a "digital divide," or inequality between those who have access to the Internet and the skills to use it and those who are less privileged (Rucht, 2005), della Porta et al. also found that movement organizations helped to socialize members in the use of the Internet (2006: 98). Beyond using the Internet to co-ordinate protests and as a source of information about the movement, activists used the Internet for online petitions, "net strikes" (in which large numbers of people jam websites at prearranged times), and similar activities (ibid., 105–6). Activists also developed their collective identities via the Internet insofar as they actively participated in online forums and mailing lists to discuss issues and ideas as well as to form new social ties (ibid., 108–11).

In the recent wave of protest that included the Arab Spring, the Internet and social media were critical in the rapid spread of protest, providing means of organizing in Tunisia, Egypt, and elsewhere despite repressive governments. Digital media facilitated spontaneous protests and, together with the occupation of public space, created autonomous political spaces for organization and debate (Castells, 2012: 106). Internet communication technologies allowed for the spread of images that created outrage and inspired protest around the world. In the case of OWS, images from Twitter, Facebook, and YouTube contrasted with more negative frames in the mainstream media (DeLuca, Lawson and Sun, 2012). Many argue that the global movement for social justice has a new form of organization and new forms of networks, one that is both global and local and one that is characterized by hotspots of actions, because of the use of new communication technologies. Castells (2012) highlights that rhizomic structures characterize recent movements. These are networks that have no formal centre and that have nodes that operate semi-autonomously in the pursuit of common goals. Such networks were key to the rapid mobilization of Occupy, Idle No More, and the Maple Spring, which relied on Twitter hashtags and Facebook to rapidly mobilize people in spontaneous flash mobs and other acts of protest.

Thus, the Internet and social media are alternatives to traditional mass media, providing social movements with another way to reach large numbers of potential constituents, and they seem to hold great potential for movement organization and development. For the global justice movement, Internet communications and social media are essential to the low-cost distribution of information and the organization of activists worldwide (Van Laer and Van Aelst, 2010). Nevertheless, the lack of quality control regarding the information posted on it is an obstacle for movements (Rucht, 2005). While the Internet facilitates the mobilization of long-term campaigns, it may also produce relatively weak social and ideological ties and collective identities (Bennett, 2003; Bennett and Segerberg, 2013; Van Laer and Van Aelst, 2010). The Internet clearly does not replace face-to-face organizing, and thus global justice campaigns and projects typically combine use of the Internet and other new technologies with more traditional forms of organizing. Independent media centres (IMCs), for example, have been established in a number of cities around the world since the first IMC was set up in Seattle to cover the WTO demonstrations in 1999. Because the mainstream mass media often focus on violence perpetrated by a minority of demonstrators and fail to present movement claims fully or fairly, IMCs decided to enlist activists to report, film, and photograph events to provide a movement perspective and information about protests (J. Smith, 2008: 134). Many IMCs are both active centres of local activity and part of the international Indymedia network of independent journalists and activists; Indymedia maintains a website (www.indymedia.org) and supports the global justice movement by providing alternative, non-corporate coverage of local, national, and international issues and movements (Halleck, 2003; Rucht, 2005).

Although the Internet and social media have been critical to global movements for social justice, conventional mass media, resources and social movement organizations remain important. Securing favourable coverage in the established press is always a challenge for social movements because, as noted above, the mass media tend to focus on drama and violence rather than on the content of movement demands. Nevertheless, mass media coverage of the global justice movement aided the movement's spread, and some coverage helped to publicize movement concerns. In the case of the Zapatistas, the dramatic 1 January 1994 actions immediately captured media attention and brought the group to world attention. The movement's articulate and charismatic spokesperson, a masked leader calling himself Subcomandante Marcos, gave many press conferences and interviews and disseminated numerous manifestos and communiqués, attracting a great deal of international media attention (Bob, 2005: 127–34). The Jubilee 2000 debt campaign, with extensive involvement of churches and other organizations, also received a great deal of media coverage (Pianta, 2003: 252). And, despite the media's generally negative reporting of disruptive public protests, coverage of movement issues in the 1999 Seattle protests was fairly extensive, owing to factors such as the novelty of the protests, then-President Clinton's statements of support for some movement demands, and the presence of unions and church organizations, which were deemed "credible media sources" (Bennett, 2003: 162). In the case of OWS, traditional mass media initially ignored the protests and later employed negative frames, but nevertheless remained important, along with social media, in eventually spreading news of the movement (DeLuca, Lawson, and Sun, 2010). Despite problems with coverage, mass media reports continue to attract people to the movement. For example, a survey of German protesters against the Iraq War in 2003 found that, among the one or more sources of information they reported, about 55 per cent heard of the demonstrations through newspapers, about 51 per cent heard through radio or television, and only about 11 per cent learned of the protest through the Internet (Rucht, 2005: 82). In a study of Australian anti-capitalist activists, twice as many saw the mainstream mass media as central to recruitment as saw the Internet as a way to expand the movement (Bramble and Minns, 2005). Moreover, the successes of movements like the Arab Spring, which require high-risk activism, are still dependent on established networks and social movement organizations (Brym et al., 2014) as well as resources. Even less risky mobilization, as in the Maple Spring, still relies on networks and resources. The actions of Quebec students, for example, were supported by older leftist organizations and unions, which helped organize and legitimize student grievances.

Movement Strategies and Outcomes

Global movements for social justice have experienced significant success, but face strategic difficulties in achieving their goals. Among the successes, large demonstrations at the meetings of international financial institutions and governmental groups have put new concerns on the public agenda. Activists have articulated a critique of neoliberal policies, created linkages among struggles around the world, and increased public awareness of the role of international trade and monetary policies in problems such as the exploitation of workers and the environment. The various movements and organizations that make up what has come to be called the global justice movement used a combination of political strategies and new cultural forms in their attempts to challenge global capitalism. Nevertheless, the movement faces major difficulties in maintaining coalitions, agreeing on solutions to the problems identified, and devising strategies that have a real impact.

The creation of a master frame opposing the neoliberal policies of state and institutional actors is, as we have seen, an important accomplishment of the movement. In combination with the Internet, counter-summits—known as parallel summits or People's Summits, held alongside international conferences such as the WTO's and G8's—are an innovative tactic for developing the critique of neoliberalism and crafting documents such as *Alternatives for the Americas* in response to the FTAA proposal. Through this process, the movement created a master frame with the "breadth and capacity to absorb and accommodate the variety of movement and region specific frames that had spurred collective action against neoliberal agreements and institutions" (Ayres, 2005: 18). Protests against neoliberal targets, such as the WTO in Seattle in 1999 and the FTAA negotiations in Quebec City in 2001, involved parallel summits as well as blockades, teach-ins, street theatre, rallies, and marches. The protests and counter-summits generated numerous discussions, position papers, and proposals for further action. The World Social Forums, held in most years since 2001, have attracted large numbers of participants and served to expand the movement geographically, involving increasing numbers of participants from the global South and helping to build a transnational collective identity (J. Smith, 2008).

While movement frames and tactics clearly mobilized the movement, it is less clear how much impact they had on targets. Part of the difficulty is that it is easier for the movement to articulate a critique of international institutions and policies than to propose workable solutions. As Ayres (2005: 20) argues, movement activists have generally agreed on a "diagnostic frame" that focuses on the shortcomings of neoliberalism, but they had more difficulty agreeing on a "prognostic frame" that would direct challenges to neoliberalism and present alternatives. Instead, a variety of different solutions were proposed, ranging from reform of institutions such as the WTO to a complete dismantling of global capitalism. Through the WSF process, however, the movement continues to generate new campaigns and alternatives to neoliberalism and global capitalism, the latter including local economic initiatives such as community-supported agriculture and co-operatives (J. Smith, 2008: 220–1).

The Seattle protests and others that followed did have some impact in altering the agendas of international institutions and intergovernmental meetings and making them more inclusive and open to public scrutiny. As a result of large-scale protests, some world leaders called for greater openness in the process of trade negotiations and other forms of global decision-making. For example, then-US president Bill Clinton met with WTO protesters in Seattle to hear the concerns of farmers and others about world trade liberalization, and in a speech afterwards, he said that people were protesting in part because they have never been allowed inside WTO deliberations. Similarly, the Canadian international trade minister at the time, said in a statement during the Seattle protests that it was time to include groups that had been shut out in the past (*National Post*, 30 November 1999). The agendas of various intergovernmental bodies targeted by protesters were also affected. For example, the G8 meeting in Genoa, Italy, in July 2001 included the issues of AIDS and African development on its agenda and invited addresses by the South African president and the head of the World Health Organization in an attempt to show concern for a broad range of global issues (*Gazette*, 20 July 2001). Public opinion in Europe and North America also showed strong support for movement positions, and in response, leaders of the G8 made some concessions on the issues of AIDS and debt relief (*Gazette,* 19 July 2001). Transnational NGOs waged a successful campaign targeted at pharmaceutical companies to win access in HIV/AIDS drugs (Olesen, 2006). Moreover, a decade after the Seattle protests, movement claims about global inequality and problems with free markets had diffused widely; activists protesting at the G20 summit in London in 2009 found "their arguments echoed, however insincerely, by prime ministers, presidents and CEOs" (Kingsnorth 2009).

Despite progress in spreading movement concerns and raising issues of accountability and democratic process with regard to international institutions and intergovernmental bodies, however, many activists began to question the value of ongoing demonstrations at international meetings—which some activists derided as "summit hopping." Policing of protests had become increasingly effective in curbing demonstrations with escalated use of force, despite the largely non-violent orientation of movement activists (della Porta et al., 2006: Ch. 6). After 9/11, a number of international meetings were held at remote locations that were inaccessible to protesters (e.g., the 2002 meeting of the G8 in Kananaskis, Alberta). Although protests and parallel summits continue to be held at the sites of international meetings, simultaneous events are also organized around the world, and activists continue to work on local and national as well as global campaigns. While searching for a long-term global strategy, activists mounted campaigns against corporate abuses of workers, against environmentally destructive projects, and in support of fair trade policies.

One of the most promising strategies of the global justice movement involves the targeting of corporations that symbolize the abuses of global capitalism. Anti-sweatshop, living wage, and fair trade movements picked up steam in the 1990s as labour unions, students, religious groups, and community organizations attempted to counter the negative effects of global capitalism on workers. In the United States, living wage campaigns led by unions and community organizations convinced a number of cities and counties to pass "living wage" legislation requiring private-sector firms with government business to provide wages above the federal minimum wage (Levi et al., 2004). Activists also pushed for a "global living wage" that would pay workers enough to allow them to live at an adequate local standard of living (Shaw, 1999). In Canada, anti-poverty movements and their allies have focused on raising provincial minimum wages. The fair trade movement, meanwhile, has flourished in countries around the world, co-ordinated by networks such as the World Fair Trade Organization (www.wfto.com). The movement works to secure fair prices for the goods of economically disadvantaged producers and to promote gender equity, environmental sustainability, and safe working conditions.

The anti-sweatshop movement, backed by unions, churches, students, and other supporters, is active in a number of industrialized countries. The movement encourages consumer boycotts of products produced in sweat-shops, pressures corporations to adopt codes of conduct for their suppliers, and attempts to monitor their compliance. In the 1990s, university stu-dents, co-ordinated by groups such as United Students against Sweatshops (USAS) in the United States and the Ethical Trading Action Group (ETAG) in Canada, pressured their universities to adopt the policy that clothing with university logos be produced in "no-sweat" conditions (Cravey, 2004; Ross, 2005). Canadian author and activist Naomi Klein provided one source of inspiration for anti-corporate activity among students and others with her book *No Logo* (1999), which analyzed the spread of brand names (e.g., Coca-Cola, McDonald's, Nike, and Starbucks) and how the production of their products is related to the exploitation of workers and the environment. Because their images are so important to them, corporations are vulnerable to attacks on their brands; thus activists target well-known corporate brands to call attention to issues of working conditions and trade practices.

In the early 1990s, activists launched one of the most significant anti-corporate campaigns ever, against Nike for sweatshop abuses by its sub-contractors in countries such as Indonesia (see Shaw, 1999, for a detailed account). As a major manufacturer of sports shoes and clothing and a company with a very positive image in North America, Nike represented an extremely important but difficult target for anti-sweatshop activists. Activists struggled for a number of years before managing to get some main-stream media coverage of Nike's abuses in publications such as the *New York Times*, no doubt aided by the extensive publicity created by revelations that the clothing line of talk-show host Kathie Lee Gifford was produced in Honduran sweatshops. Once the anti-Nike campaign received media pub-licity and benefited from the media know-how of organizations like the San Francisco-based human rights organization Global Exchange, it was able to build momentum. The campaign gained international support from unions, religious groups, students, and women's organizations, the latter playing an important role in publicizing abuses to the largely female labour force in sweatshops. The anti-Nike campaign was eventually able to secure some genuinely important concessions from Nike. Despite these conces-sions, however, and the blows to Nike's image inflicted by the campaign, organizations such as Global Exchange continued to monitor Nike practi-ces (ibid., 93).

Beginning in 2003, unions and other groups called for a boycott of Coca-Cola, accusing the company of international human rights, labour, and environmental abuses (Blanding, 2006). As part of this campaign, a number of unions and universities banned Coke and activists protested at stockholder meetings and sports events where Coke was sold. Although companies such as Nike and Coke responded to protesters with announce-ments of new workplace standards—and advertising campaigns to refur-bish their images—long-term, persistent campaigns are required to produce real and lasting change in corporate practices. Extensive resources are also needed to maintain organizations such as the Workers Rights Consortium (WRC), which was created in 2000 to monitor factories. And, despite some efforts to provide "sweat-free" alternative products, the lack of easily access-ible alternatives remains an impediment to widespread consumer boycotts of companies with questionable human rights and environmental records (La Botz, 2002). More recently, anti-sweatshop activists have switched from a focus on economic boycotts to efforts to build coalitions with labour that can pressure companies to improve working conditions in their factor-ies (J. Smith, 2008: 223).

Anti-sweatshop and fair trade organizing helped to forge alliances among unions, environmentalists, students, and community activists. Such alliances are both an important accomplishment of the global justice move-ment and an ongoing challenge. Although the anti-neoliberalism frame cre-ates some common ground among the different movements that make up the global justice movement, many ideological and strategic differences exist within the movement. These include differences over whether to reform or abolish international institutions and conflicts over tactics. Violence and the unruly tactics of some anarchists at protest events have created internal conflict, particularly after the 2001 terrorist attacks, when some of the more moderate groups in the movement were anxious to distance themselves from any form of violence. Different elements of the global justice movement also have different types of constituents and varying concerns. Although much was made of the "blue–green" alliance that seemed to emerge with the Seattle protests, symbolized by the image of "Teamsters and Turtles" com-ing together, coalition work between unions and environmentalists was not terribly extensive (Gould et al., 2005). After Seattle, environmental con-cerns became less central to the movement than social justice and global inequality themes, but to attract a broad constituency, the movement needs to develop an inclusive discourse and ideology that includes environmental concerns (Buttel and Gould, 2005). At the 2009 protests against the G20 summit in London, concerns about climate change were again linked to economic justice as activists pushed for a "Green New Deal" in response to the world economic crisis (Kingsnorth, 2009: 30). In 2010, large demon-strations at the G20 meetings in Toronto also made connections among a wide range of concerns, including human rights and environmental issues.

The global justice movement has clearly enjoyed some successes, but it continues to be divided over its political and organizational direction. Pleyers (2009) notes that the movement remains "more united in what it has been against than what it should now be for" and identifies three different ideas about how the movement should go forward. The first is the "local approach," in which activists focus on participatory self-government, following the example of the Zapatistas, or engage in local sustainability and "critical consumption" initiatives. The second is the "advocacy approach," in which activists participate in single-issue networks around issues such as the protection of water supplies from privatization that can then be used to explore larger concerns about public goods, the role of corporations, and efficiency of the public sector. The third is the "state approach," in which the movement supports the efforts of progressive government leaders to implement, for example, social programs favouring the poor. Pleyers argues that these approaches might be combined in a shared approach and suggests that the WSF can play an important role in allowing activists to formulate such a strategy.

The Occupy movement, part of the more recent global wave of democracy and social justice movements, also met with some success. The dismantling of the camps left networks of activists and some ongoing activities, even though the movement was not able to sustain widespread mobilization (Gitlin, 2013; Calhoun, 2013). Although the mass media initially ignored OWS, the movement eventually garnered extensive coverage and, as numerous commentators noted, the movement had the important impact of bringing discussion of inequality back into public discourse and influencing debate in the 2012 presidential election. Moreover, the Occupy movement was able to avoid reliance on the mass media by communicating directly to participants and by using social media, thereby avoiding "the error of making media attention the goal rather than one of many tactics in the service of a goal" (Sobieraj, 2011: 10). Despite its decline as a publicly visible movement, Occupy added to the networks, repertoire, and impact of a series of global movements for social and economic justice.

Conclusion

Global movements for social justice have generated some of the most exciting social movement activity since the decline of the protest cycle of the 1960s. Feminists, environmentalists, labour activists, students, community activists, and others joined together, in at least temporary coalitions, out of concern about the consequences of neoliberal economic policies and the practices of global capitalism. As a result of movement activities, public consciousness increased regarding the exploitation of women, workers, and the environment associated with these policies and practices, and international institutions and governmental bodies are subject to greater public scrutiny. Although large-scale demonstrations are sporadic, the movement diffused widely to many different venues, using a variety of strategies. New generations of activists, together with veterans of the movements of the 1960s, are continuing to use a repertoire of collective action to promote social change. New mobilizing structures such as the WSF, aided by the Internet and social media, have helped to maintain the movement, initiating new campaigns and providing educational space for people to learn about global issues and develop identities as transnational activists (J. Smith, 2008: 224). The extent to which the movement succeeds will depend on its ability to develop long-term campaigns offering solutions to the problems that global social justice activists have identified. As this chapter has shown, an international opportunity structure, together with movement frames, mobilizing structures, and collective action tactics, is central to that process.

Discussion Questions

1. How can collective action framing help to unite a "movement of movements" such as the global justice movement?

2. What are the central challenges facing transnational coalitions and how might these be resolved?

3. How do new waves of protest come into being and why do they decline? How much continuity is there between waves of protest such as the "Seattle cycle" and the "Occupy cycle"?

Suggested Readings

Ayres, Jeffrey M. 1998. *Defying Conventional Wisdom: Political Movements and Popular Contention against North American Free Trade*. Toronto: University of Toronto Press. This book provides a detailed history and political process analysis of the anti–free trade movement in Canada.

Castells, Manuel. 2012. *Networks of Outrage and Hope: Social Movements in the Internet Age*. Cambridge: Polity Press. This is a highly readable account of the recent wave of protests that included the Arab uprisings, the movement in Spain, and Occupy Wall Street.

Wood, Lesley. 2012. *Direct Action, Deliberation, and Diffusion: Collective Action After the WTO Protests in Seattle*. New York: Cambridge University Press. This is a systematic comparison of the spread of protest tactics after the "Battle in Seattle" and compares movements in Canada and the United States.

10 Conclusion: Social Movements and Social Change

The histories of Indigenous, women's, LGBT, environmental, and global justice movements provide but a few examples of the importance of social movements and collective action to social change. Social movements have had major impacts on social policies, cultural norms, and public opinion. They often profoundly affect the lives of movement participants and others who are touched by them. Social movement theories help to explain the extent to which movements are able to bring about social change and the nature of the obstacles they face in doing so. In this concluding chapter, we briefly revisit the successes and challenges of the movements discussed in the book in light of some of the theoretical ideas about social movements outlined in earlier chapters. We conclude by noting the ongoing challenges confronting social movements as they try to bring about social change.

Large-Scale Changes, Grievances, and Opportunities

All of the major theories of social movements point to the effects of large-scale socio-economic and political changes on the emergence and outcomes of social movements. Macro-level societal changes often create widespread grievances and political or cultural opportunities. Although grievances and opportunities alone do not mobilize collective action, they can be exploited by movement activists, who build on the organizational changes that accompany large-scale social changes. In the case of the American civil rights movement, economic changes and the resulting urbanization of southern blacks made it possible to organize a movement through the black churches. International and domestic political conditions, including the Cold War and the breakup of previous electoral alliances, created new political opportunities. Grievances had long existed, but there were now more opportunities for people to share them and new opportunities to be heard. Demographic changes were also important to the New Left student movement of the 1960s, since larger numbers of students were entering universities. In many ways, these students were privileged members of society who might not have been expected to have major grievances, but they were also part of a generation that was alarmed by nuclear arms proliferation, racism, and the Vietnam War. Once the cycle of protest of the 1960s was underway, new movements were inspired to mobilize.

Among the groups spurred by the protest cycle of the 1960s were Indigenous peoples, who responded to political opportunities through organizations such as the American Indian Movement (Nagel, 1996). In Canada their protests intensified in response to the political opportunities associated with a number of critical events, including the 1969 White Paper, which provided a common target for Indigenous groups with varying interests. Increased collective action then led to government responses, and these in turn created new political opportunities and increased available funding, which helped to generate national mobilization. The Constitution Act of 1982 and the 1987 Meech Lake Accord, which was defeated in 1990, provided further opportunities for the mobilization of Indigenous protest. Internationally, the United Nations created opportunities for worldwide mobilization of Indigenous peoples through forums such as the Working Group on Indigenous Populations, and more recently Indigenous issues have intersected with the women's movement and environmental activism.

Another movement spurred by the protest cycle of the 1960s was the women's movement, which was clearly aided by large-scale societal transformations such as shifts in labour markets and declining birth rates. Women's increased participation in the workforce and in higher education created new interests and grievances, and as women participated in more areas of social and political life, they experienced new forms of sexism in these arenas, which fuelled their participation in the women's movement. Women also found political opportunities in democratic politics as political parties came to value the women's vote. The women's movement in countries such as Canada and the United States made great advances, and in fact, its successes may partly explain the movement's lower visibility in recent years insofar that women have had fewer grievances. The maintenance of some second-wave groups and the rise of third-wave feminism, however, show that ongoing issues such as violence against women and women's reproductive rights continue to involve new generations of women in the feminist movement. Although a countermovement has opposed feminist gains on issues such as abortion, the opposition has also helped to keep the movement mobilized. Moreover, feminists in the North have increasingly joined feminists in the South in an expanded global women's movement.

Before the rise of gay liberation movements, LGBT people endured a great deal of repression and few obvious political opportunities, but cultural changes accompanying the protest cycle of the 1960s created greater public space for sexual minorities. In particular countries, political opportunities did come along with new developments, such as the adoption of the Charter of Rights and Freedoms in Canada. As in the case of the women's movement, strong opposition to the LGBT movement helped to further mobilize it, providing countermovement targets and opportunities for media exposure. In federal systems, such as the United States and Canada, political openings were provided at different levels of government in various states and provinces, whereas in more centralized systems, such as the United Kingdom, opportunities arose when sympathetic governments were in power. The creation of the European Union also brought political opportunities to Europe, where the movement has enjoyed a great deal of success in winning gay rights. In relatively tolerant countries such as Canada, the LGBT movement might, like the women's movement, be faced with perceptions that the battle has been won. Yet, ongoing struggles continue even in Canada, and international efforts to secure human rights for gay, lesbian, bisexual, and transgendered people are still needed, as violence and violations of human rights are common in many countries.

The environmental movement, like the other movements, built on the activism of the protest cycle rather than on clear political openings. Environmental threats created grievances that helped to stimulate a sense of urgency among the public in the 1960s and 1970s and that continue to arouse activists concerned with issues such as toxic waste, the destruction of forests, "dirty" and destructive energy sources (e.g., the Alberta tar sands and fracking for natural gas), and global warming. Public support has helped to create political openings, particularly in countries with successful Green parties, such as Germany. Large environmental organizations, which can boast extensive constituent support, have enjoyed some access to government officials, but they are criticized for being overly institutionalized and subject to co-optation by government and business interests. Large-scale economic structures, with their reliance on carbon-fuelled economic growth, are strong impediments to the movement's ability to deal with major environmental problems successfully. As the threats associated with climate change become more obvious, however, environmentalism is gaining momentum.

Expanding internationalism brought political opportunities for a new global justice movement, and neoliberal policies created new grievances around the world. By generating public support and some sympathy among elites, the movement was able to force some changes in the operation of international institutions and win some concessions from corporations. Widespread grievances and threats related to neoliberal policies helped to mobilize a transnational movement, but the movement faces major obstacles in tackling global capitalism and building more democratic and equitable political and economic structures. Other global social justice movements, such as the Occupy movement, continued to tackle these problems in response to the 2008 economic crisis and growing inequality. Such movements also tapped new technologies like the Internet and social media to create innovative tactics to challenge power holders.

Movement Organization and Strategy

Movements face different types of cultural and political contexts and varying opportunities. However, all opportunities must be perceived and movements have to interpret threats and grievances to mobilize people for collective action. Movements also have to use and develop mobilizing structures to bring potential constituents together and to remain mobilized over time. The agency of movement leaders and other activists is essential for effective organizing, framing, and strategizing. The protest cycle of the 1960s popularized a repertoire of strategies that appear over and over in subsequent social movements as activists engage in many contentious performances (Tilly, 2008). For example, movements continue to use mass demonstrations and street theatre, various types of teach-ins, and sit-ins (with creative variations such as "kiss-ins" by gay activists, "tree-sits" by environmentalists, and "die-ins," first by anti–nuclear war and later by AIDS activists). Activists from the sixties generation have continued to join with new generations of activists, most recently in global social justice movements. Some long-standing organizational structures have been maintained and new movement organizations have formed. Collective action frames, such as the civil rights master frame, have been adapted by various movements, and new frames, such as the master frame opposing neoliberalism and austerity measures, have been developed. The successes of movements depend on their ability to innovate strategies and frame grievances as well as to take advantage of political and cultural opportunities.

In the case of Indigenous protest, activist groups built on the frames and tactics of the 1960s as they called for "Red Power" and demanded justice by occupying spaces. Although some critical events were the result of government actions, these events did not automatically mobilize nationwide protest; the frames and tactics used by activists in response to such events were essential to the spread of the movement. Indigenous activists used both institutional tactics, such as lawsuits, and radical protest tactics to build new organizations and create national and international movements. In more recent years they have used social media and past treaties to spark the Idle No More movement and advocate for an investigation of murdered and missing Indigenous women and against environmental destruction of traditional lands.

The women's movement successfully transformed rape and domestic violence, once seen as private concerns, into political issues, framing "the personal as political." The movement targeted numerous types of authorities and issues and gained influence within many institutions, such as

universities and churches. Although many second-wave women's movement organizations declined, some remained active and new organizations
formed. Contemporary feminists have developed new cultural projects and
used new media for spreading movement ideas, including zines and websites. Globally, the women's movement organized through UN mobilizing
structures and developed international women's rights networks. Despite
the difficulties involved in creating international coalitions, the movement
has developed frames that unite feminists around problems such as poverty
and violence against women.

The LGBT movement adapted to the decline of the 1960s protest cycle
by building community structures and a collective identity that helped to
maintain the movement. Although the movement had difficulty pursuing
some of the liberationist goals of its early years, gay rights activists made
great gains by using a civil rights frame and a quasi-ethnic group identity
to pursue legal rights. New forms of activism, such as Queer Nation, helped
the movement expand to include more bisexual and transgender people.
With victories such as the right to marriage or civil unions in a number of
countries, the movement has had an important cultural influence. Finding
strategies to tackle repression in many countries around the world, however,
remains a major challenge for the movement.

The environmental movement has used a range of organizational forms
and strategies to pursue its goals, including large formalized organizations
capable of lobbying governments and decentralized radical groups able to
engage in risky direct-action tactics. The formalized organizations have
helped to maintain the movement over many years, and the radical groups
have prodded the movement to innovate strategically. Grassroots environmentalists have invigorated the movement with anti-logging blockades,
protest camps, and bike-ins to reclaim city streets from cars. Owing to the
urgency of climate change, formalized and grassroots organizations have
more and more incentive to work together, as they did to bring hundreds
of thousands of people to New York City for the People's Climate March
in 2014. Public support for environmentalism is strong, and consumer boycotts have at times been used effectively, but the movement faces obstacles
in attempting to change consumer lifestyles and in addressing complicated
issues through the mass media. The environmental movement also faces
countermovement opposition to lifestyle changes and corporate opposition
to the structural changes needed to address global warming and other major
issues. Environmentalists have formed alliances with unions and Indigenous
peoples and have worked to promote new understandings of sustainable
development in searching for solutions to environmental problems.

The global justice movement created a unifying collective action frame
that connected various types of problems and inequities with global capitalism and neoliberal economic policies. The movement made excellent use of

the Internet and social media to organize activists around the world. Although it is difficult to sustain global alliances, the movement created some durable coalitions and other mobilizing structures, such as independent media centres. The movement developed some innovative strategies, such as parallel summits, anti-sweatshop boycotts, and fair trade initiatives. Public awareness of issues associated with global economic policies increased as a result of its initiatives, but the movement struggled to maintain its momentum and to come up with workable solutions to the large-scale problems identified. The movement also faces the challenge of maintaining the interest of local activists during lulls in global campaigns. New social justice movements such as the Occupy movement have emerged around the world, continuing to struggle for social and economic equality.

Conclusion

Social movements help to bring about many political and cultural transformations, but they also face numerous challenges in effecting change. Movements typically confront powerful adversaries and long-standing structural arrangements, and they rely on cultural and political openings to afford the possibility of success. In democratic polities, mobilization of public support helps movements influence government officials and other elites. The traditional mass media are critical in reaching new supporters, but movements have to use dramatic tactics and attractive packages to get their messages conveyed through it. The use of new communication technologies, such as smart phones and social media, are increasingly important to social movements and help them broadcast their messages unfiltered by news agencies and other power holders. Coalitions of different types of constituents strengthen movements, but they are difficult to form and maintain. Movements need leadership and vision in order to create the collective action frames, organizational vehicles, and strategies and tactics necessary for ongoing and effective campaigns. Despite the many obstacles facing social movements, the movements discussed in this book provide examples of how significant change can be achieved through collective action.

Notes

Chapter 5

1. Dickason (2002: 375–6) notes that anthropologist Harry B. Hawthorn was appointed by the federal government in 1963 to study and report on the social, educational, and economic conditions of Canada's Aboriginal peoples. His report appeared in 1966, listing 151 recommendations, one of which emphasized that Canadian Indians were Canadian citizens "plus"—that is, they also had additional Aboriginal rights.
2. This organization was also referred to as the Indian and Eskimo Association in a number of documents.
3. Corporal Marcel Lemay was the Sûreté du Québec officer who lost his life during the Oka standoff.
4. Some sources cite him as Lyall James. It is unclear which spelling is accurate.

Chapter 7

1. Much scholarship (e.g., Adam, 1995; Armstrong, 2002; Engel, 2001; Raeburn, 2004; Rayside, 1998; Smith, 1999) focuses on the efforts of the "gay and lesbian movement" to advance the rights of sexual minorities because, historically, gay and lesbian identity-based activism became dominant in the 1970s and remains important (cf. Armstrong, 2002: xix; Engel, 2001: xii–xiii). However, LGBT is now widely used to include lesbian, gay, bisexual, and transgender people and the latter two groups are increasingly active in the movement. We use LGBT to refer to the movement generally, while using "gay and lesbian" when more historically accurate.

Chapter 9

1. The Group of Eight, known as the G8, is an annual gathering of the heads of eight major industrialized democracies—Canada, France, Germany, Italy, Japan, Russia, the United Kingdom, and the United States. The group began as the G6 in 1975, becoming the G7 with the addition of Canada in 1976 and the G8 with the addition of Russia in 1997.

Glossary

abeyance A period in which a movement is not highly visible or very active but is maintained by an organization or other processes (Taylor, 1989).

adherents Those who believe in a cause and want to see movement goals achieved.

beneficiary constituents Aggrieved persons or groups that stand to benefit from the successes of a movement.

bureaucratization (formalization) Characteristic of movement organizations with established procedures for decision-making, a developed division of labour, explicit criteria for membership, and rules governing subunits such as standing committees or chapters.

bystander public A public that defines issues from a bystander's perspective but may become involved in a conflict.

centralization Characteristic of movement organizations in which there is a single centre of decision-making power.

charivari A traditional form of collective action directed towards individuals who have transgressed community norms.

claim-making performances Public gatherings of collective actors who use familiar tactics in making claims on the interests of targets (Tilly, 2008).

collective action frames Interpretations of issues and events that inspire and legitimate collective action.

collective behaviour theory A theoretical approach to social movements that focuses on the grievances or strains that are seen as leading to collective behaviours outside of established institutions and politics.

collective campaign An "aggregate of collective events or activities that appear to be oriented toward some relatively specific goal or good, and that occur within some proximity in space and time" (Marwell and Oliver, 1984: 12).

collective good A public good that cannot be withheld from any members of a group or population regardless of whether or not they work to achieve it.

collective identity A sense of shared experiences and values connecting individuals to movements and making them feel capable of effecting change through collective action.

conscience constituents Persons or groups who contribute to movements but do not personally benefit from their achievements.

constituents Supporters who contribute resources to a movement.

contentious politics Episodic public interactions of claim-makers and their targets, typically government authorities, based on claims related to the interests of social movement actors or other claim-makers; includes both *contained contention* by established political actors and *transgressive contention*, which involves at least some "newly self-identified political actors" and/or "innovative collective action" by at least some parties (McAdam et al., 2001: 7–8).

countermovement A "set of opinions and beliefs in a population opposed to a social movement" (McCarthy and Zald, 1977: 1217–18).

critical events Events that focus the attention of movement supporters, members of the public, and authorities on particular issues, creating threats and opportunities that influence movement mobilization and outcomes.

cultural opportunity structure Elements of cultural environments, such as ideologies, that facilitate and constrain collective action.

cycle of contention (protest cycle) A period of heightened conflict when a number of social movements are mobilized and engaged in collective action.

diffusion The spread of forms of contention from one site to others.

discourse analysis Textual analysis of language and meanings in rhetoric and documents.

discursive opportunity structure Factors, such as cultural context and mass media norms, that shape movement discourse.

externalization "[T]he vertical projection of domestic claims onto international institutions or foreign actors" (Tarrow, 2005: 32).

formalization See **bureaucratization.**

frame bridging Extension of collective action frames to connect together the concerns of different groups or movements.

framing perspective Emphasizes the role of movements in constructing cultural meanings. Movement leaders and organizations frame issues in particular ways to identify injustices, attribute blame, propose solutions, and motivate collective action.

free rider problem The problem of getting individuals to participate in social movements or other collective action when they will reap the benefits of the collective action regardless of their personal participation or contributions.

global framing The use of international symbols in the framing of domestic issues.

ideologically structured action Activities inspired by or promoting movement ideology that take place in everyday life and within organizations and institutions.

initiator movement A movement that comes early in a cycle of protest and demonstrates to others that protest tactics can be used effectively.

institutionalization The tendency of movement organizations that survive over many years to develop bureaucratic structures, rely on professional staff, and cultivate relations with government officials and other elites.

internalization A "response to foreign or international pressures within domestic politics" (Tarrow, 2005: 32).

internationalism The "structure of relations among states, non-state actors, and international institutions, and the opportunities this produces for actors to engage in collective action at different levels of this system" (Tarrow, 2005: 25).

international opportunity structure The international space created by international institutions.

mass society theory The theory that collective behaviour is a response to the social isolation that occurs in societies lacking in the secondary groups needed to bind people together and keep them attached to the mainstream society.

master frames Generic types of frames available for use by a number of different social movements.

material incentives Selective incentives that involve tangible rewards such as money.

mesomobilization actors Co-ordinating groups that integrate participating groups into a movement or campaign.

micromobilization actors The various groups that mobilize individuals to participate in protest.

mobilization The process whereby a group that shares grievances or interests gains collective control over tangible and intangible resources.

mobilizing structures The formal and informal networks, groups, and organizational vehicles that movements use to recruit participants and organize action campaigns.

movement entrepreneurs Social movement leaders who take the initiative to mobilize people with similar preferences into a movement or movement organization.

multi-organizational field The total set of organizations with which movement organizations might interact, including those that might either oppose or support the movement.

new social movement theory A theoretical approach focusing on the new types of social movements emerging in "post-industrial" or "advanced capitalist" society thought to differ in structure, type of constituents, and ideology from older movements.

political opportunities Features of the political environment that influence

movement emergence and success, including the extent of openness in the polity, shifts in political alignments, divisions among elites, the availability of influential allies, and repression or facilitation by the state.

political opportunity structure See **political opportunities**

political process theory A theoretical approach focusing on the interactions of social movement actors with the state and the role of political opportunities in the mobilization and outcomes of social movements.

professionalized movements Movements that have leaders who are paid to work full-time for movement organizations, that often attract conscience constituents rather than beneficiaries, and that rely on financial contributions rather than activism from large numbers of participants.

protest cycle See **cycle of contention.**

purposive incentives Selective incentives that come from the sense of satisfaction at having contributed to the attainment of a worthwhile cause.

rational choice theory A theoretical approach that focuses on the costs and benefits of collective action for individuals.

recruitment The process of getting individuals to commit resources such as time, money, and skills to a movement.

relative deprivation theory A theory that collective behaviour is most likely when conditions start to improve and expectations rise, but the rate of improvement does not match expectations and people feel deprived relative to others.

repertoire of collective action The limited set of protest forms familiar during a given time.

resource mobilization theory A theoretical approach focusing on the resources, organization, and opportunities needed for social movement mobilization and collective action.

resources The tangible and intangible assets available to social movement organizations and other actors.

scale shift The shifting of co-ordination of collective action to a different level.

selective incentives Benefits available exclusively to those who participate in collective action.

social movement Alternatively defined as "collective challenges, based on common purposes and social solidarities, in sustained interaction with elites, opponents, and authorities" (Tarrow, 1998: 4) or "a set of opinions and beliefs in a population which represents preferences for changing some elements of the social structure and/or reward distribution of a society" (McCarthy and Zald, 1977: 1217–18).

social movement community Networks of political movement organizations, individuals, cultural groups, alternative institutions, and institutional supporters in a social movement.

social movement industry The collection of social movement organizations within a movement.

social movement organization (SMO) A "complex, or formal, organization which identifies its goals with the preferences of a social movement or a countermovement and attempts to implement those goals" (McCarthy and Zald, 1977: 1218).

social movement sector All of the social movement industries in a society.

solidary incentives Selective incentives that come from associating with a group.

spinoff movement A movement that comes late in a protest cycle, modelled on earlier movements.

symbolic interactionism A social-psychological theory that focuses on the ways in which actors construct meanings through social interaction.

transnational coalition formation The creation of a network or coalition among actors from different countries.

References

Ackland, Robert, and Mathieu O'Neil. 2011. "Online Collective Identity: The Case of the Environmental Movement," *Social Networks* 33, 3: 177–90.

Adam, Barry D. 1995. *The Rise of a Gay and Lesbian Movement*, rev. edn. New York: Twayne.

Adamson, Nancy, Linda McPhail, and Margaret Briskin. 1988. *Feminist Organizing for Change: The Contemporary Women's Movement in Canada*. Toronto: Oxford University Press.

Adkin, Laurie E. 1992. "Counter-Hegemony and Environmental Politics in Canada," in William K. Carroll, ed., *Organizing Dissent*. Toronto: Garamond Press, 135–56.

———. 1998. *Politics of Sustainable Development: Citizens, Unions and the Corporations*. Montreal: Black Rose Books.

AFN (Assembly of First Nations). 2007. "Questions and Answers: National Day of Action." http://www.afn.ca/nda/q-a.htm.

———. 2011. *Assembly of First Nations: Our Story*. http://www.afn.ca/index.php. en.about-afn/our-story.

Agyeman, Julian, Peter Cole, Randolph Haluza-Delay, and Pat O'Riley, eds. 2009. *Speaking for Ourselves: Environmental Justice in Canada*. Vancouver: UBC Press.

Alfred, Taiaiake. 1999. *Peace, Power, Righteousness: An Indigenous Manifesto*. Toronto: Oxford University Press.

Almeida, Paul. 2003. "Opportunity Organizations and Threat-Induced Contention: Protest Waves in Authoritarian Settings," *American Journal of Sociology* 109, 2: 345–400.

———. 2008. *Waves of Protest: Popular Struggle in El Salvador, 1925–2005*. Minneapolis: University of Minnesota Press.

Amnesty International. 2004. *Stolen Sisters: A Human Rights Response to Discrimination and Violence Against Indigenous Women in Canada*. AI Index: AMR 20/003/2004.

Anaya, James. 2014. "Report of the Special Rapporteur on the Rights of Indigenous Peoples," United Nations Human Rights Commission. A/HRC/27/52/Add.2.

Ancelovici, Marcos. 2002. "Organizing against Globalization: The Case of ATTAC in France," *Politics & Society* 30, 3: 427–63.

Anderson, Benedict. 1991. *Imagined Communities: Reflections on the Origin and Spread of Nationalism*, rev. edn. New York: Verso.

Andrews, Kenneth T. 2004. *Freedom Is a Constant Struggle*. Chicago: University of Chicago Press.

Angus Reid Public Opinion. 2010. "Americans and Britons Becoming More Skeptical of Climate Change." http://www.visioncritical.com/category/global-opinions-and-trends.

Antrobus, Peggy. 2004. *The Global Women's Movement: Origins, Issues and Strategies*. London: Zed Books.

APTN (Aboriginal Peoples Television Network). 2014. "1,186 Murdered and Missing Indigenous Women Over Past 30 Years: RCMP," *APTN National News*. http://aptn.ca/news/2014/05/01/oppos-ition-renew-calls-national-inquiry-mis-sing-murdered-indigenous-women-girls/ [01/07/2014 10:06:34].

Armstrong, Elizabeth A. 2002. *Forging Gay Identities: Organizing Sexuality in San Francisco, 1950–1994*. Chicago: University of Chicago Press.

———, and Suzanna M. Crage. 2006. "Movements and Memory: The Making of the Stonewall Myth," *American Sociological Review* 71: 724–51.

Austin, David. 2007. "All Roads Led to Montreal: Black Power, the Caribbean, and the Black Radical Tradition in Canada," *The Journal of African American History* 92, 4: 516–39.

Ayres, Jeffrey M. 1998. *Defying Conventional Wisdom: Political Movements and Popular Contention against North American Free Trade*. Toronto: University of Toronto Press.

———. 1999. "From the Streets to the Internet: The Cyber-Diffusion of Contention," *Annals, Academy of Political and Social Sciences* 566: 132–43.

———. 2004. "Framing Collective Action against Neoliberalism: The Case of the 'Anti-Globalization' Movement," *Journal of World-Systems Research* 10, 1: 11–34.

———. 2005. "From 'Anti-Globalization' to the Global Justice Movement: Framing Collective Action against Neoliberalism," in Podobnik and Reifer (2005: 9–27).

Barakso, Maryann. 2004. *Governing NOW.* Ithaca, NY: Cornell University Press.

Barker, Joanne. 2006. "Gender, Sovereignty, and the Discourse of Rights in Native Women's Activism," *Meridians: Feminism, Race, Transnationalism* 7, 1: 127–61.

Barker-Plummer, Bernadette. 2002. "Producing Public Voice: Resource Mobilization and Media Access in the National Organization for Women," *Journalism and Mass Communication Quarterly* 79, 1: 188–205.

Barrera, Jorge. 2013. "New Treaty Alliance to Demand Meeting with Harper," *Aboriginal Peoples Television Network (National News).* http://aptn.ca/ news/2013/07/18/new-treaty-alliance-to-demand-meeting-with-harper/.

Barker-Plummer, Bernadette. 2002. "Producing Public Voice: Resource Mobilization and Media Access in the National Organization for Women," *Journalism & Mass Communication Quarterly* 79: 188–205.

Bashevkin, Sylvia. "Free Trade and Canadian Feminism: The Case of the National Action Committee on the Status of Women," *Canadian Public Policy* 15, 4: 363–75.

1998. *Women on the Defensive: Living through Conservative Times.* Toronto: University of Toronto Press.

———. 2009. *Women, Power, Politics: The Hidden Story of Canada's Unfinished Democracy.* Don Mills, ON: Oxford University Press.

Baumgardner, Jennifer, and Amy Richards. 2000. *Manifesta: Young Women, Feminism and the Future.* New York: Farrar, Straus and Giroux.

Beder, Sharon. 2002. *Global Spin: The Corporate Assault on Environmentalism,* rev. edn. Totnes, UK: Green Books.

Bégin, Monique. 1992. "The Royal Commission on the Status of Women in Canada: Twenty Years Later," in Constance Backhouse and David H. Flaherty, eds, *Challenging Times: The Women's Movement in Canada and the United States.* Montreal & Kingston: McGill-Queen's University Press, 21–38.

Bégin-Caouette, Olivier and Glen A. Jones. 2014. "Student Organization in Canada and Quebec's 'Maple Spring'," *Studies in Higher Education* 39, 3: 412–25.

Bell, Joyce M. 2014. *The Black Power Movement and American Social Work.* New York: Columbia University Press.

Benford, Robert D. 1993. "Frame Disputes within the Nuclear Disarmament Movement," *Social Forces* 71, 3: 677–701.

———, and David A. Snow. 2000. "Framing Processes and Social Movements: An Overview and Assessment," *Annual Review of Sociology* 26: 611–39.

Bennett, W. Lance. 2003. "Communicating Global Activism: Strengths and Vulnerabilities of Networked Politics," *Information, Communication & Society* 6, 2: 143–68.

———, and Alexandra Segerberg. 2013. *The Logic of Connective Action: Digital Media and the Personalization of Contentious Politics.* New York: Cambridge University Press.

Berger, Dan. 2010. "Introduction: Exploding Limits in the 1970s," in D. Berger, ed., *The Hidden 1970s: Histories of Radicalism.* New York: Rutgers, 1-18.

Bernstein, Mary. 1997. "Celebration and Suppression: The Strategic Uses of Identity by the Lesbian and Gay Movement," *American Journal of Sociology* 103, 3: 531–65.

Beyerlein, Kraig, and John R Hipp. 2006. "From Pews to Participation: The Effect of Congregation Activity and Context on Bridging Civic Engagement," *Social Problems* 53, 1: 97–117.

Biro, Andrew. 2010. "Environmental Prospects in Canada," *Environmental Politics* 19: 303–9.

Bisset, Kevin. 2014. "Debate Over Access to Abortion in Prince Edward Island Intensifies," *Globe and Mail.* http://www. theglobeandmail.com/news/national/ debate-over-access-to-abortion-in-prince-edward-island-intensifies/ article18877480/.

Black, Naomi. 1993. "The Canadian Women's Movement: The Second Wave," in Sandra Burt, Lorraine Code, and Lindsay Dorney, eds, *Changing Patterns: Women in Canada*, 2nd edn. Toronto: McClelland & Stewart, 151–75.

Blais, Melissa and Francis Dupis-Déri. 2012. "Masculinism and the Antifeminist Countermovement," *Social Movement Studies* 11, 1: 21–39.

Blanding, Michael. 2006. "The Case against Coca-Cola," *Nation* 282, 17: 13–17.

Blee, Kathleen M., and Verta Taylor. 2002. "Semi-Structured Interviewing in Social Movement Research," in Klandermans and Staggenborg (2002: 92–117).

Blumer, Herbert. 1951. "Collective Behavior," in A.M. Lee, ed., *Principles of Sociology*. New York: Barnes and Noble, 166–222.

Bob, Clifford. 2005. *The Marketing of Rebellion: Insurgents, Media, and International Activism*. New York: Cambridge University Press.

Bond, Patrick and Michael K. Dorsey. 2010. "Anatomies of Environmental Knowledge and Resistance: Diverse Climate Justice Movements and Waning Eco-Neoliberalism," *Journal of Australian Political Economy* 66: 286–316.

Bosso, Christopher J. 2005. *Environment, Inc.: From Grassroots to Beltway*. Lawrence: University Press of Kansas.

Boxer, Marilyn Jacoby. 1998. *When Women Ask the Questions: Creating Women's Studies in America*. Baltimore: John Hopkins University Press.

Bramble, Tom, and John Minns. 2005. "Whose Streets? Our Streets! Activist Perspectives on the Australian Anti-capitalist Movement," *Social Movement Studies* 4, 2: 105–21.

Branch, Taylor. 1988. *Parting the Waters: America in the King Years, 1954–63*. New York: Simon & Schuster.

Braungart, Margaret M. and Richard G. Braungart. 1991. "The Effects of the 1960s Political Generation on Former Left- and Right-Wing Youth Activist Leaders," *Social Problems* 38, 3: 297–315.

Brick, Philip, and R. McGreggor Cawley. 2008. "Producing Political Climate Change: The Hidden Life of US Environmentalism," *Environmental Politics* 17, 2: 200–18.

BBC (British Broadcasting Corporation). 2014. "Where is it Illegal to Be Gay?' *BBC News*. http://www.bbc.com/news/world-25927595.

Brodie, Janine, Shelley A.M. Gavigan, and Jane Jenson. 1992. *The Politics of Abortion*. Toronto: Oxford University Press.

Brown, Michael, and John May. 1991. *The Greenpeace Story*. New York: Dorling Kindersley.

Brown, Michael P. 1997. *Replacing Citizenship:* AIDS *Activism and Radical Democracy*. New York: Guilford Press.

Brownmiller, Susan. 1975. *Against Our Will: Men, Women, and Rape*. New York: Bantam Books.

Brulle, Robert J. 2000. *Agency, Democracy, and Nature: The U.S. Environmental Movement from a Critical Theory Perspective*. Cambridge, Mass.: MIT Press.

———. 2015. "The US National Climate Change Movement," in *Changing Climate Politics*, edited by Yael Wolinsky-Nahmias. Los Angeles: Sage/CQ Press, 146–70

———, and J. Craig Jenkins. 2006. "Spinning Our Way to Sustainability," *Organization & Environment* 19, 1: 82–7.

———, and David N. Pellow. 2006. "Environmental Justice: Human Health and Environmental Inequalities," *Annual Review of Public Health* 27: 103–24.

Brushett, Kevin. 2009. "Making Shit Disturbers: The Selection and Training of the Company of Young Canadian Volunteers, 1965–1970,' in M. A. Palaeologu [ed], *The Sixties in Canada: A Turbulent and Creative Decade*. Montreal: Blackrose, 246–69.

Bryner, Gary. 2008. "Failure and Opportunity: Environmental Groups in the US Climate Change Policy," *Environmental Politics* 17, 2: 319–36.

Brym, Robert, Melisa Godbout, Andreas Hoffbauer, Gabe Menard, and Tony Huiqan Zhang. 2014. "Social Media in the 2011 Egyptian Uprising," *The British Journal of Sociology* 65, 2: 266–92.

Brysk, Alison, and Carol Wise. 1997. "Liberalization and Ethnic Conflict in Latin America," *Studies in Comparative International Development* 32, 2: 76–104.

Bucek, Jan, and Brian Smith. 2000. "New Approaches to Local Democracy: Direct Democracy Participation and the 'Third Sector'," *Environment and Planning C: Government and Policy* 18: 3–16.

Buechler, Steven M. 1990. *Women's Movements in the United States*. New Brunswick, NJ: Rutgers University Press.

———. 1995. "New Social Movement Theories," *Sociological Quarterly* 36, 3: 441–64.

———. 2000. *Social Movements in Advanced Capitalism*. New York: Oxford University Press.

———. 2002. "Toward a Structural Approach to Social Movements," *Research in Political Sociology* 10: 1–45.

———. 2011. *Understanding Social Movements: Theories from the Classical Era to the Present*. Boulder, CO: Paradigm Publishers.

Burstein, Paul, Rachel L. Einwohner, and Jocelyn A. Hollander. 1995. "The Success of Political Movements: A Bargaining Perspective," in J.C. Jenkins and B. Klandermans, eds, *The Politics of Social Protest*. Minneapolis: University of Minnesota Press, 275–95.

Bush, Evelyn, and Pete Simi. 2001. "European Farmers and Their Protests," in D. Imig and S. Tarrow, eds, *Contentious Europeans*. Lanham, Md: Rowman & Littlefield, 97–121.

Bush, Rod. 1999. *We Are Not What We Seem: Black Nationalism and Class Struggle in the American Century*. New York: New York University Press.

Butler, Jennifer S. 2006. *Born Again: The Christian Right Globalized*. London: Pluto Press.

Buttel, Frederik, and Kenneth Gould. 2005. "Global Social Movements at the Crossroads: An Investigation of Relations between the Anti-corporate Globalization and Environmental Movements," in Podobnik and Reifer (2005: 139–55).

CAFE (Canadian Association for Equality) 2014. Mandate. http://equalitycanada.com/about/mandate/.

Cairns, Alan C. 2000. *Citizens Plus: Aboriginal Peoples and the Canadian State*. Vancouver: UBC Press.

Calhoun, Craig. 1993. "'New Social Movements' of the Early Nineteenth Century," *Social Science History* 17, 3: 385–427.

———. 2013. "Occupy Wall Street in Perspective," *British Journal of Sociology* 64, 1: 26–37.

Canadian Heritage. 2005. "Evaluation of the Aboriginal Representative Organizations Program."

Canadian Press. 1951. "Calls Indian Bill Dictatorial," *Globe and Mail*, 3 Mar., 8.

———. 1972. "Iroquois Says Ottawa Seeks to Split Indians," *Globe and Mail*, 27 July, 9.

———. 1980. "Violence Is Last Thing They Want, Indians Say of Ottawa Journey," *Globe and Mail*, 27 Nov., 12.

———. 1981. "Native Group Reviewing BNA Stand," *Globe and Mail*, 21 Apr., 8.

———. 2014. "Report of 1,000 Murdered or Missing Aboriginal Women Spurs Call for Inquiry." http://www.cbc.ca/news/politics/report-of-1-000-murdered-or-missing-aboriginal-women-spurs-calls-for-inquiry-1.2628372.

Carden, Maren Lockwood. 1974. *The New Feminist Movement*. New York: Russell Sage Foundation.

Cardinal, Harold. 1999. *The Unjust Society*. Vancouver: Douglas & McIntyre.

Carmin, Joann, and Deborah B. Balser. 2002. "Selecting Repertoires of Action in Environmental Movement Organizations," *Organization & Environment* 15, 4: 365–88.

Carroll, William K., and R.S. Ratner. 1995. "Old Unions and New Social Movements," *Labour/Le Travail* 35 (Spring): 195–221.

———. 1996. "Master Framing and Cross-Movement Networking in Contemporary Social Movements," *Sociological Quarterly* 37, 4: 601–25.

———. 1999. "Media Strategies and Political Projects: A Comparative Study of Social Movements," *Canadian Journal of Sociology* 24, 1: 1–34.

Carson, Clayborne. 1981. *In Struggle: sncc and the Black Awakening of the 1960s*. Cambridge, Mass.: Harvard University Press.

Carson, Rachel. 1962. *Silent Spring*. Boston: Houghton Mifflin.

Cartwright, John. 2003. "Environmental Groups, Ontario's Lands for Life Process and the Forest Accord'. *Environmental Politics* 12: 115–32.

Cassidy, Sean. 1992. "The Environment and the Media: Two Strategies for Challenging Hegemony," in J. Wasko and V. Mosco, eds, *Democratic Communications in the Information Age*. Toronto: Garamond Press, 159–74.

Castells, Manuel. 2004. *The Power of Identity*. Malden, Mass: Blackwell Pub.

———. 2007. "Communication, Power and Counter-power in the Network Society," *International Journal of Communications* 1: 238–66.

———. 2012. *Networks of Outrage and Hope: Social Movements in the Internet Age*. Polity Press.

Castle, Stephen, and Steven Erlanger. 2009. "Riots Erupt Near Bridge That Links 2 Countries," *New York Times*, 5 April.

Caute, David. 1988. *The Year of the Barricades: A Journey through 1968*. New York: Harper and Row.

Caven, Febna. 2013. "Being Idle No More: The Women Behind the Movement," *Cultural Survival* 37(1). http://www.culturalsurvival.org/publications/cultural-survival-quarterly/being-idle-no-more-women-behind-movement.

CBC (Canadian Broadcasting Corporation). 2006. "Caledonia Land Claim: Timeline." http://www.cbc.ca/news/background/caledonia-landclaim/index.html.

———. "Massive Student Tuition March Paralyzes Montreal," CBC *News*. http://www.cbc.ca/news/canada/montreal/massive-student-tuition-march-paralyzes-montreal-1.1165575.

———. 2014. "Environmentalists Stage Day of Action to Protest Pipelines," CBC *News*. http://www.cbc.ca/news/canada/montreal/environmentalists-stage-day-of-action-to-protest-pipelines-1.2638583.

Chafetz, Janet S., and Anthony G. Dworkin. 1986. *Female Revolt: The Rise of Women's Movements in World and Historical Perspective*. Totowa, NJ: Rowman & Littlefield.

Chappell, Lousie. 2000. "Interacting with the State: Feminist Strategies and Political Opportunities,' *International Feminist Journal of Politics* 2, 2: 244–75.

Chauncey, George. 2004. *Why Marriage?* New York: Basic Books.

Cherniak, Donna, and Allan Feingold. 1972. "Birth Control Handbook," in *Women Unite!* Toronto: Canadian Women's Educational Press, 109–13.

Churchill, David S. 2010. "Supa, Selma, and Stevenson: The Politics of Solidarity in the Mid-1960s Toronto," *Journal of Canadian Studies* 44, 2: 32–69.

Clément, Dominique. 2008. *Canada's Rights Revolution: Social Movements and Social Change, 1937–1982*. Vancouver: UBC Press.

Cleveland, John. 2009. "'Berkley North': Why Simon Fraser Had the Strongest 1960s Student Power Movement," in M. A. Palaeologu [ed] *The Sixties in Canada: A Turbulent and Creative Decade*. Montreal: Black Rose, 193–232.

Coates, Ken. 2000. *The Marshall Decision and Native Rights*. Montreal & Kingston: McGill-Queen's University Press.

Coleman, William D. 1984. *The Independence Movement in Quebec: 1945–1980*. Toronto: University of Toronto Press.

Collier, George A., and Jane F. Collier. 2005. "The Zapatista Rebellion in the Context of Globalization," *Journal of Peasant Studies* 32, 3 and 4: 450–60.

Connell, Robert W. 1990. "A Whole New World: Remaking Masculinity in the Context of the Environmental Movement," *Gender & Society* 4, 4: 452–78.

Conway, Janet M. 2004. *Identity, Place, Knowledge: Social Movements Contesting Globalization*. Halifax: Fernwood Publishing.

Corrigall-Brown, Catherine. 2012. *Patterns of Protest: Trajectories of Participation in Social Movements*. Stanford, CA: Stanford University Press.

Cornell, Stephen. 1988. *The Return of the Native: American Indian Political Resurgence*. New York: Oxford University Press.

Costain, Anne N. 1992. *Inviting Women's Rebellion: A Political Process Interpretation of the Women's Movement*. Baltimore: Johns Hopkins University Press.

Cravey, Altha J. 2004. "Students and the Anti-sweatshop Movement," *Antipode* 36, 2: 203–8.

Crossley, Nick. 2003. "From Reproduction to Transformation: Social Movement Fields and the Radical Habitus," *Theory, Culture, and Society* 20, 6: 43–68.

CTV. 2007. "Chiefs Want Railways to Shut Down on Day of Action." http://stressed.ctv.ca/CTVNews/Business/20070524/AFN_railways_070524/.

Cummings, Joan Grant. 2001. "From Natty Dreads to Grey Ponytails: The Revolution is Multi-generational," in Mitchell et al. (2001: 309–14).

Cuneo, Michael W. 1989. *Catholics against the State: Anti-abortion Protest in Toronto.* Toronto: University of Toronto Press.

Curtis, Russell L., Jr, and Louis Zurcher Jr. 1973. "Stable Resources of Protest Movements: The Multi-organizational Field," *Social Forces* 52: 53–61.

Dale, Stephen. 1996. *McLuhan's Children: The Greenpeace Message and the Media.* Toronto: Between the Lines.

Dalton, Russell J. 2005. "The Greening of the Globe? Cross-national Levels of Environmental Group Membership," *Environmental Politics* 14, 4: 441–59.

Davies, James C. 1962. "Toward a Theory of Revolution," *American Sociological Review* 27: 5–19.

———. 1971. *When Men Revolt and Why.* New York: Free Press.

Dayan, Daniel, and Elihu Katz. 1992. *Media Events: The Live Broadcasting of History.* Cambridge, Mass.: Harvard University Press.

Decima Research. 2007. "Environment on the Agenda," press release, 4 Jan.

della Porta, Donatella. 1995. *Social Movements, Political Violence, and the State.* Cambridge: Cambridge University Press.

———, Massimiliano Andretta, Lorenzo Mosca, and Herbert Reiter. 2006. *Globalization from Below: Transnational Activists and Protest Networks.* Minneapolis: University of Minnesota Press.

———, and Olivier Fillieule. 2004. "Policing Social Protest," in Snow et al. (2004: 217–41).

DeLuca, Kevin M., Sean Lawson, and Ye Sun. 2012. "Occupy Wall Street on the Public Screens of Social Media: The Many Framings of the Birth of a Protest Movement," *Communication, Culture & Critique* 5: 483–509.

D'Emilio, John. 1983. *Sexual Politics, Sexual Communities: The Making of a Homosexual Minority in the United States, 1940–1970.* Chicago: University of Chicago Press.

Devall, Bill. 1992. "Deep Ecology and Radical Environmentalism," in Riley E. Dunlap and Angela G. Mertig, eds, *American Environmentalism: The U.S. Environmental Movement, 1970–1990.* Philadelphia: Taylor and Francis, 51–62.

Diani, Mario. 1992. "The Concept of Social Movement," *Sociological Review* 40, 1: 1–25.

Dickason, Olive Patricia. 2002. *Canada's First Nations: A History of Founding Peoples from Earliest Times,* 3rd edn. Toronto: Oxford University Press.

Dickerson, Carrie A., and William J. Campbell. 2008. "Strange Bedfellows: Youth Activists, Government Sponsorship, and the Company of Young Canadians (CYC), 1965–1970," *European Journal of American Studies* 68: DOI: 10.4000/ejas.2862.

Doherty, Brian. 1999. "Paving the Way: The Rise of Direct Action against Road-Building and the Changing Character of British Environmentalism," *Political Studies* 47, 2: 275–91.

Dorf, Michael C., and Sidney Tarrow. 2014. "Strange Bedfellows: How an Anticipatory Countermovement Brought Same-Sex Marriage into the Public Arena," *Law & Social Inquiry* 39: 449–73.

Dowie, Mark. 1995. *Losing Ground: American Environmentalism at the Close of the Twentieth Century.* Cambridge, Mass.: MIT Press.

Downs, Anthony. 1972. "Up and Down with Ecology—The 'Issue-Attention Cycle'," *Public Interest* 28: 38–50.

Downton, James V., Jr, and Paul E. Wehr. 1991. "Peace Movements: The Role of Commitment and Community in Sustaining Member Participation," *Research in Social Movements, Conflicts and Change* 13: 113–34.

Duberman, Martin B. 1993. *Stonewall.* New York: Dutton.

Duchen, Claire. 1994. *Women's Rights and Women's Lives in France, 1944–1968.* New York: Routledge.

Dufour, Pascale, and Janet Conway. 2010. "Emerging Visions of Another World? Tensions and Collaboration at the Quebec Social Forum," *Journal of World-Systems Research* 16: 29–47.

Dufour, Pascale, and Isabelle Giraud. 2007a. "The Continuity of

Transnational Solidarities in the World March of Women, 2000 and 2005: A Collective Identity-Building Approach," *Mobilization* 12: 307–22.

———. 2007b. "Globalization and Political Change in the Women's Movement: The Politics of Scale and Political Empowerment in the World March of Women," *Social Science Quarterly* 88: 1152–73.

Dunlap, Riley E. 2006. "Show Us the Data," *Organization & Environment* 19, 1: 88–102.

———, and Richard York. 2008. "The Globalization of Environmental Concern and the Limits of the Postmaterialist Values Explan-ation: Evidence from Four Multinational Surveys," *Sociological Quarterly* 49: 529–63.

Dunlap, Riley E., and Aaron M. McCright. 2011. "Organized Climate Change Denial," in J. S. Dryzek, R. B. Norgaard, and D. Schlosberg, eds, *Climate Change and Society*. New York: Oxford University Press, 144–60.

Earl, Jennifer. 2004. "The Cultural Consequences of Social Movements," in Snow et al. (2004: 508–30).

———, and Alan Schussman. 2003. "The New Site of Activism: On-Line Organizations, Movement Entrepreneurs, and the Changing Location of Social Movement Decision Making," *Research in Social Movements, Conflicts and Change* 24: 155–87.

———, and Katrina Kimport. 2011. *Digitally Enabled Social Change: Activism in the Internet Age*. Cambridge, MA: MIT Press.

Echols, Alice. 1989. *Daring to Be Bad: Radical Feminism in America, 1967–1975*. Minneapolis: University of Minnesota Press.

Edwards, Bob, and John D. McCarthy. 2004. "Resources and Social Movement Mobilization," in Snow et al. (2004: 116–52).

Egale. 2014. "About Egale.' *Egale*. http://egale.ca/about-egale/.

Engel, Stephen M. 2001. *The Unfinished Revolution: Social Movement Theory and the Gay and Lesbian Movement*. Cambridge: Cambridge University Press.

Enke, Anne. 2007. *Finding the Movement: Sexuality, Contested Space, and Feminist Activism*. Durham, NC: Duke University Press.

Environics Institute. 2013. *Focus Canada 2010: Public Opinion on the Record Serving the Public Interest*. Ottawa: Environics Institute.

Epstein, Barbara. 1991. *Political Protest and Cultural Revolution: Nonviolent Direct Action in the 1970s and 1980s*. Berkeley: University of California Press.

———. 2001. "What Happened to the Women's Movement?," *Monthly Review* 53, 1: 1–13.

Epstein, Steven. 1999. "Gay and Lesbian Movements in the United States: Dilemmas of Identity, Diversity, and Political Strategy," in B.D. Adam, J.W. Duyvendak, and A. Krouwel, eds, *The Global Emergence of Gay and Lesbian Politics*. Philadelphia: Temple University Press, 30–90.

Erwin, Lorna. 1993. "Neoconservatism and the Canadian Pro-family Movement," *Canadian Review of Sociology and Anthropology* 30, 3: 401–20.

Evans, Sara. 1979. *Personal Politics: The Roots of Women's Liberation in the Civil Rights Movement and the New Left*. New York: Vintage Books.

———. 2003. *Tidal Wave: How Women Changed America at Century's End*. New York: Free Press.

Eyerman, Ron, and Andrew Jamison. 1989. "Environmental Knowledge as an Organizational Weapon: The Case of Greenpeace," *Social Science Information* 28, 1: 99–119.

Deacon, Leith and Jamie Baxter. 2013. "No Opportunity to Say No: A Case Study of Procedural Environmental Injustice in Canada," *Journal of Environmental Planning and Management* 56, 5: 607–23.

Fairclough, Adam. 1987. *To Redeem the Soul of America: The Southern Christian Leadership Conference and Martin Luther King, Jr*. Athens: University of Georgia Press.

Ferree, Myra Marx . 2006. "Globalization and Feminism: Opportunities and Obstacles for Activism in the Global Arena," in M. Marx Feree and A.M. Tripp, eds, *Global Feminism: Transnational Women's Activism, Organizing, and Human Rights*. New York: New York University Press, 3–23.

————.William Anthony Gamson, Jürgen Gerhards, and Dieter Rucht. 2002. *Shaping Abortion Discourse: Democracy and the Public Sphere in Germany and the United States*. Cambridge: Cambridge University Press.

————, and Carol McClurg Mueller. 2004. "Feminism and the Women's Movement: A Global Perspective," in Snow et al. (2004: 576–607).

Fetner, Tina. "Working Anita Bryant: The Impact of Christian Anti-Gay Activism on Lesbian and Gay Movement Claims," *Social Problems* 48, 3: 411–28.

————.2008. *How the Religious Right Shaped Lesbian and Gay Activism*. Minneapolis: University of Minnesota Press.

Findlen, Barbara, ed. 2001. *Listen Up: Voices from the Next Feminist Generation*, 2nd edn. Emeryville, Calif.: Seal Press.

Fireman, Bruce, and William A. Gamson. 1979. "Utilitarian Logic in the Resource Mobilization Perspective," in M.N. Zald and J.D. McCarthy, eds, *The Dynamics of Social Movements: Resource Mobilization, Social Control, and Tactics*. Cambridge, Mass.: Winthrop, 8–44.

Flacks, Richard. 2005. "The Question of Relevance in Social Movement Studies," in D. Croteau, W. Hoynes, and C. Ryan, eds, *Rhyming Hope and History: Activists, Academics, and Social Movement Scholarship*. Minneapolis: University of Minnesota Press, 3–19.

Flanagan, Tom. 2000. *First Nations? Second Thoughts*. Montreal & Kingston: McGill-Queen's University Press.

Fleras, Augie, and Jean Leonard Elliott. 1992. *The "Nations Within": Aboriginal–State Relations in Canada, the United States, and New Zealand*. Toronto. Oxford University Press.

————. 2003. *Unequal Relations: An Introduction to Race and Ethnic Dynamics in Canada*, 4th edn. Toronto: Prentice-Hall.

Fligstein, Neil, and Doug McAdam. 2013. *A Theory of Fields*. New York: Oxford University Press.

————. 2011. "Toward a General Theory of Strategic Action Fields," *Sociological Theory* 29, 1: 1–26.

Francome, Colin. 1984. *Abortion Freedom: A Worldwide Movement*. Winchester, Mass.: Allen and Unwin.

Fraser, Ronald. 1988. *1968: A Student Generation in Revolt*. London: Chatto & Windus.

Freeman, Barbara M. 2001. *The Satellite Sex: The Media and Women's Issues in English Canada, 1966–1971*. Waterloo, Ont.: Wilfrid Laurier University Press.

Freeman, Jo. 1972. "The Tyranny of Structurelessness," in A. Koedt, E. Levine, and A. Rapone, eds, *Radical Feminism*. New York: Quadrangle Press, 285–99.

————. 1975. *The Politics of Women's Liberation*. New York: Longman.

————. 1979. "Resource Mobilization and Strategy: A Model for Analyzing Social Movement Organization Actions," in M.N. Zald and J.D. McCarthy, eds, *The Dynamics of Social Movements: Resource Mobilization, Social Control, and Tactics*. Cambridge, Mass.: Winthrop, 167–89.

Gagné, Marie-Anik. 1994. *A Nation within a Nation: Dependency and the Cree*. Montreal: Black Rose Books.

Gamson, Josh. 1989. "Silence, Death, and the Invisible Enemy: AIDS Activism and Social Movement 'Newness'," *Social Problems* 36, 4: 351–67.

Gamson, William A. 1990. *The Strategy of Social Protest*, 2nd edn. Belmont, Calif.: Wadsworth.

————. 1998. "Social Movements and Cultural Change," in Marco G. Giugni, Doug McAdam, and Charles Tilly, eds, *From Contention to Democracy*. Lanham, Md.: Rowman & Littlefield, 57–77.

————. 2004. "Bystanders, Public Opinion, and the Media," in Snow et al. (2004: 242–61).

————, and David S. Meyer. 1996. "Framing Political Opportunity," in McAdam et al. (1996: 275–90).

————, and Gadi Wolfsfeld. 1993. "Movements and Media as Interacting Systems," *Annals, Academy of Political and Social Science* 528: 114–25.

Gans, Herbert J. 1979. *Deciding What's News: A Study of CBS Evening News, NBC Nightly News, Newsweek and Time*. New York: Vintage Books.

Ganz, Marshall. 2000. "Resources and Resourcefulness: Strategic Capacity in the Unionization of California Agriculture, 1959–1966," *American Journal of Sociology* 105, 4: 1003–62.

Garrow, David J. 1986. *Bearing the Cross: Martin Luther King, Jr., and the Southern Christian Leadership Conference*. New York: Vintage Books.

Gazette (Montreal). 2001. "Protesters Make Dent in Agenda," 19 July.

————. 2001. "Unlikely Allies Descend on Italy," 20 July.

Gerhards, Jürgen, and Dieter Rucht. 1992. "Mesomobilization: Organizing and Framing in Two Protest Campaigns in West Germany," *American Journal of Sociology* 98, 3: 555–95.

Gerlach, Luther, and Virginia H. Hine. 1970. *People, Power, Change: Movements of Social Transformation*. Indianapolis: Bobbs-Merrill.

Gilchrist, Kristen. 2010. "Newsworthy' Victims?" *Feminist Media Studies* 10, 4: 373–90.

Gillham, Patrick F., and John A. Noakes. 2007. "'More Than a March in a Circle': Transgressive Protests and the Limits of Negotiated Management," *Mobilization* 12, 4: 341–57.

Gilmore, Stephanie. 2005. "Bridging the Waves: Sex and Sexuality in a Second Wave Organization," in Reger (2005: 97–116).

Giroux, Henry A. 2013. "The Quebec Student Protest Movement in the Age of Neoliberal Terror," *Social Identities: Journal for the Study of Race, Nation, and Culture* 19, 5: 515–35.

Gitlin, Todd. 1980. *The Whole World Is Watching: Mass Media and the Making of the New Left*. Berkeley: University of California Press.

————. 1987. *The Sixties: Years of Hope, Days of Rage*. New York: Bantam Books.

————. 2012. *Occupy Nation: The Roots, the Spirit, and the Promise of Occupy Wall Street*. New York: IT Books.

————. 2013. "Occupy's Predicament: The Moment and the Prospects for the Movement," *The British Journal of Sociology* 64: 3–25.

Giugni, Marco G. 1998. "Was It Worth the Effort? The Outcomes and Consequences of Social Movements," *Annual Review of Sociology* 98: 371–93.

Globe and Mail. 1972. "Ontario Group Wants Ottawa to 'Live Up to Commitment': Indians Occupy Federal Office to Protest Holding Back of Grants," 18 July, 5.

————. 1990a. "CBC News/Poll," 9 July, A4.

————. 1990b. "Ontario Natives Blockade Roads, Rail Line," 6 Sept., A6.

————. 1994. "Myth of Eternal Forest Toppled," 14 July, A1, A3.

Goddu, Jenn. 1999. "'Powerless, Public-Spirited Women,' 'Angry Feminists,' and 'The Muffin Lobby': Newspaper and Magazine Coverage of Three National Women's Groups from 1980 to 1995," *Canadian Journal of Communication* 24: 105–26.

Gore, Al. 2014. "The Turning Point,' *Rolling Stone*, July 3.

Goodwin, Jeff, and James M. Jasper, and Francesca Polletta, eds. 2001. *Passionate Politics: Emotions and Social Movements*. Chicago: University of Chicago Press.

Gould, Deborah B. 2002. "Life during Wartime: Emotions and the Development of ACT UP," *Mobilization* 7, 2: 177–200.

————. 2009. *Moving Politics: Emotion and ACT UP's Fight against aids*. Chicago: University of Chicago Press.

Gould, Kenneth, Tammy Lewis, and J. Timmons Roberts. 2005. "Blue–Green Coalitions: Constraints and Possibilities in the Post 9/11 Political Environment," in Podobnik and Reifer (2005: 123–38).

Gould, Roger V. 1993. "Collective Action and Network Structure," *American Sociological Review* 58, 2: 182–96.

Graff, E.J. 1999. "Same-Sex Spouses in Canada," *Nation* 269, 2 (12 July): 23–4.

Grand Council of the Crees. 1998. *Never without Consent: James Bay Crees' Stand against Forcible Inclusion into an Independent Québec*. Toronto: ECW Press.

Gundy, John and Miriam Smith. 2005. "The Politics of Multiscalar Citizenship: The Case of Lesbian and Gay Organizing in Canada," *Citizenship Studies* 9, 4: 389–404.

Gurney, Joan Neff, and Kathleen J. Tierney. 1982. "Relative Deprivation and Social Movements: A Critical Look at Twenty Years of Theory and Research," *Sociological Quarterly* 23, 1: 33–47.

Gurr, Ted Robert. 1970. *Why Men Rebel*. Princeton, NJ: Princeton University Press.

Gusfield, Joseph R. 1981. "Social Movements and Social Change: Perspectives of Linearity and Fluidity,"

Social Movements, Conflicts and Change 4: 317–39.

Habermas, Jürgen. 1984. *The Theory of Communicative Action*, vol. 1, trans. Thomas McCarthy. Boston: Beacon Press.

———. 1987. *The Theory of Communicative Action*, vol. 2, trans. Thomas McCarthy. Boston: Beacon Press.

Hacket, Robert A., and Richard Gruneau. 2000. *The Missing News: Filters and the Blind Spots in Canada's Press*. Aurora, Ont.: Garamond Press.

Hagan, John. 2001. *Northern Passage: American Vietnam War Resisters in Canada*. Cambridge, Mass.: Harvard University Press.

Haig-Brown, Celia. 1988. *Resistance and Renewal: Surviving the Indian Residential School*. Vancouver: Arsenal Pulp Press.

Halleck, DeeDee. 2003. "Gathering Storm: Cyberactivism after Seattle," in J. Harper and T. Yantek, eds, *Media, Profit, and Politics: Competing Priorities in an Open Society*. Kent, Ohio: Kent State University Press, 202–14.

Hallin, Daniel C. 1989. *The "Uncensored War": The Media and Vietnam*. Berkeley: University of California Press.

Hampson, Sarah. 2015. "How the Dentistry-School Scandal Has Let Loose a Torrent of Anger at Dalhousie." *Globe and Mail*. http://www.theglobeandmail.com/news/national/education/how-the-dentistry-school-scandal-has-let-loose-a-torrent-of-anger-at-dalhousie/article23344495/.

Haluza-Delay, Randolph. 2007. "Environmental Justice in Canada," *Local Environment* 12: 557–63.

———. 2015. "Alberta Internalizing Oilsands Opposition: A Test of the Social Movement Society Thesis," in H. Ramos and K. Rodgers, *Protest and Politics: The Promise of Social Movement Societies*. Vancouver: UBC Press.

———, and Angela V. Carter. 2014. "Joining Up and Scaling Up: Analyzing Resistance to Canada's 'Dirty Oil'," In L. Bencze and S. Alsop, eds, *Activist Science and Technology Education, Cultural Studies of Science Education* 9, DOI 10.1007/978-94-007-4360-1_19.

Harris, Chris. 2009. "Canadian Black Power, Organic Intellectuals and the War of Position in Toronto, 1967–1975," in M.A. Palaeologu, ed, *The Sixties in Canada: A Turbulent and Creative Decade*. Montreal: Blackrose, 324–39.

Harrison, Kathryn. 2007. "The Road Not Taken: Climate Change Policy in Canada and the United States," *Global Environmental Politics* 7: 92–117.

Hartmann, Susan M. 1998. *The Other Feminists: Activists in the Liberal Establishment*. New Haven, Conn.: Yale University Press.

Hawkesworth, Mary. 2004. "The Semiotics of Premature Burial: Feminism in a Postfeminist Age," *Signs* 29, 4: 961–85.

Heirich, Max. 1968. *The Spiral of Conflict: Berkeley, 1964*. New York: Columbia University Press.

Henry, Astrid. 2004. *Not My Mother's Sister: Generational Conflict and Third-Wave Feminism*. Bloomington: Indiana University Press.

———. 2005. "Solitary Sisterhood: Individualism Meets Collectivity in Feminism's Third Wave," in Reger (2005: 81–96).

Heywood, Leslie, and Jennifer Drake, eds. 1997. *Third Wave Agenda: Being Feminist, Doing Feminism*. Minneapolis: University of Minnesota Press.

Hoffer, Eric. 1951. *The True Believer*. New York: Harper.

Hoffbauer, Andreas, and Howard Ramos. 2014. "Social and Political Convergence on Environmental Events: The Roles of Simplicity and Visuality in the BP Oil Spill," *Canadian Review of Sociology* 51, 3: 216–38.

Hole, Judith, and Ellen Levine. 1971. *Rebirth of Feminism*. New York: Quadrangle Books.

Howlett, Michael, and Sima Joshi-Koop. 2010. "Canadian Environmental Politics and Policy," in J.C. Courtney and D.E. Smith, eds, *The Oxford Handbook of Canadian Politics*. New York: Oxford University Press, 469–87.

Hull, Kathleen E. 2006. *Same-Sex Marriage: The Cultural Politics of Love and Law*. Cambridge: Cambridge University Press.

Hunter, Robert. 2004. *The Greenpeace to Amchitka: An Environmental Odyssey*. Vancouver: Arsenal Pulp Press.

INAC (Indian and Northern Affairs Canada). 1996a. *Report of the Royal*

Commission on Aboriginal Peoples. Ottawa: Indian and Northern Affairs Canada. http://www.ainc-inac.gc.ca/ch/rcap/sg/sgmm_e.html.

———. 1996b. *Report of the Royal Commission on Aboriginal Peoples*, section 9.12 ("Indian Voting Rights"). Ottawa: Indian and Northern Affairs Canada. http://www.ainc-inac.gc.ca/ ch/rcap/sg/sg26_e.html#92.

———. 1996c. *Report of the Royal Commission on Aboriginal Peoples*, section 9.5 ("Attacks on Traditional Culture"). Ottawa: Indian and Northern Affairs Canada. http://www.ainc-inac.gc.ca/ch/rcap/sg/sg25_e.html#85.

———. n.d. *The James Bay and Northern Quebec Agreement and the Northeastern Quebec Agreement: History*. Ottawa: Indian and Northern Affairs Canada. http://www.aincinac.gc.ca/pr/info/info14_e.html.

———. 2009. *Summative Evaluation of Consultation and Policy Development and Basic Organizational Capacity Funding. Final Report.* CIDM: 1939910.

———. 2010a. "Fact Sheet: The Nisga'a Treaty." http://www.ainc-inac.gc.ca/ai/mr/is/nit-eng.asp.

———. 2010b. "At a Glance: The Specific Claims Tribunal Act." http://www.ainc-inac.gc.ca/al/ldc/spc/jal/fct3-eng.asp.

Inglehart, Ronald. 1990. *Culture Shift in Advanced Industrial Society*. Princeton, NJ: Princeton University Press.

———. 1995. "Public Support for Environmental Protection: Objective Problems and Subjective Values in 43 Societies," PS: *Political Science and Politics* 28, 1: 57–72.

Inman, Derek, Stefan Smis, and Dorothée Cambou. 2013. "'We Will Remain Idle No More': The Shortcoming of Canada's 'Duty to Consult' Indigenous Peoples," *Goettingen Journal of International Law* 5, 1: 251–85.

Jackson, Kenneth. 2014. "1,186 Murdered and Missing Indigenous Women Over the Past 30 Years: RCMP." *Aboriginal Peoples Television Network*. http://aptn.ca/news/2014/05/01/opposition-renew-calls-national-inquiry-missing-murdered-indigenous-women-girls/.

Jasper, James M. 1998. "The Emotions of Protest: Affective and Reactive Emotions in and around Social Movements," *Sociological Forum* 13, 3: 397–424.

———, and Jane Poulsen. 1993. "Fighting Back: Vulnerabilities, Blunders, and Countermobilization by the Targets in Three Animal Rights Campaigns," *Sociological Forum* 8, 4: 639–57.

Jennings, M. Kent. 1987. "Residues of a Movement: The Aging of the American Protest Generation," *The American Political Science Review* 81, 2: 367–82.

———. 2002. "Generation Units and the Student Protest Movement in the United States: An Intra- and Intergenerational Analysis," *Political Psychology* 23, 2: 303–24.

Jenkins, J. Craig. 1981. "Sociopolitical Movements," in S.L. Long, ed., *Handbook of Political Behavior*, vol. 4. New York: Plenum, 81–154.

———. 1983. "Resource Mobilization Theory and the Study of Social Movements," *Annual Review of Sociology* 9: 527–53.

———, David Jacobs, and Jon Agnone. 2003. "Political Opportunities and African-American Protest, 1948–1997," *American Journal of Sociology* 109, 2: 277–303.

———, and Charles Perrow. 1977. "Insurgency of the Powerless: Farm Workers Movements, 1946–1972," *American Sociological Review* 42: 249–68.

———, Michael Wallace, and Andrew S. Fullerton. 2008. "A Social Movement Society?: A Cross-National Analysis of Protest Potential," *International Journal of Sociology* 38, 3: 12–35.

Jenson, Jane. 1992. "Getting to Morgentaler: From One Representation to Another," in Brodie et al. (1992: 15–55).

———, and Martin Papillon. 2000. "Challenging the Citizenship Regime: The James Bay Cree and Transnational Action," *Politics & Society* 28, 2: 245–64.

Johnson, Troy R. 1996. *The Occupation of Alcatraz Island: Indian Self-Determination and the Rise of Indian Activism*. Urbana: University of Illinois Press.

Johnston, Josée and Judith Taylor. 2008. "Feminist Consumerism and Fat Activists: A Comparative Study of Grassroots Activism and the Dove Real Beauty Campaign," *Signs* 33, 4: 941–66.

Josephy, Alvin M., Jr, Joane Nagel, and Troy Johnson. 1999. *Red Power: The American Indians' Fight for Freedom*, 2nd edn. Lincoln: University of Nebraska Press.

Kaplan, Laura. 1995. *The Story of Jane: The Legendary Underground Feminist Abortion Service*. New York: Pantheon Books.

Katzenstein, Mary Fainsod. 1998. *Faithful and Fearless: Moving Feminist Protest inside the Church and Military*. Princeton, NJ: Princeton University Press.

Keck, Margaret E., and Kathryn Sikkink. 1998. *Activists beyond Borders: Advocacy Networks in International Politics*. Ithaca, NY: Cornell University Press.

Kennedy, Elizabeth L., and Madeline D. Davis. 1993. *Boots of Leather, Slippers of Gold: The History of a Lesbian Community*. New York: Penguin Books.

Khasnabish, Alex. 2004. "Moments of Co-incidence: Exploring the Intersection of Zapatismo and Independent Labour in Mexico," *Critique of Anthropology* 24, 3: 256–76.

———. 2010. *Zapatistas: Rebellion from the Grassroots to the Global*. London and Halifax: Zed Press and Fernwood Publishing.

Kielbowicz, Richard B., and Clifford Scherer. 1986. "The Role of the Press in the Dynamics of Social Movements," *Research in Social Movements, Conflicts and Change* 9: 71–96.

Killian, Lewis M. 1994. "Are Social Movements Irrational or Are They Collective Behavior?," in R.R. Dynes and K.J. Tierney, eds, *Disasters, Collective Behavior, and Social Organization*. Newark: University of Delaware Press, 273–80.

Kingsnorth, Paul. 2009. "London Calls the Street Rebels," *New Statesman*, 30 Mar., 30–1.

Kinsman, Gary. 1996. *The Regulation of Desire: Homo and Hetero Sexualities*. Montreal: Black Rose.

———. 2001. "Challenging Canadian and Queer Nationalism," in T. Goldie, ed., *In a Queer Country: Gay and Lesbian Studies in the Canadian Context*. Vancouver: Arsenal Pulp Press, 209–34.

Klandermans, Bert. 1986. "New Social Movements and Resource Mobilization: The European and American Approach," *International Journal of Mass Emergencies and Disasters* 4: 13–37.

———. 1992. "The Social Construction of Protest and Multiorganizational Fields," in A.D. Morris and C.M. Mueller, eds, *Frontiers in Social Movement Theory*. New Haven, Conn.: Yale University Press, 77–103.

———. 1994. "Transient Identities: Changes in Collective Identity in the Dutch Peace Movement," in H. Johnston, J. Gusfield, and E. Larana, eds, *New Social Movements: From Ideology to Identity*. Philadelphia: Temple University Press, 168–85.

———. 1997. *The Social Psychology of Protest*. Oxford: Blackwell.

———, and Jackie Smith. 2002. "Survey Research: A Case for Comparative Designs," in Klandermans and Staggenborg (2002, 3–31).

———, and Suzanne Staggenborg, eds. 2002. *Methods of Social Movement Research*. Minneapolis: University of Minnesota Press.

Kleidman, Robert. 1993. *Organizing for Peace: Neutrality, the Test Ban, and the Freeze*. Syracuse, NY: Syracuse University Press.

Klein, Naomi. 1999. *No Logo*. New York: Picador.

Knegt, Peter. 2011. *About Canada: Queer Rights*. Halifax: Fernwood.

Koopmans, Ruud, and Dieter Rucht. 2002. "Protest Event Analysis," in Klandermans and Staggenborg (2002, 231–59).

Kornhauser, William. 1959. *The Politics of a Mass Society*. New York: Free Press.

Kostash, Myrna. 1980. *Long Way from Home: The Story of the Sixties Generation in Canada*. Toronto: James Lorimer.

Krieber, Janine. 1989. "Protest and Fringe Groups in Québec," in C.E.S. Franks, ed., *Dissent and the State*. Toronto: Oxford University Press, 211–23.

Kriesi, Hanspeter, Rudd Koopmans, Jan Willem Duyvendak, and Marco G. Giugni. 1995. *New Social Movements in Western Europe: A Comparative Analysis*. Minneapolis: University of Minnesota Press.

Kurzman, Charles. 2004. "The Poststructuralist Consensus in Social Movement Theory," in Jeff Goodwin and James M. Jasper, eds, *Rethinking Social Movements*. Lanham, Md.: Rowman & Littlefield, 111–20.

Kutchins, Herb, and Stuart A. Kirk. 1997. *Making Us Crazy*. New York: Free Press.

La Botz, Dan. 2002. "After a Decade of Antisweatshop Organizing, Activists Say It's Time They Pulled Together," 28 June. http://www.organicconsumers.org/clothes/sweatshop_movement.cfm.

Lambertus, Sandra. 2004. *Wartime Images, Peacetime Wounds: The Media and the Gustafsen Lake Standoff*. Toronto: University of Toronto Press.

Lang, Kurt, and Gladys E. Lang. 1961. *Collective Dynamics*. New York: Thomas Y. Crowell.

Langman, L. 2013. "Occupy: A New New Social Movement," *Current Sociology* 61, 4: 510–24.

Lawrence, Bonita. 2003. "Gender, Race, and the Regulation of Native Identity in Canada and the United States: An Overview," *Hypatia* 18, 2: 3–31.

Le Bon, Gustav. 1895. *The Crowd*. New York: Viking.

Légaré, André. 2008. "Canada's Experiment with Aboriginal Self-Determination in Nunavut From Vision to Illusion," *Inter-national Journal on Minority Group Rights* 15: 335–67.

Leiserowitz, Anthony A. 2007. "International public perception, opinion, and understanding of climate change: Current patterns, trends, and limitations." Thematic paper for: *Human Development Report 2007: Climate Change and Human Development*. Rising to the Challenge. United Nations Development Program. http://hdr.undp.org/en/reports/global/hdr2007-2008/papers/leiserowitz_anthony.pdf.

———, Robert W. Kates, and Thomas M. Parris. 2005. "Do Global Attitudes and Behaviors Support Sustainable Development?," *Environment* 47, 9: 22–38.

Lent, Adam. 2003. "The Transformation of Gay and Lesbian Politics in Britain," *British Journal of Politics and International Relations* 5, 1: 24–49.

Levi, Margaret, David J. Olson, and Erich Steinman. 2004. "Living Wage Movement," in I. Ness, ed., *Encyclopedia of American Social Movements*, vol. 4. Armonk, NY: Sharpe Reference.

Levitt, Cyril. 1984. *Children of Privilege: Student Revolt in the Sixties: A Study of Student Movements in Canada, the United States, and West Germany*. Toronto: University of Toronto Press.

Lexier, Roberta. 2007. "'The Backdrop Against Which Everything Happened': English-Canadian Student Movements and Off-Campus Movements for Change," *History of Intellectual Culture* 7, 1: 1–18.

———. 2012. "To Struggle Together or Fracture Apart: The Sixties Student Movements at English-Canadian Universities," in L Campbelle, D. Clément and G. Kealy [eds] *Debating Dissent: Canada and the 1960s*. Toronto: UTP, 81–95.

Lichterman, Paul. 1996. *The Search for Political Community: American Activists Reinventing Commitment*. Cambridge: Cambridge University Press.

———. 2002. "Seeing Structure Happen: Theory-Driven Participant Observation," in Klandermans and Staggenborg (2002, 118–45).

Linden, Sidney. 2007. "Investigation and Findings, Volume 1: Executive Summary." *Ipperwash Inquiry*. Attorney General of Ontario.

Lo, Clarence. 1990. *Small Property Versus Big Government: Social Origins of the Property Tax Revolt*. Berkeley: University of California Press.

Lofland, John. 1979. "White-Hot Mobilization: Strategies of a Millenarian Movement," in M.N. Zald and J.D. McCarthy, eds, *The Dynamics of Social Movements*. Cambridge, Mass.: Winthrop, 157–66.

Long, David. 1992. "Culture, Ideology, and Militancy: The Movement of Native Indians in Canada, 1969–1991," in W.K.Carroll, ed., *Organizing Dissent: Contemporary Social Movements in Theory and Practice*. Toronto: Garamond Press, 118–34.

Longhofer, Wesley, and Evan Schofer. 2010. "National and Global Origins of Environmental Association," *American Sociological Review* 75: 505–33.

Lowe, Philip, and Jane Goyder. 1983. *Environmental Groups in Politics*. London: George Allen & Unwin.

Luders, Joseph. 2006. "The Economics of Movement Success: Business Responses to Civil Rights Mobilization," *American Journal of Sociology* 111, 4: 963–98.

———. 2010. *The Civil Rights Movement and the Logic of Social Change*. New York: Cambridge University Press.

McAdam, Doug. 1983. "Tactical Innovation and the Pace of Insurgency," *American Sociological Review* 48, 6: 735–54.

———. 1986. "Recruitment to High-Risk Activism: The Case of Freedom Summer," *American Journal of Sociology* 92, 1: 64–90.

———. 1988. *Freedom Summer.* New York: Oxford University Press.

———. 1994. "Culture and Social Movements," in E. Larana, H. Johnston, and J.R. Gusfield, eds, *New Social Movements: From Ideology to Identity.* Philadelphia: Temple University Press, 36–57.

———. 1995. "'Initiator' and 'Spin-off' Movements: Diffusion Processes in Protest Cycles," in M. Traugott, ed., *Repertoires and Cycles of Collective Action.* Durham, NC: Duke University Press, 217–39.

———. 1996. "The Framing Function of Movement Tactics: Strategic Dramaturgy in the American Civil Rights Movement," in McAdam et al. (1996: 338–55).

———. 1999. *Political Process and the Development of Black Insurgency,* 2nd edn. Chicago: University of Chicago Press.

———, and Hilary S. Boudet. 2012. *Putting Movements in Their Place: Explaining Variation in Community Response to the Siting of Proposed Energy Projects.* New York: Cambridge University Press.

———, and Debra Friedman. 1992. "Collective Identity and Activism: Networks, Choices, and the Life of a Social Movement," in Aldon D. Morris and Carol M. Mueller, eds, *Frontiers in Social Movement Theory.* New Haven, Conn.: Yale University Press, 156–73.

———, John D. McCarthy, and Mayer N. Zald. 1988. "Social Movements," in N.J. Smelser, ed., *Handbook of Sociology.* Newbury Park, CA: Sage, 695–737.

———, John D. McCarthy, and Mayer N. Zald, eds. 1996. *Comparative Perspectives on Social Movements.* New York: Cambridge University Press.

———, and Dieter Rucht. 1993. "The Cross-national Diffusion of Movement Ideas," *Annals, American Academy of Political and Social Science* 528: 56–74.

———, and William Sewell Jr. 2001. "It's about Time: Temporality in the Study of Social Movements and Revolutions," in R. Aminzade, J. Goldstone, D. McAdam, E. Perry, W. Sewell, S. Tarrow, and C. Tilly, eds, *Silence and Voice in Contentious Politics.* Cambridge: Cambridge University Press, 89–125.

———, Sidney Tarrow, and Charles Tilly. 2001. *Dynamics of Contention.* Cambridge: Cambridge University Press.

McCammon, Holly J. 2001. "Stirring Up Suffrage Sentiment: The Formation of the State Women's Suffrage Organizations, 1866–1914," *Social Forces* 80, 2: 449–80.

McCarthy, John D., and Mayer N. Zald. 1973. *The Trend of Social Movements in America: Professionalization and Resource Mobilization.* Morristown, NJ: General Learning Press.

———. 1977. "Resource Mobilization and Social Movements: A Partial Theory," *American Journal of Sociology* 82, 6: 1212–41.

———. 2002. "The Enduring Vitality of the Resource Mobilization Theory of Social Movements," in H.T. Jonathan, ed., *Handbook of Sociological Theory.* New York: Kluwer Academic/Plenum, 533–65.

McCarthy, Shawn, and Oliver Moore. 2012. "David Suzuki Laments Tory-Imposed 'Chill' on Green Groups," *Globe and Mail,* 25 April. http://ecestats.theglobeandmail.com/news/politics/david-suzuki-laments-tory-imposed-chill-on-green-groups/article2400300/?service=mobile.

McCloskey, Michael. 1992. "Twenty Years of Change in the Environmental Movement: An Insider's View," in Riley E. Dunlap and Angela G. Mertig, eds, *American Environmentalism: The U.S. Environmental Movement, 1970–1990.* Philadelphia: Taylor and Francis, 77–88.

McComas, Katherine, and James Shanahan. 1999. "Telling Stories about Global Climate Change," *Communication Research* 26, 1: 30–57.

McKenzie, Judith I. 2002. *Environmental Politics in Canada: Managing the Commons into the Twenty-first Century.* Toronto: Oxford University Press.

McKibben, Bill. 2013. "The Fossil Fuel Resistance," *Rolling Stone,* 25 April.

McMillan, Jane; Janelle Young and Molly Peters. 2013. "Commentary: The 'Idle No More' Movement in Eastern Canada," *Canadian Journal of Law and Society* 28, 3: 429–31.

McRobbie, Angela. 2009. *The Aftermath of Feminism: Gender, Culture, and Social Change*. Thousand Oaks, CA: Sage.

McRoberts, Kenneth. 1993. *Quebec: Social Change and Political Crisis*, 3rd edn. Toronto: Oxford University Press.

MacDonald, Christine. 2008. *Green Inc: An Environmental Insider Reveals How a Good Cause Has Gone Bad*. Guilford, CT: The Globe Pequot Press.

Mann, Ruth M. 2008. "Men's Rights and Feminist Advocacy in Canadian Domestic Violence Policy Arenas: Contexts, Dynamics, and Outcomes of Antifeminist Backlash," *Feminist Criminology* 3, 1: 44–75.

Maney, Gregory M. 2001. "Rival Transnational Networks and Indigenous Rights: The San Blas Kuna in Panama and the Yanomami in Brazil," *Social Movements, Conflicts and Change* 23: 103–44.

Mansbridge, Jane J. 1986. *Why We Lost the era*. Chicago: University of Chicago Press.

Masson, Dominique. "Constructing Scale/Contesting Scale: Women's Movement and Rescaling Politics in Québec," *Social Politics* 21, 3: 462–86.

———. "Politique(s) Des Échelles et Transnationalisation: Perspectives Géographiques," *Politique et Sociétés* 28, 1: 113–33.

Marwell, Gerald, and Pamela Oliver. 1984. "Collective Action Theory and Social Movements Research," *Research in Social Movements, Conflicts and Change* 7: 1–27.

———. 1993. *The Critical Mass in Collective Action: A Micro-Social Theory*. Cambridge: Cambridge University Press.

Marwick, Arthur. 1998. *The Sixties: Cultural Revolution in Britain, France, Italy, and the United States*. New York: Oxford University Press.

Marx, Gary T., and James L. Wood. 1975. "Strands of Theory and Research in Collective Behavior," *Annual Review of Sociology* 1: 363–428.

Matthews, J. Scott. 2005. "The Political Foundations of Support for Same-Sex Marriage in Canada," *Canadian Journal of Political Science* 38, 4: 841–66.

Mayo, Marjorie. 2005. *Global Citizens: Social Movements and the Challenge of Globalization*. New York: Zed Books.

Meier, August, and Elliott Rudwick. 1973. CORE: *A Study of the Civil Rights Movement, 1942–1968*. Urbana: University of Illinois Press.

Melucci, Alberto. 1988. "Getting Involved: Identity and Mobilization in Social Movements," *International Social Movement Research* 1: 329–48.

———. 1989. *Nomads of the Present: Social Movements and Individual Needs in Contemporary Society*, ed. John Keane and Paul Mier. Philadelphia: Temple University Press.

———. 1996. *Challenging Codes: Collective Action in the Information Age*. Cambridge: Cambridge University Press.

Meyer, David S., and Suzanne Staggenborg. 1996. "Movements, Countermovements, and the Structure of Political Opportunity," *American Journal of Sociology* 101, 6: 1628–60.

———, and Suzanne Staggenborg. 1998. "Countermovement Dynamics in Federal Systems: A Comparison of Abortion Politics in Canada and the United States," *Research in Political Sociology* 8: 209–40.

———, and Sidney R. Tarrow. 1998b. "A Movement Society: Contentious Politics for a New Century," in D. Meyer and S. Tarrow, eds, *The Social Movement Society: Contentious Politics for a New Century*. Oxford: Rowman and Littlefield, 1–28.

———, and Nancy Whittier. 1994. "Social Movement Spillover," *Social Problems* 41, 2: 277–98.

Messer-Davidow, Ellen. 2002. *Disciplining feminism: From Social Activism to Academic Discourse*. Durham, NC: Duke University Press.

Milkman, Ruth, Stephanie Luce, and Penny Lewis. 2013. "Changing the Subject: A Bottom-Up Account of Occupy Wall Street in New York City." New York: The Murphy Institute, City University of New York.

Miller, James R. 1989. *Skyscrapers Hide the Heavens: A History of Indian–White Relations in Canada*. Toronto: University of Toronto Press.

Mitchell, Allyson, Lisa Bryn Rundle, and Lara Karaian, eds. 2001. *Turbo Chicks: Talking Young Feminisms*. Toronto: Sumach Press.

Mitchell, Robert Cameron. 1979. "National Environmental Lobbies and the Apparent Illogic of Collective Action," in C.S. Russell, *Collective Decision Making: Applications from Public Choice Theory*. Baltimore: Johns Hopkins University Press, 87–136.

———. 1984. "Public Opinion and Environmental Politics in the 1970s and 1980s," in J.V. Norman and M.E. Kraft, eds, *Environmental Policy in the 1980s: Reagan's New Agenda*. Washington, DC: Congressional Quarterly Press, 51–74.

———, Angela G. Mertig, and Riley E. Dunlap. 1992. "Twenty Years of Environmental Mobilization: Trends among National Environmental Organizations," in Riley E. Dunlap and Angela G. Mertig, eds, *American Environmentalism: The U.S. Environmental Movement, 1970–1990*. Philadelphia: Taylor and Francis, 11–26.

Moghadam, Valentine M. 2005. *Globalizing Women*. Baltimore: Johns Hopkins University Press.

Mohai, Paul, David Pellow, and J. Timmons Roberts. 2009. "Environmental Justice," *Annual Review of Environment and Resources* 34: 405–30.

Morden, Michael. 2013. "Telling Stories about Conflict: Symbolic Politics and the Ipperwash Land Transfer Agreement," *Canadian Journal of Political Science* 46, 3: 505–24.

Morgan, Rhiannon. 2004. "Advancing Indigenous Rights at the United Nations: Strategic Framing and Its Impact on the Normative Development of International Law," *Social and Legal Studies* 13, 4: 481–500.

Morris, Aldon D. 1981. "Black Southern Student Sit-in Movement: An Analysis of Internal Organization," *American Sociological Review* 46, 4: 744–67.

———. 1984. *The Origins of the Civil Rights Movement: Black Communities Organizing for Change*. New York: Free Press.

———. 1999. "A Retrospective on the Civil Rights Movement: Political and Intellectual Landmarks," *Annual Review of Sociology* 25: 517–39.

———. 2000. "Reflections on Social Movement Theory: Criticisms and Proposals," *Contemporary Sociology* 29: 445–54.

———, and Cedric Herring. 1987. "Theory and Research in Social Movements: A Critical Review," *Annual Review in Political Science* 2: 137–98.

———, and Suzanne Staggenborg. 2004. "Leadership in Social Movements," in Snow et al. (2004: 171–96).

Morris, Stephen D. 2001. "Between Neo-Liberal and Neo-Indigenismo: Reconstructing National Identity in Mexico," *National Identities* 3, 3: 239–55.

Morris, William. 1969. "Ottawa Plans to Abolish Treaties, Move Out of Indian Affairs in 5 Years," *Globe and Mail*, 26 June, 1–2.

Morton, F.L. 1992. *Morgentaler v. Borowski: Abortion, the Charter, and the Courts*. Toronto: McClelland & Stewart.

Moser, Susanne C. 2007. "In the Long Shadows of Inaction: The Quiet Building of a Climate Protection Movement in the United States," *Global Environmental Politics* 7, 2: 124–44.

Mueller, Carol McClurg. 1987. "Collective Consciousness, Identity Transformation, and the Rise of Women in Public Office in the United States," in M. Mary Fainsod Katzenstein and Carol McClurg, eds, *The Women's Movements in the United States and Western Europe: Consciousness, Political Opportunity and Public Policy*. Philadelphia: Temple University Press, 89–108.

———. 1994. "Conflict Networks and the Origins of Women's Liberation," in E. Laraña, H. Johnston, and J.R. Gusfield, eds, *New Social Movements*. Philadelphia: Temple University Press, 234–63.

Mueller, Carol. 1999. "Claim 'Radicalization?' The 1989 Protest Cycle in the GDR," *Social Problems* 46, 4: 528–47.

Munro, Lyle. 2005. "Strategies, Action Repertoires and DIY Activism in the Animal Rights Movement," *Social Movement Studies* 4, 1: 75–94.

Myers, Daniel J. 1994. "Communication Technology and Social Movements: Contributions of Computer Networks to Activism," *Social Science Computer Review* 12, 2: 250–60.

Nagel, Joane. 1994. "Constructing Ethnicity: Creating and Recreating Ethnic Identity and Culture," *Social Problems* 41, 1: 152–76.

———. 1995. "American Indian Ethnic Renewal: Politics and the Resurgence of Identity," *American Sociological Review* 60, 6: 947–65.

———. 1996. *American Indian Ethnic Renewal: Red Power and the Resurgence of Identity and Culture.* New York: Oxford University Press.

Nepstad, Sharon Erickson, and Christian Smith. 2001. "The Social Structure of Moral Outrage in Recruitment to the U.S. Central America Peace Movement," in J. Goodwin, J. M. Jasper, and F. Polletta, eds, *Passionate Politics: Emotions and Social Movements.* Chicago: University of Chicago Press, 158–74.

New York Times. 1999. "Loggers Find Canadian Rain Forest Flush with Foes," 22 Oct.

Niezen, Ronald. 2000. "Recognizing Indigenism: Canadian Unity and the International Movement of Indigenous Peoples," *Comparative Studies in Society and History* 42, 1: 119–48.

Nisga'a Lisims Government. 2010. http://www.nisgaalisims.ca/ nisgaa-final-agreement.

Noonan, Rita K. 1995. "Women against the State: Political Opportunities and Collective Action Frames in Chile's Transition to Democracy," *Sociological Forum* 10, 1: 81–111.

NWAC (Native Women's Association of Canada). 2010. *Fact Sheet: Root Causes of Vilence Against Aboriginal Women and the Impact of Colonization.* http://www. nwac.ca/files/download/NWAC_3F_ Toolkit_e_0.pdf.

———. 2010. *What Their Stories Tell Us: Research Findings from the Sisters in Spirit Initiative.*

Oberschall, Anthony. 1973. *Social Conflict and Social Movements.* Englewood Cliffs, NJ: Prentice-Hall.

———. 1978. "The Decline of the 1960s Social Movements," *Research in Social Movements, Conflicts and Change* 1: 257–89.

Obonsawin, Roger, and Heather Howard-Bobiwash. 1997. "The Native Canadian Centre of Toronto: The Meeting Place for the Aboriginal Community for 35 Years," in Frances Sanderson and Heather Howard-Bobiwash, eds, *The Meeting Place: Aboriginal Life in Toronto.* Toronto: Native Canadian Centre of Toronto.

Office of the High Commission of Human Rights. "Fact Sheet No. 9 (Rev. 1), The Rights of Indigenous Peoples." New York: Office of the High Commission of Human Rights. http://www.unhchr.ch/ html/menu6/2/fs9.htm.

Oliver, Pamela E., Jorge Cadena-Roa, and Kelley D. Strawn. 2003. "Emerging Trends in the Study of Protest and Social Movements," *Research in Political Sociology* 12: 213–44.

Olson, Mancur. 1965. *The Logic of Collective Action: Public Goods and the Theory of Groups.* Cambridge, Mass.: Harvard University Press.

Ostrander, Madeline. 2014. "Bluegrass Uprising," *The Nation*, 6 January.

Owram, Doug. 1996. *Born at the Right Time: A History of the Baby-Boom Generation.* Toronto: University of Toronto Press.

Paehlke, Robert. 1997. "Green Politics and the Rise of the Environmental Movement," in Thomas Fleming, ed., *The Environment and Canadian Society.* Scarborough, Ont.: ITP Nelson, 252–74.

Pal, Leslie. 1993. *Interests of State: The Politics of Language, Multiculturalism, and Feminism in Canada.* Montreal & Kingston: McGill-Queen's University Press.

Park, Robert E., and Ernest W. Burgess. 1921. *Introduction to the Science of Sociology.* Chicago: University of Chicago Press.

Patterson, Lisa. 2006. "Aboriginal Roundtable to Kelowna Accord: Aboriginal Policy Negotiations, 2004–2005," Library of Parliament. prb 06-04E. http://www2.parl.gc.ca/content/ lop/researchpublications/prb0604-e. htm.

Peckham, Michael. 1998. "New Dimensions of Social Movement/Countermovement Interaction: The Case of Scientology and Its Internet Critics," *Canadian Journal of Sociology* 23, 4: 317–47.

Perrow, Charles. 1979. "The Sixties Observed," in Mayer N. Zald and John D. McCarthy, eds, *The Dynamics of Social Movements.* Cambridge, Mass.: Winthrop, 192–211.

Pew. 2013. "Protecting the Environment Ranks in the Middle of Public's Priorities for 2013,' *Pew Research Centre*. http://www.pewresearch.org/daily-number/protecting-the-environment-ranks-in-the-middle-of-publics-priorities-for-2013/.

Pianta, Mario. 2003. "Democracy vs Globalization: The Growth of Parallel Summits and Global Movements," in D. Archibugi, ed., *Debating Cosmopolitics*. London: Verso, 232–56.

Pichardo, Nelson A. 1997. "New Social Movements: A Critical Review," *Annual Review of Sociology* 23: 411–30.

Pierceson, Jason. 2005. *Courts, Liberalism, and Rights: Gay Law and Politics in the United States and Canada*. Philadelphia: Temple University Press.

Pinard, Maurice. 2011. *Motivational Dimensions in Social Movements and Contentious Collective Action*. Montreal: McGill-Queens University Press.

Pinello, Daniel R. 2006. *America's Struggle for Same-Sex Marriage*. New York: Cambridge University Press.

Piven, Frances Fox, and Richard A. Cloward. 1977. *Poor People's Movements: Why They Succeed, How They Fail*. New York: Vintage Books.

Platiel, Rudy. 1970. "Indians Warn Battles over Treaties May Fill the Courts," *Globe and Mail*, 15 Apr., 5.

Pleyers, Geoffrey. 2009. "World Social Forum 2009: A Generation's Challenge," *Open Democracy*. http://www.opendemocracy.net.

Podobnik, Bruce. 2005. "Resistance to Globalization: Cycles and Trends in the Globalization Protest Movement," in Podobnik and Reifer (2005: 51–68).

———, and T. Reifer, eds. 2005. *Transforming Globalization*. Leiden, Netherlands: Brill.

Poirier, Patricia. 1990. "Mohawks Prepared for Talks to Resume: Hint at Proposals to Reopen Bridge," *Globe and Mail*, 27 Aug., A1, A3.

Polletta, Francesca. 1997. "Culture and Its Discontents: Recent Theorizing on the Cultural Dimensions of Protest," *Sociological Inquiry* 67, 4: 431–50.

———. 2002. *Freedom Is an Endless Meeting*. Chicago: University of Chicago Press.

———. 2004. "Culture in and Outside of Institutions," *Research in Social Movements, Conflicts and Change* 25: 161–83.

———, and M. Kai Ho. 2006. "Frames and Their Consequences," in R.E. Goodin and C. Tilly, eds, *The Oxford Handbook of Contextual Political Analysis*. Oxford: Oxford University Press, 187–209.

———, and James M. Jasper. 2001. "Collective Identity and Social Movements," *Annual Review of Sociology* 27: 283–305.

Ponting, J. Rick. 2000. "Public Opinion on Canadian Aboriginal Issues, 1976–98: Persistence, Change, and Cohort Analysis," *Canadian Ethnic Studies* 32, 3: 44–75.

Pride, Richard A. 1995. "How Activists and Media Frame Social Problems: Critical Events versus Performance Trends for Schools," *Political Communication* 12, 1: 5–26.

Raeburn, Nicole C. 2004. *Changing Corporate America from Inside Out: Lesbian and Gay Workplace Organizing*. Minneapolis: University of Minnesota Press.

Rahman, Fauzia. 2014. "We Are Not All Malala: Children and Citizenship in the Age of Internet and Drones," in L. Herrara,ed., *Wired Citizenship: Youth Learning and Activism in the Middle East*. London: Rutledge.

Ramos, Howard. 2004. "Divergent Paths: Aboriginal Mobilization in Canada, 1951–2000," PhD thesis, McGill University.

———. 2006. "What Causes Canadian Aboriginal Protest? Examining Resources, Opportunities and Identity, 1951–2000," *Canadian Journal of Sociology* 31, 2: 211–34.

———. 2007. "Special Plus and Special Negative: The Conflict between Perceptions and Applications of 'Special Status' in Canada," in Genevieve Fuji Johnson and Randy Enomoto, eds, *Race, Racialization, and Antiracism in Canada and Beyond*. Toronto: University of Toronto Press, 131–50.

———. 2008. "Opportunity for Whom?: Political Opportunity and Critical Events in Canadian Aboriginal Mobilization, 1951–2000," *Social Forces* 87, 2: 795–824.

———, and Kathleen Rodgers. 2015. "Introduction," in H. Ramos and K.

Rodgers, *Protest and Politics: The Promise of Social Movement Societies.* Vancouver: UBC Press.

Ratner, R.S., and Andrew Woolford. 2008. "Mesomobilization and Fragile Coalitions: Aboriginal Politics and Treaty-Making in British Columbia," *Research in Social Movements, Conflicts and Change* 28: 113–36.

Rayside, David. 1998. *On the Fringe: Gays and Lesbians in Politics.* Ithaca, NY: Cornell University Press.

Rebick, Judy. 2005. *Ten Thousand Roses: The Making of a Feminist Revolution.* Toronto: Penguin Canada.

Reger, Jo, ed. 2005. *Different Wavelengths: Studies of the Contemporary Women's Movement.* New York: Routledge.

———. 2014. "Debating US Contemporary Feminism," *Sociology Compass* 8, 1: 43–51.

———. 2014b. "The Story of a Slut Walk: Sexuality, Race, and Generational Divisions in Contemporary Feminist Activism," *Journal of Contemporary Ethnography* DOI: 10.1177/0891241614526434.

———, and Lacey Story. 2005. "Talking about My Vagina: Two College Campuses and *The Vagina Monologues,*" in Reger (2005: 139–60).

Revkin, Andrew C. 2009. "Environmental Issues Slide in Poll of Public's Concerns," *New York Times,* 22 Jan.

RCMP (Royal Canadian Mounted Police). 2014. *Missing and Murdered Aboriginal Women: A National Operation Overview.* http://www.rcmp-grc.gc.ca/pubs/mmaw-faapd-eng.pdf.

Ricard, François. 1994. *The Lyric Generation: The Life and Times of the Baby Boomers,* trans. Donald Winkler. Toronto: Stoddart.

Rice, Waubgeshig. 2010. "Oka Helped Us Find Our Voice," *Globe and Mail,* 15 July. http://www.theglobeand-mail.com/life/facts-and-arguments/oka-helped-us-find-our-voice/article1641527/.

Rimmerman, Craig A. 2002. *From Identity to Politics: The Lesbian and Gay Movements in the United States.* Philadelphia: Temple University Press.

Robinson. Don G. 2013. "Malala Yousafzai: A Voice Worth Hearing," *Journal of Applied Instructional Design* 3, 2: 5–6.

Rodgers, Kathleen, and Melanie Knight. 2011. "'You Just Felt the Collective Wind Being Knocked Out of Us:' The Deinstitutionalization of Feminism and the Survival of Women's Organizing in Canada," *Women's Studies International Forum* 34: 570–81.

Rohlinger, Deana A. 2002. "Framing the Abortion Debate: Organizational Resources, Media Strategies, and Movement-Countermovement Dynamics," *Sociological Quarterly* 43, 4: 479–507.

———. 2007. "American Media and Deliberative Democratic Processes," *Sociological Theory* 25, 2: 122–48.

Rojas, Fabio. 2007. *From Black Power to Black Studies.* Baltimore: John Hopkins University Press.

Rome, Adam. 2003. "'Give Earth a Chance": The Environmental Movement and the Sixties," *Journal of American History* 90, 2: 525–54.

Rome, Adam. 2013. *The Genius of Earth Day: How a 1970 Teach-In Unexpectedly Made the First Green Generation.* New York: Hill and Wang.

Rootes, Christopher. 1999. *Environmental Movements: Local, National and Global.* London: Frank Cass.

———. 2004. "Environmental Movements," in Snow et al. (2004: 608–40).

———, and Robert Brulle. 2013. "Environmental Movements," in D. A. Snow, D. della Porta, B. Klandermans, and D. McAdam, eds, *The Wiley-Blackwell Encyclopedia of Social and Political Movements.* Malden, MA: Wiley Blackwell. DOI: 10.1002/9780470999103.

Rosen, Ruth. 2000. *The World Split Open: How the Modern Women's Movement Changed America.* New York: Penguin Books.

Ross, Robert J.S. 2005. "From Anti-sweatshop, to Global Justice, to Anti-war: Student Participation in Globalization Protests," in Podobnik and Reifer (2005: 112–21).

Roth, Benita. 2004. *Separate Roads to Feminism: Black, Chicana, and White Feminist Movements in America's Second Wave.* Cambridge: Cambridge University Press.

Rucht, Dieter. 1988. "Themes, Logics, and Arenas of Social Movements: A

Structural Approach," *International Social Movement Research* 1: 305–28.

———. 1995. "Ecological Protest as Calculated Law-Breaking: Greenpeace and Earth First! in Comparative Perspective," in R. Wolfgang, ed., *Green Politics Three*. Edinburgh: Edinburgh University Press, 66–89.

———. 2004. "Movement Allies, Adversaries, and Third Parties," in Snow et al. (2004: 197–216).

———. 2005. "The Internet as a New Opportunity for Transnational Protest Groups," in M. Kousis and C. Tilly, eds, *Economic and Political Contention in Comparative Perspective*. Boulder, Colo.: Paradigm, 70–85.

Rucht, Dieter, and Jochen Roose. 1999. "The German Environmental Movement at a Crossroads?," *Environmental Politics* 8, 1: 59–80.

———. 2001. "Neither Decline nor Sclerosis: The Organizational Structure of the German Environmental Movement," *West European Politics* 24, 4: 55–81.

Rupp, Leila J. 1997. *Worlds of Women: The Making of an International Women's Movement*. Princeton, NJ: Princeton University Press.

Rupp, Leila J., and Verta Taylor. 1987. *Survival in the Doldrums: The American Women's Rights Movement, 1945 to the 1960s*. New York: Oxford University Press.

———. 1999. "Forging Feminist Identity in an International Movement: A Collective Identity Approach to Twentieth-Century Feminism," *Signs* 24, 2: 363–86.

Ryan, Charlotte, Kevin M. Carragee and William Meinhofer. 2001. "Theory into Practice: Framing, the News Media, and Collective Action," *Journal of Broadcasting & Electronic Media* 45, 1: 175–82.

Saad, Lydia. 2006. "Americans Still Not Highly Concerned about Global Warming," Gallup Poll, Apr., 20–2.

Sale, Kirkpatrick. 1973. *SDS*. New York: Random House.

———. 1993. *The Green Revolution*. New York: Hill and Wang.

Schlosberg, David. 2007. *Defining Environmental Justice: Theories, Movements, and Nature*. Oxford: Oxford University Press.

Schudson, Michael. 2003. *The Sociology of News*. New York: Norton.

Schulz, Markus S. 1998. "Collective Action across Borders: Opportunity Structures, Network Capacities, and Communicative Praxis in the Age of Advanced Globalization," *Sociological Perspectives* 41, 3: 587–616.

SCT (Specific Claims Tribunal). 2009. "Registry of the Specific Claims Tribunal: Frequently Asked Questions." http://www.sct-trp.ca/freq/index_e.htm.

Sears, Alan. 2005. "Queer Anti-Capitalism: What's Left of Lesbian and Gay Liberation?," in *Science and Society* 69, 1: 92–112.

Seidman, Gay W. 2000. "Adjusting the Lens: What Do Globalizations, Transnationalism, and the Anti-apartheid Movement Mean for Social Movement Theory?," in J.A. Guidry, M.D. Kennedy, and M.N. Zald, eds, *Globalizations and Social Movements*. Ann Arbor: University of Michigan Press, 339–57.

Shaw, Randy. 1999. *Reclaiming America: Nike, Clean Air, and the New National Activism*. Berkeley: University of California Press.

Shellenberger, Michael, and Ted Nordhaus. 2004. "The Death of Environmentalism: Global Warming Politics in a Post-Environmental World." http://www.thebreakthrough.org/images/Death_of_Environmentalism.pdf.

Shorter, Edward. 1975. *The Making of the Modern Family*. New York: Basic Books.

Sigal, Leon V. 1973. *Reporters and Officials: The Organization and Politics of Newsmaking*. Lexington, Mass.: D.C. Heath.

Sklair, Leslie. 1994. "Capitalism and Development in Global Perspective," In L. Sklair, ed., *Capitalism and Development*. New York: Rutledge, 165–88.

———. 2002. *Globalization: Capitalism and its Alternatives*. New York: Oxford University Press.

Skrentny, John D. 1998. "The Effect of the Cold War on African-American Civil Rights: America and the World Audience, 1945–1968," *Theory and Society* 27: 237–85.

SlutWalk Toronto. 2014. "Because We've Had Enough," *SlutWalk Toronto*. http://www.slutwalktoronto.com.

Smelser, Neil J. 1962. *Theory of Collective Behavior*. New York: Free Press.

———. 1970. "Two Critics in Search of a Bias: A Response to Currie and Skolnick," *Annals, American Academy of Political and Social Science* 391: 46–55.

Smith, Jackie. 2001. "Globalizing Resistance: The Battle of Seattle and the Future of Social Movements," *Mobilization* 6, 1: 1–19.

———. 2008. *Social Movements for Global Democracy*. Baltimore: Johns Hopkins University Press.

———, et al. 2008. *Global Democracy and the World Social Forums*. Boulder, Colo.: Paradigm Publishers.

Smith, Miriam. 1998. "Social Movements and Equality Seeking: The Case of Gay Liberation in Canada," *Canadian Journal of Political Science* 31, 2: 285–309.

———. 1999. *Lesbian and Gay Rights in Canada*. Toronto: University of Toronto Press.

———. 2004. "Segmented Network: Linguistic Practices in Canadian Lesbian and Gay Rights Organizing," *Ethnicities* 4, 1: 99–124.

———. 2005. "Social Movements and Judicial Empowerment: Courts, Public Policy, and Lesbian and Gay Organizing in Canada," *Politics and Society* 33, 2: 327–53.

———. 2007. "Framing Same-Sex Marriage in Canada and the United States: *Goodridge, Halpern* and the National Boundaries of Political Discourse," *Social and Legal Studies* 16, 1: 5–26.

———. 2008. *Political Institutions and Lesbian and Gay Rights in the United States and Canada*. New York: Routledge.

Snow, David A. 2001. "Collective Identity," in Neil J. Smelser and Paul B. Baltes, eds, *International Encyclopedia of the Social and Behavioral Sciences*. London: Elsevier, 2212–19.

———. 2004. "Social Movements as Challenges to Authority: Resistance to an Emerging Conceptual Hegemony," *Research in Social Movements, Conflicts and Change* 25: 3–25.

———, and Robert D. Benford. 1992. "Ideology, Frame Resonance and Participant Mobilization," *International Social Movement Research* 1: 197–217.

———, E. Burke Rochford Jr, Steven K. Worden, and Robert D. Benford. 1986. "Frame Alignment Processes, Micromobilization, and Movement Participation," *American Sociological Review* 51, 4: 464–81.

———, Sarah A. Soule, and Hanspeter Kriesi, eds. 2004. *The Blackwell Companion to Social Movements*. Malden, Mass.: Blackwell.

———, Sarah A. Soule and Daniel M. Cress. 2005. "Identifying the Precipitants of Homeless Protest Across 17 U.S. Cities, 1980 to 1990," *Social Forces* 83, 3: 1183–210.

Snyder, David, and William R. Kelly. 1979. "Strategies for Investigating Violence and Social Change: Illustrations from Analyses of Racial Disorders and Implications for Mobilization Research," in M.N. Zald and J.D. McCarthy, eds, *The Dynamics of Social Movements: Resource Mobilization, Social Control, and Tactics*. Cambridge, Mass.: Winthrop, 212–37.

Sobieraj, Sarah. 2011. *Soundbitten: The Perils of Media-Centered Political Activism*. New York: New York University Press.

———. 2011. "A Sociologist's View of the 'Occupy' Camps: Movements in a Shifting Media Landscape," *Footnotes* 39, 9: 9–10.

Solomon, Evan, and Kristen Everson. 2014. "7 Environmental Charities Face Canada Revenue Agency Audits,' *CBC News*. http://www.cbc.ca/news/politics/7-environmental-charities-face-canada-revenue-agency-audits-1.2526330.

Soule, Sarah A. 2004. "Going to the Chapel? Same-Sex Marriage Bans in the United States, 1973–20," *Social Problems* 51, 4: 453–77.

———, and Susan Olzak. 2004. "When Do Movements Matter? The Politics of Contingency and the Equal Rights Amendment," *American Sociological Review* 69: 473–97.

Speed, Shannon, and Jane F. Collier. 2000. "Limiting Indigenous Autonomy in Chiapas, Mexico: The State Government's Use of Human Rights," *Human Rights Quarterly* 22: 877–905.

Springer, Kimberly. 2005. *Living for the Revolution: Black Feminist Organizations, 1968–1980*. Durham, NC: Duke University Press.

Staggenborg, Suzanne. 1986. "Coalition Work in the Pro-Choice Movement: Organizational and Environmental Opportunities and Obstacles," *Social Problems* 33, 5: 374–90.

———. 1988. "The Consequences of Professionalization and Formalization in the Pro-Choice Movement," *American Sociological Review* 53: 585–605.

———. 1989. "Stability and Innovation in the Women's Movement: A Comparison of Two Movement Organizations," *Social Problems* 36, 1: 75–92.

———. 1991. *The Pro-Choice Movement: Organization and Activism in the Abortion Conflict*. New York: Oxford University Press.

———. 1993. "Critical Events and the Mobilization of the Pro-Choice Movement," *Research in Political Sociology* 6: 319–45.

———. 1995. "Can Feminist Organizations Be Effective?," in Myra Marx Ferree and Patricia Yancey Martin, eds, *Feminist Organizations: Harvest of the New Women's Movement*. Philadelphia: Temple University Press, 339–55.

———. 1998. "Social Movement Communities and Cycles of Protest: The Emergence and Maintenance of a Local Women's Movement," *Social Problems* 45, 2: 180–204.

———. 2001. "Beyond Culture versus Politics: A Case Study of a Local Women's Movement," *Gender & Society* 15, 4: 507–30.

———, and Josée Lecomte. 2009. "Social Movement Campaigns: Mobilization and Outcomes in the Montreal Women's Movement Community," *Mobilization* 14, 2: 405–22.

———, and Verta Taylor. 2005. "Whatever Happened to the Women's Movement?," *Mobilization* 10, 1: 37–52.

Stanbridge, Karen, and J. Scott Kenney. 2009. "Emotions and the Campaign for Victims' Rights in Canada," *Canadian Journal of Criminology and Criminal Justice* 51: 473–509.

Starr, Amory. 2005. *Global Revolt: A Guide to the Movements against Globalization*. New York: Zed Books.

———, Luis Fernandez, and Christian Scholl. 2011. *Shutting Down the Streets: Political Violence and Social Control in the Global Era*. New York: New York University Press.

Steinberg, Marc W. 1998. "Tilting the Frame: Considerations on Collective Action Framing from a Discursive Turn," *Theory and Society* 27, 6: 845–72.

Steinhart, Peter. 1987. "The Longer View," *Audubon* 89, 2: 10–13.

Steinman, Erich. 2012. "Settler Colonial Power and the American Indian Sovereignty Movement: Forms of Domination, Strategies of Transformation," *American Journal of Sociology* 117, 4: 1073–130.

Stewart, Keith. 2003. "If I Can't Dance: Reformism, Anti-Capitalism and the Canadian Environmental Movement," *Canadian Dimension* 37, 5: 41–3.

Stoddart Mark C.J. 2012. *Making Meaning Out of Mountains: The Political Ecology of Skiing*. Vancouver: UBC Press.

———, and Howard Ramos. 2013. "Going Local: Calls for Local Democracy and Environmental Governance at Jumbo Pass and the Tobeatic Wilderness Area," *Interface* 5, 1: 229–52.

———, Howard Ramos, and David B. Tindall. 2013. "Environmentalists' Media-Work for Jumbo Pass and the Tobeatic Wilderness, Canada: Combining Text-Centred and Activist-Centred Approaches to News Media and Social Movements," *Social Movement Studies* (http://dx.doi.org/10.1080/14742837.2013.831344): 1–17.

———, and Laura MacDonald. 2011. "'Keep it Wild, Keep it Local': Comparing News Media and the Internet as Sites for Environmental Movement Activism for Jumbo Pass, British Columbia," *Canadian Journal of Sociology* 36, 4: 313–35.

Stone, Amy L. 2012. *Gay Rights at the Ballot Box*. Minneapolis: University of Minnesota Press.

———. 2013. "Winning for LGBT Rights Laws, Losing for Same-Sex Marriage," in Mary Bernstein and Verta Taylor, eds, *The Marrying Kind? Debating Same-Sex Marriage within the Lesbian and Gay Movement*. Minneapolis: University of Minnesota Press.

Strapagiel, Lauren. 2014. "Do New Brunswick's Abortion Restrictions Violate Women's Rights," *Canada.com*. http://o.canada.com/health/do-new-brunswicks-abortion-restrictions-vio-late-womens-rights.

Stryker, Susan. 2008. "Transgender History, Homonormativity, and Disciplinarity," *Radical History Review* 100: 145–57.

Swerdlow, Amy. 1993. *Women's Strike for Peace*. Chicago: University of Chicago Press.

Switzer, Jacqueline Vaughn. 1997. *Green Backlash: The History and Politics of Environmental Opposition in the U.S.* Boulder, Colo.: Lynne Rienner.

Szasz, Andrew. 1994. *Ecopopulism: Toxic Waste and the Movement for Environmental Justice*. Minneapolis: University of Minnesota Press.

Taras, David. 1990. *The Newsmakers: The Media's Influence on Canadian Politics*. Scarborough, Ont.: Nelson.

Tarrow, Sidney. 1989. *Democracy and Disorder: Protest and Politics in Italy, 1965–1975*. Oxford: Oxford University Press.

———. 2005. *The New Transnational Activism*. New York: Cambridge University Press.

———. 2011. *Power in Movement: Social Movements and Contentious Politics, Revised and Updated Third Edition*. New York: Cambridge University Press.

Tattrie, Jon. 2010. *The Hermit of Africville: The Life of Eddie Carvery*. Halifax: Pottersfield.

Taylor, Judith. 2015. "No to Protests, Yes to Festivals: How the Creative Class Organizes in the *Social Movement Society*," in H. Ramos and K. Rodgers, eds, *Protest and Politics: The Promise of Social Movement Societies*. Vancouver: UBC Press.

Taylor, Judith, Josée Johnston, and Krista Whitehead. 2014. "A Corporation in Feminist Clothing? Young Women Discuss the Dove 'Real Beauty' Campaign," *Critical Sociology* 20, 10: 1–22.

Taylor, Verta. 1989. "Social Movement Continuity: The Women's Movement in Abeyance," *American Sociological Review* 54: 761–75.

———, and Leila J. Rupp. 1993. "Women's Culture and Lesbian Feminist Activism: A Reconsideration of Cultural Feminism," *Signs* 19, 1: 32–61.

———, and Nancy E. Whittier. 1992. "Collective Identity in Social Movement Communities: Lesbian Feminist Mobilization," in A.D. Morris and C.M. Mueller, eds, *Frontiers in Social Movement Theory*. New Haven, Conn.: Yale University Press, 104–29.

———, Katrina Kimport, Nella Van Dyke, and Ellen Ann Andersen. 2009. "Culture and Mobilization: Tactical Repertoires, Same-Sex Weddings, and the Impact on Gay Activism," *American Sociological Review* 74, 6: 865–90.

Tennant, Paul. 1990. *Aboriginal Peoples and Politics: The Indian Land Question in British Columbia, 1849–1989*. Vancouver: UBC Press.

Tierney, Kathleen J. 1982. "The Battered Women Movement and the Creation of the Wife Beating Problem," *Social Problems* 29, 3: 207–20.

Tilly, Charles. 1978. *From Mobilization to Revolution*. Reading, Mass.: Addison-Wesley.

———. 1984. "Social Movements and National Politics," in H. Charles Bright and Susan Harding, eds, *Statemaking and Social Movements*. Ann Arbor: University of Michigan Press, 297–317.

———. 1986. "European Violence and Collective Action Since 1700," *Social Research* 53, 1: 159–84.

———. 1988. "Social Movements, Old and New," *Research in Social Movements, Conflicts and Change* 10: 1–18.

———. 1995. *Popular Contention in Great Britain, 1758–1834*. Cambridge, Mass.: Harvard University Press.

———. 2004. *Contention and Democracy in Europe, 1650–2000*. New York: Cambridge University Press.

———. 2008. *Contentious Performances*. New York: Cambridge University Press.

———, and Sidney Tarrow. 2006. *Contentious Politics*. Boulder, CO: Paradigm.

———, and Lesley J. Wood. 2013. *Social Movements, 1768–2012*, 3rd edn. Boulder, CO: Paradigm Publishers.

Tindall, David B. 2002. "Social Networks, Identification and Participation in an Environmental Movement: Low-Medium Cost Activism within the British Columbia Wilderness Preservation Movement," *Canadian Review of Sociology and Anthropology* 39, 4: 413–52.

Toronto Star. 1999. "Logging on to Protest," 29 Nov.

Touraine, Alain. 1971. *The May Movement: Revolt and Reform*. New York: Random House.

Tuchman, Gaye. 1978. *Making News: A Study in the Construction of Reality.* New York: Free Press.

Turner, Ralph. 1981. "Collective Behavior and Resource Mobilization as Approaches to Social Movements: Issues and Continuities," *Social Movements, Conflicts and Change* 4: 1–24.

———, and Lewis M. Killian. 1957. *Collective Behavior.* Englewood Cliffs, NJ: Prentice-Hall.

———. 1972. *Collective Behavior*, 2nd edn. Englewood Cliffs, NJ: Prentice-Hall.

———. 1987. *Collective Behavior*, 3rd edn. Englewood Cliffs, NJ: Prentice-Hall.

Uldam, Julie, and Tina Askanius. 2013. "Online Civic Cultures: Debating Climate Change Activism on YouTube," *International Journal of Communication* 7: 1185–204.

Useem, Michael. 1975. *Protest Movements in America.* Indianapolis: Bobbs-Merrill.

Valocchi, Steve. 1999. "Riding the Crest of a Protest Wave? Collective Action Frames in the Gay Liberation Movement, 1969–1973," *Mobilization* 4, 1: 59–73.

———. 2001. "Individual Identities, Collective Identities, and Organizational Structure: The Relationship of the Political Left and Gay Liberation in the United States," *Sociological Perspectives* 44, 4: 445–67.

Van Cott, Donna Lee. 2007. "Latin America's Indigenous Peoples," *Journal of Democracy* 18, 4: 127–42.

———. 2010. "Indigenous Peoples' Politics in Latin America," *Annual Review of Political Science* 13: 385–405.

Van Deburg, William L. 1992. *New Day in Babylon: The Black Power Movement and American Culture, 1965–1975.* Chicago: University of Chicago Press.

Van Dyke, Nella. 2003. "Crossing Movement Boundaries: Factors that Facilitate Coalition Protest by American College Students, 1930–1990," *Social Problems* 50, 2: 226–50.

Van Gelder, Sarah. 2013. "Speaking with the Founders of Idle No More," *Huffington Post.* http://www.huffington-post.ca/sarah-van-gelder/idle-no-more-founders_b_2708644.html.

Van Laer, Jeroen, and Peter Van Aelst. 2010. "Internet and Social Movement Action Repertoires: Opportunities and Limitations," *Information, Communication, & Society* 13: 1146–71.

Vasi, Ion Bogdan. 2007. "Thinking Globally, Planning Nationally and Acting Locally: Nested Organizational Fields and the Adoption of Environmental Practices," *Social Forces* 86, 1: 113–36.

Vickers, Jill. 2010. "A Two-Way Street: Federalism and Women's Politics in Canada and the United States," *Journal of Federalism* 40: 412–35.

———, Pauline Rankin, and Christine Appelle. 1993. *Politics As If Women Mattered: A Political Analysis of the National Action Committee on the Status of Women.* Toronto: University of Toronto Press.

Vipond, Robert. 2004. "The Civil Rights Movement Comes to Winnipeg: American Influence on "Rights Talk" in Canada, 1968–71," in S.L. Newman, ed., *Constitutional Politics in Canada and the United States.* Albany: State University of New York Press, 89–107.

Voss, Kim, and Rachel Sherman. 2000. "Breaking the Iron Law of Oligarchy: Union Revitalization in the American Labor Movement," *American Journal of Sociology* 106, 2: 303–49.

Walker, Gillian A. 1990. *Family Violence and the Women's Movement.* Toronto: University of Toronto Press.

Walker, James W. St G. 2012. "Black Confrontation in Sixties Halifax," in L Campbelle, D. Clément and G. Kealy, eds, *Debating Dissent: Canada and the 1960s.* Toronto: UTP, 173–92.

Walker, Rebecca, ed. 1995. *To Be Real: Telling the Truth and Changing the Face of Feminism.* New York: Anchor Books.

Wall, Derek. 1999. *Earth First! and the Anti-Roads Movement: Radical Environmentalism and the Comparative Social Movements.* London: Routledge.

Walsh, Edward J. 1988. *Democracy in the Shadows: Citizen Mobilization in the Wake of the Accident at Three Mile Island.* Westport, Conn.: Greenwood Press.

Wapner, Paul. 2002. "Horizontal Politics: Environmental Activism and Global Cultural Change," *Global Environmental Politics* 2, 2: 37–62.

Warner, Tom. 2002. *Never Going Back: A History of Queer Activism in Canada.* Toronto: University of Toronto Press.

Webster, Norman. 1979. "Indians to Petition the Queen on Constitution," *Globe and Mail,* 2 July, 4.

Webster, Paul. 2006. "Canadian Aboriginal people's health and the Kelowna deal," *The Lancet* 368, 9532: 275–6.

Werum, Regina, and Bill Winders. 2001. "Who's 'In' and Who's 'Out': State Fragmentation and the Struggle over Gay Rights, 1974–1999," *Social Problems* 48, 3: 386–410.

Weyler, Rex. 2004. *Greenpeace: How a Group of Ecologists, Journalists and Visionaries Changed the World*. Vancouver: Raincoast Books.

Whittier, Nancy. 1995. *Feminist Generations: The Persistence of the Radical Women's Movement*. Philadelphia: Temple University Press.

———. 1997. "Political Generations, Micro-Cohorts, and the Transformation of Social Movements," *American Sociological Review* 62, 5: 760–78.

Wilkes, Rima. 2004a. "First Nation Politics: Deprivation, Resources, and Participation in Collective Action," *Sociological Inquiry* 74, 4: 570–89.

———. 2004b. "A Systematic Approach to Studying Indigenous Politics: Band-Level Mobilization in Canada, 1981–2000," *Social Science Journal* 41: 447–57.

———. 2006. "The Protest Actions of Indigenous Peoples: A Canadian–U.S. Comparison of Social Movement Emergence," *American Behavioral Scientist* 50, 4: 510–25.

———, Catherine Cornigall-Brown, and Daniel Myers. 2010. "Packaging Protest: Media Coverage of Indigenous People's Collective Action," *Canadian Review of Sociology* 47, 4: 327–57.

———, Catherine Corrigall-Brown. 2012. "Picturing Protest: The Visual Framing of Collective Action by First Nations in Canada," *American Behavioral Scientist* 56, 2: 223–43.

———, and Michael Kehl. 2014. "One image, multiple nationalisms: Face to Face and the Siege at Kanehsatà:ke," *Nations and Nationalisms*. DOI: 10.1111/nana.12067.

Wilms, Jessie. 2015. "Timeline of Jian Ghomeshi Story," *Toronto Star*, 8 January, http://www.thestar.com/news/gta/2015/01/08/timeline_of_jian_ghomeshi_story.html.

Wilson, Jeremy. 1992. "Green Lobbies: Pressure Groups and Environmental Policy," in R. Boardman, ed., *Canadian Environmental Policy: Ecosystems, Politics, and Process*. Toronto: Oxford University Press, 109–25.

———. 2001. "Continuity and Change in the Canadian Environmental Movement: Assessing the Effects of Institutionalization," in D.L. VanNijnatten and R. Boardman, eds, *Canadian Environmental Policy: Context and Cases*. Toronto: Oxford University Press, 46–65.

Wilson, John. 1973. *Introduction to Social Movements*. New York: Basic Books.

Wines, Michael. 2014. "Environmental Groups Focus on Change by Strengthening Their Political Operations," *The New York Times*, 1 June.

Wood, Lesley J. 2005a. "Taking to the Streets against Neoliberalism: Global Days of Action and Other Strategies," in Podobnik and Reifer (2005: 69–81).

———. 2005b. "Bridging the Chasms: The Case of Peoples' Global Action," in J. Bandy and J. Sith, eds, *Coalitions across Borders: Transnational Protest and the Neoliberal Order*. Lanham, Md.: Rowman & Littlefield, 95–117.

———. 2012. *Direct Action, Deliberation, and Diffusion*. New York: Cambridge University Press.

———. 2015. "Uncooperative Movements, Militarized Policing and the Social Movement Society," in H. Ramos and K. Rodgers, eds, *Protest and Politics: The Promise of Social Movement Societies*. Vancouver: UBC Press.

Woons, Marc. 2013. "Commentary: The 'Idle No More' Movement and Global Indifference to Indigenous Nationalism," *AlterNative: An International Journal of Indigenous Peoples* 9, 2: 172–7.

Wotherspoon, Terry, and John Hansen. 2013. "The 'Idle No More' Movement: Paradoxes of First Nations Inclusion in the Canadian Context," *Social Inclusion* 1, 1: 21–36.

Yousafzai, Malala (with Christina Lamb). 2013. *I am Malala: The Girl Who Stood Up for Education and Was Shot by the Taliban*. New York: Little, Brown and Company.

Young, Nathan and Eric Dugas. 2011. "Representations of Climate Change in Canadian National Print Media:

The Banalization of Global Warming,"
Canadian Review of Sociology 48, 1:
1–22.

———, and Aline Coutinho. 2013.
"Government, Anti-Reflexivity, and the
Construction of Public Ignorance About
Climate Change: Australia and Canada
Compared," *Global Environmental
Politics* 13, 2: 89–108.

Young, Scott. 1969. "A Strange Feeling at
the Centre of Indian Discontent," *Globe
and Mail*, 11 July, 7.

Zald, Mayer N. 2000. "Ideologically
Structured Action: An Enlarged
Agenda for Social Movement Research,"
Mobilization 5, 1: 1–16.

———, and Bert Useem. 1987. "Movement
and Countermovement Interaction:
Mobilization, Tactics, and State
Involvement," in M.N. Zald and
J.D. McCarthy, eds, *Social Movements
in an Organizational Society*. New

Brunswick, NJ: Transaction Books,
247–72.

Zelko, Frank. 2013. *Make it a Green
Peace! The Rise of Countercultural
Environmentalism*. New York: Oxford
University Press.

Zhao, Dingxin. 1998. "Ecologies of Social
Movements: Student Mobilization
During the 1989 Prodemocracy
Movement in Beijing," *American Journal
of Sociology* 103, 6: 1493–529.

———. 2000. "State-Society Relations and
the Discourses and Activities of the 1989
Beijing Student Movement," *American
Journal of Sociology* 105, 6: 1592–632.

Zhou, Min. 2013. "A Multidimensional
Analysis of Public Environmental
Concern in Canada," *Canadian Review
of Sociology* 50, 4: 454–81.

Zogby International. 2006. "Zogby Post-
Election Poll: Dems Gained from Global
Warming Debate," press release, 16 Nov.

Index